SHARED RESPONSIBILITY

Contents

Acronyms   ix

Foreword   xiii

PART I   OVERVIEW   I

1 Introduction   3

2 United Nations: Organization and Methods of Work   23

3 The Secretariat   45

PART II   PEACE AND SECURITY   67

4 The Security Council   69

5 Peacekeeping Operations   89

6 Peacebuilding   111

PART III   FREEDOM   131

7 Human Rights   133

8 Genocide and War Crimes   159

PART IV   DEVELOPMENT   183

9 Global Development Goals   185

10 Operational Activities for Development   207

11 Sustainable Development   233

PART V   PERSPECTIVES   257

12 Perspectives   259

UN System Organizational Chart   271
Notes   273
Suggestions for Further Reading   291
Bibliography   297
Index   309

Acronyms

ACABQ	Advisory Committee on Administrative and Budgetary Questions
AGECC	Advisory Group on Energy and Climate Change
AGF	Advisory Group on Climate Change Financing
AL	Arab League
ALBA	Alianza Boliviana para los Pueblos de Nuestra América
AMISOM	African Union Mission in Somalia
ASEAN	Association of Southeast Asian Nations
ASG	assistant secretary-general
AU	African Union
BCPR	Bureau of Crisis Prevention and Recovery
BRICS	Brazil, Russia, India, China, South Africa
CANZ	Canada, Australia, New Zealand
CAT	Committee Against Torture
CEB	Chief Executives Board for Coordination
CFC	chlorofluorocarbons
COP	Conference of the Parties
CSD	Commission on Sustainable Development
DAC	Development Assistance Committee
DAO	Delivering as One
DESA	Department of Economic and Social Affairs
DFS	Department of Field Support
DGACM	Department for General Assembly and Conference Management
DIIS	Danish Institute for International Studies
DPA	Department of Political Affairs

DPI	Department of Public Information
DPKO	Department of Peacekeeping Operations
DSS	Department of Safety and Security
ECCC	Extraordinary Chambers in the Court of Cambodia
ECHR	European Convention on Human Rights
ECLAC	Economic Commission for Latin America and the Caribbean
ECOSOC	Economic and Social Council
ECOWAS	Economic Community of West African States
EOSG	Executive Office of the Secretary-General
EPTA	Expanded Programme of Technical Assistance
EU	European Union
FAO	Food and Agriculture Organization
GATT	General Agreement on Tariffs and Trade
GEF	Global Environmental Facility
GFATM	Global Fund to Fight AIDS, Tuberculosis and Malaria
G4	Group of 4
G8	Group of 8
G20	Group of 20
G77	Group of 77
HDI	Human Development Index
HRC	Human Rights Council
IAEA	International Atomic Energy Agency
ICC	International Criminal Court
ICCPR	International Covenant on Civil and Political Rights
ICESCR	International Covenant on Economic, Social and Cultural Rights
ICISS	International Commission on Intervention and State Sovereignty
ICPD	International Conference on Population and Development
ICTR	International Criminal Tribunal for Rwanda
ICTY	International Criminal Tribunal for the former Yugoslavia
IEA	International Energy Agency
IGAD	Intergovernmental Authority on Development (in Eastern Africa)
ILO	International Labor Organization
IMF	International Monetary Fund
IPCC	Intergovernmental Panel on Climate Change

Shared Responsibility

The United Nations in the Age of Globalization

CARSTEN STAUR

Translated by
STEVEN HARRIS

McGill-Queen's University Press
Montreal & Kingston • Ithaca

© McGill-Queen's University Press 2013

ISBN 978-0-7735-4293-8 (cloth)
ISBN 978-0-7735-4294-5 (paper)
ISBN 978-0-7735-9015-1 (ePDF)
ISBN 978-0-7735-9016-8 (ePUB)

Legal deposit fourth quarter 2013
Bibliothèque nationale du Québec

Printed in Canada on acid-free paper that is 100% ancient forest free
(100% post-consumer recycled), processed chlorine free.

Published simultaneously in the United Kingdom, Eire, and Europe in
paper back by DJØF Publishing, Copenhagen.

This revised translation by Steven Harris of the original Danish edition
Den globale udfordring. FN mellem relevans, legitimitet og handlekraft,
DJØF Publishing, Copenhagen 2011, is financed by the *Hermod
Lannung Foundation*, Copenhagen, Denmark.

McGill-Queen's University Press acknowledges the support of the
Canada Council for the Arts for our publishing program. We also
acknowledge the financial support of the Government of Canada
through the Canada Book Fund for our publishing activities.

Library and Archives Canada Cataloguing in Publication

Staur, Carsten, 1954–
    [Globale udfordring. English]
    Shared responsibility : the United Nations in the age of
globalization / Carsten Staur ; translated by Steven Harris.

Translation of: Den globale udfordring.
Includes bibliographical references and index.
Issued in print and electronic formats.
ISBN 978-0-7735-4293-8 (bound). – ISBN 978-0-7735-4294-5 (pbk.). –
ISBN 978-0-7735-9015-1 (ePDF). – ISBN 978-0-7735-9016-8 (ePUB)

    1. United Nations – History – 21st century. 2. Peace-building.
3. Human rights. 4. Sustainable development. I. Title.
II. Title: Globale udfordring. English

JZ4984.5.S7313 2013   341.23   C2013-904677-1
                                             C2013-904678-x

This book was typeset by True to Type in 10.5/13 Sabon

To Marie-Louise

ISAF	International Security Assistance Force
MDG	Millennium Development Goals
MINURCAT	United Nations Mission in the Central African Republic and Chad
MINUSTAH	United Nations Stabilization Mission in Haiti
MONUSCO	United Nations Organization Stabilization Mission in the Democratic Republic of the Congo
NAM	Non-Aligned Movement
NATO	North Atlantic Treaty Organization
NGO	non-governmental organizations
NIEO	new international economic order
NPT	Treaty on the Non-Proliferation of Nuclear Weapons
OAS	Organization of American States
OCHA	Office for the Coordination of Humanitarian Affairs
ODA	Official Development Assistance
OECD	Organisation for Economic Co-operation and Development
OHCHR	Office of the UN High Commissioner for Human Rights
OIC	Organization of Islamic Cooperation
OLA	Office of Legal Affairs
ONUC	United Nations Operation in Congo
PBC	Peacebuilding Commission
PBF	Peacebuilding Fund
PBSO	Peacebuilding Support Office
R2P	Responsibility to Protect
RC	Resident Coordinator
SADC	Southern African Development Community
SARS	severe acute respiratory syndrome
SCSL	Special Court for Sierra Leone
SE4ALL	Sustainable Energy for All
SHIRBRIG	Multinational Standby High Readiness Brigade for United Nations Operations
SRSG	special representative of the secretary-general
TCCS	troop-contributing countries
UN	United Nations
UNAIDS	Joint United Nations Programme on HIV/AIDS
UNAMID	UN–African Union Hybrid Operation in Darfur
UNAMIR	United Nations Assistance Mission for Rwanda
UNCLOS	United Nations Convention on the Law of the Sea

UNCTAD	United Nations Conference on Trade and Development
UNDG	United Nations Development Group
UNDP	United Nations Development Programme
UNDOF	United Nations Disengagement Observer Force
UNEF	United Nations Emergency Force
UNEP	United Nations Environmental Programme
UNESCO	United Nations Educational, Scientific and Cultural Organization
UNFCCC	United Nations Framework Convention on Climate Change
UNFICYP	United Nations Force in Cyprus
UNFPA	United Nations Fund for Population Activities
UNHCR	United Nations High Commissioner for Refugees
UNHSP	United Nations Human Settlement Programme
UNICEF	United Nations Children's Fund
UNIDO	United Nations Industrial Development Organization
UNIFIL	United Nations Interim Force in Lebanon
UNITAF	Unified Task Force
UNMIL	United Nations Mission in Liberia
UNMIS	United Nations Mission in Sudan
UNMISS	United Nations Mission in South Sudan
UNMOGIP	United Nations Military Observer Group in India and Pakistan
UNODC	United Nations Office on Drugs and Crime
UNOPS	United Nations Office for Project Services
UNPROFOR	United Nations Protection Force
UNRWA	United Nations Relief and Works Agency
USG	under-secretary-general
UNTSO	United Nations Truce Supervision Organization
WEOG	Western European and Others Group
WFP	World Food Programme
WHO	World Health Organization
WMO	World Meteorological Organization
WTO	World Trade Organization
WWF	World Wide Fund for Nature

Foreword

Nothing at the UN is as simple and straightforward as it looks.
Mark Malloch-Brown, former UNDP Administrator, 2011

On a wall on the third floor of the UN General Assembly Building in New York there is a short quote from the second secretary-general of the United Nations, Dag Hammarskjöld, which states: "The UN was not created to take humanity to heaven, but to save it from hell." Another quote from Winston Churchill says: "It is better to jaw-jaw than to war-war." Both quotes are from the 1950s when the Cold War was doing its best to conjure up fear of a catastrophic Third World War. An organization that could help prevent the ultimate disaster needed no further justification for its existence.

The situation today is different. Even though wars, armed conflicts, and terrorism are still evident threats to mankind, the looming global disaster no longer takes the form of a nuclear world war.

Present-day fears relate to climate change and to global sustainability in the long term, and the solution to these issues involves strengthened global collaboration on the trans-boundary problems that can only be solved by working together. The question is whether the United Nations is still relevant to these existential challenges in the twenty-first century. Does the UN have the strength and drive necessary to make the decisions and implement the solutions?

The simple answer is that the United Nations represents opportunities – opportunities for solving armed conflicts and for helping victims back on their feet, opportunities for preventing mass atrocities against civilians and creating free societies everywhere in the world, opportunities for steering the globalization process in the right direction and for reducing global poverty. It is not a given that the world will or can make use of these opportunities. This will depend on the political will of the member states and on the skill and ability with which they pursue these opportunities.

On a number of occasions over recent years I have discussed the challenges facing the United Nations with visitors to New York. I have noted considerable sympathy and goodwill toward the UN, but also some scepticism. The discussions have often focused on what the United Nations' most important tasks would be over the next ten to fifteen years.

This book is an attempt to answer this question in more detail and to sketch out the problems faced by the United Nations, and the organization's possibilities for presenting itself as relevant, legitimate, and action-oriented in the twenty-first century. The picture is not black and white; there are many nuances.

That it has been possible to take this project from a vague idea and turn it into a book in a fairly short time is due not least to the great support I have had from my outstanding and experienced colleagues at the Permanent Mission of Denmark to the United Nations. Some have commented on the manuscript along the way, and all have followed the project with great enthusiasm. For this reason I owe heartfelt thanks to Erik Laursen; Michael Hyldgaard; Jette Michelsen; Eva Raabyemagle; Mia Steninge; Asif Parbst Amin; Steen Malthe Hansen; Maria Nilaus Tarp; Ulf Melgaard; Karsten Kolding; Kristina Bendtzen Rashid; Marcus Carter Mathiasen; and to my secretary, Margit Rasmussen, for her assistance during the writing of the book. The analyses and conclusions presented here are, of course, my own, and do not necessarily express the views of either the Permanent Mission of Denmark to the United Nations or the Danish Ministry of Foreign Affairs.

I also want to thank Nanna Hvidt, Bo Lidegaard, Ellen Margrethe Løj, Anne-Birgitte Albrectsen, and Jakob Simonsen for discussions and comments on the manuscript; as well as Sten Rynning, Anders Wivel, and Casper Sylvest for criticisms and suggestions. Naturally, the responsibility for any mistakes or omissions is mine alone. I also owe a debt of gratitude to a number of senior UN officials and fellow Permanent Representatives to the United Nations whom I have engaged in conversations on some of the main topics of the book.

This book was published in Danish in late 2011. A number of colleagues continued to suggest that it should also be published in English, and McGill-Queen's University Press heeded the call. My sincere thanks to Steven Harris, who translated the book; to the Hermod Lannung Foundation in Copenhagen, which generously funded the translation; and to Adrian Galwin at McGill-Queen's who took on the project. Also sincere thanks to Wilfried Roloff, my editor at DJØF Publishing in Copenhagen, who facilitated the project, and to Carol Harrison, who copy-edited the manuscript.

Last, but not least, I thank Marie-Louise for her encouragement, indulgence, and candid comments on the manuscript throughout the process. Without you I could not have done it.

New York
May 2013

PART I

Overview

The UN headquarters, and especially the impressive high Secretariat Building that lies on the banks of the East River in midtown Manhattan, has become a New York City landmark. This means that it is not possible just to tear down the sixty-year-old buildings, even though they have become almost unusable, with rain pouring through the roof and the plumbing often in disorder. Instead the United Nations has embarked on a comprehensive renovation project from 2008 to 2014 to bring the buildings up to twenty-first-century standards and to create a modern, energy-efficient headquarters complex for the world organization.

Meanwhile, several thousand staff members have been temporarily moved to new offices elsewhere in midtown. On 14 February 2011 the Secretariat Building is buzzing with construction workers removing all non-load-bearing walls and the old windows.

We are on the thirty-eighth floor, where the secretary-general's office used to be located – and where it will be soon again, once the renovation is completed. Now we only see the bare concrete floor, the structural elements, and a mass of pallets loaded with new panes of glass. The old windows are being replaced with modern ones that are both energy-efficient and blast proof. The building is completely open to the wind on all sides, and one can clearly see how narrow it is. This is not for people with a fear of heights.

The secretary-general's office was in the northeast corner of the building, but the only remnant is an old safe, which was probably too heavy to move. The door is ajar and the safe is empty save for its share of stories to tell, if it only could, of life on the thirty-eighth floor and the crises and successes of the United Nations through more than sixty-five years.

This book is not about the past but about the present and the future. Still, what the United Nations is, and what the organization might become in the years ahead will always be rooted in the vision of the founding fathers of the United Nations when they drafted the UN Charter.

Past, present, and future will therefore all be part of this story of the UN in the age of globalization.

I

Introduction

We the peoples of the United Nations, determined to save succeeding generations from the scourge of war ... do hereby establish an international organization to be known as the United Nations.

Charter of the United Nations

THE BEGINNING

In the summer of 1945, at the time of the United Nations' creation, there was no need to justify or defend the new world organization.

Already in the preamble to the UN Charter it was made clear that the participating countries were acting with urgency and out of a deeply felt determination "to save succeeding generations from the scourge of war, which twice in our lifetime has brought untold sorrow to mankind."

The victors of the Second World War – the United States, the Soviet Union (USSR), and the United Kingdom – wanted to build a new world organization in which these great powers (together with France and China) played a decisive role in securing international peace and security. The creation of the UN Security Council and the granting of veto powers to the five permanent members of the council was the cornerstone of the new global security system.

At the same time the members of the United Nations reaffirmed their "faith in fundamental human rights, in the dignity and worth of the human person [and] in the equal rights of men and women and of nations large and small" and their determination "to promote social progress and better standards of life in larger freedom ... and to employ international machinery for the promotion of the economic and social advancement of all peoples."

The language of the UN Charter is solemn, but its meaning, and the basic values that it expresses, could not have been clearer. The Charter was signed in San Francisco on 26 June 1945. The surrender of Germany in early May had ended the Second World War in Europe, but in Asia the nuclear bombings of Hiroshima and Nagasaki were still to come, and Japan's surrender was far from given. In the final reckoning, the Second World War had cost the lives of more than 60 million people, most of them civilians. Whatever divided the world in 1945, there was general agreement that loss of human life on this scale should never be allowed to happen again.

In 1945, the United Nations had fifty-one member states, mainly the victors of the war and those countries which, like some Latin American and smaller European nations, had succeeded politically in positioning themselves advantageously in the war's final phase. With the admission of South Sudan as a new member in July 2011, the United Nations now has 193 member states. Most of the increase in membership has been due to the admission of former colonies, primarily in Africa and Asia, which gained their independence in the 1950s and 1960s. The breakup of the Soviet Union and of Yugoslavia in the 1990s also led to the establishment of a number of new independent states and hence new members of the UN.

Today's United Nations is a very different political institution from what it was in 1945. In so many other respects, the world has changed dramatically since then as well.

There are many more people on Earth. In 1945, the world population stood at 2.5 billion people. In 2011, it reached 7 billion, and it will probably be more than 9 billion by 2050, and exceed 10 billion before the population curve breaks at the turn of the twenty-first century. Almost all future population growth will take place in developing countries. In many industrialized countries, not least in Europe, population numbers will fall.

Since 1945, there have been truly formidable economic and technological developments, initially in industrialized countries in North America, Western Europe, and Japan, but in recent decades also in some developing countries which are becoming new global economic powers – "emerging economies" such as China, India, Brazil, Mexico, Indonesia, Turkey, and others. In a few years' time China and India will join the United States as the world's three leading economies. A Chinese growth rate of almost 8 per cent per year compared to an

American growth rate of just 2.5 per cent would mean that China would overtake the United States as world's largest economy in 2018. However, the average income of an American would still be almost three times as large as the average income of a Chinese.

These demographic and economic developments have had major consequences, not least for European countries, which are today much less globally important than they were in 1945. European growth has simply been too sluggish compared with the growth in other regions. The poorest developing countries, including many countries in sub-Saharan Africa, have experienced increased economic growth in recent years and are likely to continue on that track, with economic growth rates of more than 5 per cent per year. At the same time, it is obvious that poor countries that are affected by internal conflict, violence, and personal insecurity are in severe danger of missing out on the region's economic upturn. Achieving increased economic growth and development in developing countries, and avoiding the risk of this prospect being derailed by increased inequality, conflict, and strife, will be one of the main global challenges in the years to come.[1]

The world has seen equally impressive political developments, not least over the last twenty years since the end of the Cold War in 1989, which left the United States unchallenged as the world's paramount superpower. During the Clinton administration (1993–2001) America's unique position in the world created the basis for increased international co-operation, including at the United Nations. But the establishment of a much more positive climate of international co-operation was not always followed by new and more concrete forms of collaboration between countries or by the involvement of new actors, which would have been necessary to achieve significant results. The end of the Cold War, therefore, did not lead to substantial changes in the postwar international system.

At the start of the new millennium, a new global situation began to emerge, with the emerging economies gaining further economic momentum and becoming increasingly self-aware and politically confident. The emerging economies and a more assertive Russia no longer give the United States the same free hand in global affairs as they did in the 1990s. At the same time, the European Union is seeking to intensify its economic and political co-operation, and reclaim a more central position for Europe on the world stage.

THE UNITED NATIONS
IN THE INTERNATIONAL SYSTEM

This book is about the United Nations and its potential to serve, over the next ten to fifteen years, at the core of the system of international organizations and agreements which is often referred to as "global governance."

Global governance is the global management system that consists of the sets of rules, norms, institutions, and forms of co-operation through which the world formally or informally, and in co-operation, tries to manage the many international actors and their different – and often conflicting – interests. The term *global governance* should not be confused with *global government*, i.e., a world government. A global government does not exist and it is very unlikely that it will ever be established. The UN General Assembly is not a "global parliament" and the UN secretary-general is not a "world president."[2]

The three core themes of this book are: the UN's relevance to solving the most important global problems; the organization's legitimacy as a framework for widely accepted international solutions; and its effectiveness in implementing the solutions which its member states decide to pursue. Taken together, these three core themes will determine whether the United Nations has the potential to be a key player in future global governance.

Of course, global governance is relevant to much more than just the United Nations. There are more than 240 international organizations; some are global (e.g., the UN and the World Bank), others regional (e.g.. the European Union [EU] and the African Union [AU]), and some have very few members while others have almost universal membership. In sheer numbers, the United Nations and its various organizations in the UN system represent less than one-fifth of all international organizations, but in terms of status and legitimacy, the UN often surpasses other international organizations (see chapter 2 for an overview).

As the preamble to the UN Charter demonstrates, the UN has a clear mandate to maintain international peace and security, strengthen respect for human rights, and enable social and economic development. The key questions asked in this book are: How will the UN handle these challenges up to the year 2025? What specific means of global governance will the UN need to employ, and why and how? And what will be the correlation between the relevance of the UN, its legitimacy, and its effectiveness?

An integral element of these issues is the various views of the 193 member states that essentially "own" the UN and thus ultimately determine the parameters within which the organization can operate and the goals it should pursue.

There are many views on the United Nations. Governments and peoples in Europe tend to have a fairly positive view of the organization. This is especially true for the smaller Northern European countries which have been among the strongest and most consistent supporters of the UN system from the very beginning. This support is a reflection of a fundamental belief in international co-operation, identification with the United Nations' core values, and a clear recognition that a more rule-based international system benefits smaller countries that would otherwise suffer greatly in a world in which might is right.[3]

Other member states have historically had a more distant and less enthusiastic relationship with the UN. The great powers in particular often assess their co-operation with the UN in light of their successes in pursuing their more narrowly defined national interests within the organization.

The former (Republican) US ambassador to the United Nations (2005–06), John Bolton, predominantly saw the United Nations as a hotbed of anti-Western and anti-American criticism and as fundamentally inefficient. Bolton's perhaps most widely quoted observation was that it would not make the slightest difference if you took away the top ten of the thirty-eight floors of the UN Secretariat Building. But Bolton was not the first US ambassador to the UN to regard the organization with scepticism and frustration. Some of his predecessors, including Democrat political icons such as Adlai Stevenson (1961–65) and especially Daniel Patrick Moynihan (1973–75) were also fairly critical of the UN in relation to the pursuit of American interests.[4]

The fact that all countries can be, and ideally should be, members of the United Nations (provided that they are approved by the Security Council and the General Assembly) occasionally leads some people to question whether other, more limited, forms of international co-operation would not be more effective than the all-inclusive UN. The creation of a global League of Democracies, as an alternative to the United Nations, has been one of the most consistent proposals in this respect. It was supported by the Republican candidate, John McCain, during the US presidential election campaign in 2008, and it

also received support from some Democrats. The basic argument
for such a League of Democracies is that co-operation between "politically like-minded" (democratic) countries would provide a better
framework for effective decision making. The league would be able to
agree on issues more profoundly and more speedily if it did not have
to take into account the views of non-democratic states, which tend to
drive all international co-operation down toward the lowest common
denominator.[5]

The counter-argument has been that a global organization which
only included a selection of countries would, by definition, no longer
be global. Such an organization might perhaps be able to make better
and faster decisions than the UN on some global issues, but it would
not be able to implement them, precisely because its membership
would not be global and countries left out of such an organization
would not feel any ownership of the decisions or any obligation to
implement them. Moreover, by their very nature a significant number
of global co-operation issues are simply not very political in scope.
The former Chinese leader Deng Xiaoping (1904–1997) is often quoted as having said that he did not care whether the cat was black or
white, as long as it caught mice. The same applies to issues such as
global measures to avert bird flu and other pandemics. Here democracies and dictatorships very often work seamlessly side by side, and if
countries disagree, their conflicting views usually have little to do
with their governmental status. Another important argument against
the "League of Democracies" is that talking with and trying to influence those with whom you disagree in order to achieve solutions that
can take international co-operation forward is at the heart of international collaboration.

It is a truism that global challenges require global solutions, and that
all countries should be involved in the pursuit of such solutions. The
strength of the UN system is that it has universal membership and that
the decisions which are made in the United Nations can be implemented in all 193 member states. This is clearly most crucial and
urgent in relation to global pandemics such as avian flu, severe acute
respiratory syndrome (SARS), and H1N1 flu, where the World Health
Organization (WHO) sets the international standards and ensures coordination between national health authorities. That co-operation
between *all* countries is necessary in such situations is recognized by
all, and it has even been possible to find a model for the practical participation of Taiwan in this regard, with Chinese agreement.

Thus, with all its deficiencies and shortcomings (which are addressed later in this book), the fact remains that the United Nations continues to be the best and effectively the only international organization for managing the complexities of globalization. The basic structure of the United Nations provides for a more effective partnership between "rich" and "poor" than other forums for international co-operation which are less formal, less universal, less equal, and thus, in some sense, also less legitimate. But the UN is not a homogeneous partnership.

The Security Council is more like a limited company or corporation, where power is distributed according to share capital, and where all the five major "shareholders" have a blocking minority (veto powers). In contrast, the General Assembly most resembles a co-operative, where all participants (member states) have one vote, and where each of the many small members therefore wields the same influence as the much fewer bigger members, much as was the case in the co-operative agricultural movements across Europe in the nineteenth and early twentieth centuries.

It is far more difficult and time-consuming to manage a co-operative and keep all its members happy than it is to be a major shareholder in a corporation. As anyone living in a housing co-operative will know, sentiments often run high when important decisions are to be made. There are often substantial differences between the interests of those who are about to sell their apartment and those who have just bought one (often at much too high a price). There can be intense discussions about issues large and small, such as how much neighbours should be able to interfere in each other's doings, rules for the keeping of animals (or not), and for noise levels in the evening. But most of the time the members do manage to find compromises and practical solutions which everyone can live with, or at least grudgingly obey – solutions that everyone recognizes as legitimate because they have been involved in the negotiating and decision making. The same principle applies to the "ownership" of solutions reached in the UN General Assembly. Broadly agreed decisions are arrived at through protracted negotiations, defining a common set of standards which all member states, or the vast majority of member states, adhere to. This applies to everything from the UN Convention on the Law of the Sea (UNCLOS) to the Treaty on the Non-Proliferation of Nuclear Weapons (NPT).

The raisons d'être of the United Nations are the many problems that transcend national borders, and the management of global commons or global public goods. These issues require the establishment of framework conditions or goals in which all countries have a stake, and which can only be achieved through the collaboration of all countries.

The three main sections of this book, on peace and security, freedom, and development, all refer to topics that relate to such more broadly defined global public goods. But the concept of global public goods can obviously also be defined and implemented more specifically. Global co-operation in combatting infectious diseases, in combatting global warming and climate change or in fighting terrorism are all examples of global public goods. In all these areas the United Nations has the potential capacity to combine normative interventions (i.e., negotiations of international rules and standards that are accepted by all) with operational initiatives and practical assistance, particularly for countries with a limited capacity to introduce and implement these rules and standards.

The United Nations remains at the centre of the international system. It may be a cliché to say that if the UN did not exist it would have to be invented, but it is true nonetheless.

GLOBAL MEGA-TRENDS TOWARD 2025

What kinds of global developments will have the most impact over the next ten to fifteen years – thereby setting the stage on which the United Nations will have to perform and succeed? It is always difficult to make long-term predictions, and no such predictions will hold true in full. Therefore, no medium- to long-term plans can be effectively implemented without making the necessary corrections along the way. But the more effort that is put into developing various kinds of scenario planning and elaborating likely global trends, the better the United Nations and other international organizations will be able to anticipate and adapt to new conditions; and the better positioned they will be to stay the course.[6]

The analyses and reflections in this book are based on the assumption that over the next ten to fifteen years, and probably longer, four specific global paradigm shifts will have a decisive effect on international co-operation in general and on the UN in particular. These four quite different global paradigm shifts will all contribute to the complexities of the contexts in which the UN member states and other actors try to assess, balance, and pursue their various interests in continued and intensified international co-operation. The four new paradigms highlighted here will not change the basic fact that international co-operation is of fundamental benefit to all countries. But these various paradigm shifts will have an impact on the demands of some of the actors, either positively or negatively, and they will influence the behaviour of different actors with regard to alliances and forms of collaboration.

The four major paradigm shifts, or mega-trends, which will be of particular importance to the United Nations are the following.

1 A Fundamental Change in the Global Power Structure, with Some Emerging Economies Developing into New Key Players

The first paradigm shift is the ongoing fundamental change in the global power structure. In this context "power" is seen in relative terms and therefore as a zero-sum game between countries and regions. This means that while UN member states will continue to negotiate and work together on specific issues, their respective negotiating powers will gradually change as will the entire informal framework for co-operation, creating uncertainty as to where individual member states stand in the global power structure. This will be more pronounced in the future than in past decades, and the UN will become a forum in which competing powers will try to stake their claims to more prominent places in the global power structure. Countries moving up the ladder will seek to assert themselves and make sure that their new status is recognized, and countries that are in relative decline will try to delay this process as much as they can. Having the United Nations and other international organizations as the battleground for this global power struggle has the great advantage that the fight will be fought by peaceful means, but a fight it will be, nonetheless.

This global power struggle will primarily reflect the expected changes over the next few decades in economic growth, level of development, regional position, demographic trends, increased urbanization, and the emergence of a much larger middle class in individual countries and regions. All these changes will fundamentally challenge the postwar global power structure of 1945, on which the United Nations was built. China, India, Brazil, Mexico, South Africa, Nigeria, Indonesia, Turkey, Iran, and Egypt are among those seeking greater recognition as key regional and global players, and a higher position in the informal hierarchy of nations. A number of these countries are therefore also seeking a more permanent presence in the UN Security Council (see chapter 4).

Brazil, Russia, India, China, and South Africa, known jointly by the acronym BRICS, are also developing closer political co-operation and supporting each other's increased involvement in issues which figure high on the international agenda. This means further pressure on Europe, Japan, and the United States to accommodate these new and more ambitious global actors. Fareed Zakaria has politely described this fundamental change as being about "the rise of the rest" rather than the decline of the West. However, in a zero-sum game this description is more soothing than real.[7]

Briefly, the extensive changes in the global power structure that we are witnessing, and which will only increase over the coming years, are likely to generate considerable tensions in the United Nations as well as in other international organizations. Such tensions could be further compounded by increased national self-esteem or outright nationalism in some countries as they either move up or down the global power ladder. Even so, it is unlikely that such tensions will lead to a breakdown of global governance or global institutions. The interests of all states in the maintenance of the international system for the pursuit of their own interests and for seeking agreements with other states are simply too important. Globalization has made the international system, including the United Nations, a "must keep."

2 A More Pronounced Struggle
between Different Global Value Systems

The United Nations is a values-based organization, particularly when dealing with human rights issues. The key values of the UN Charter and the Universal Declaration of Human Rights and the emphasis on individual – and universal – human rights are strongly supported by Western countries. At the same time these values are under increased scrutiny and pressure from a number of developing countries. In particular, some developing countries see UN monitoring of human rights in individual member states as interfering in their domestic affairs. Their concerns particularly apply to critical reports of UN special rapporteurs and others looking at a number of specific human rights issues, including the use of torture. The involvement of non-governmental human rights organizations in the human rights work of the United Nations has also created major difficulties between those member states which support increased participation of civil society and those which remain sceptical or are opposed to it outright.

In addition, there is an ongoing debate about various parts of the established concepts of human rights and their interrelationships, where different member states also hold different views. From a Western perspective, the emphasis is on civil and political rights and fundamental freedoms, and on the protection of individual citizens against abuses of state power. This view is challenged both by newer human rights concepts such as the right to development, which also has a collective dimension in which the state rather than merely individuals have rights, and by the strong emphasis on economic and social rights, such as the right to food, right to water, et cetera, to which other UN members tend to attach greater emphasis. Thus, different member states emphasize different parts of the human rights agenda, as set out in the Charter, the Declaration, and subsequent human rights conventions. The political struggles over this at the UN can be quite fierce, and so far neither the end of the Cold War nor the Arab Spring has provided much relief in this regard.

In recent years, there has been considerable focus on the issue of defamation of religions, where some Islamic countries have presented proposals that would effectively restrict freedom of expression in relation to religion and religious issues. Most recently, the issue of sexual orientation, including lesbian, gay, bisexual, and transgender rights (the LGBT agenda) has been a point of contention at the UN. Some countries have systematically sought to purge all references to the importance of combatting discrimination based on sexual orientation from all human rights resolutions adopted by the UN General Assembly.

3 New Non-state Actors Wanting a Greater Say in the Decision-Making Processes Alongside the Member States

The United Nations was created by its member states and for its member states. It is the nation-states that are the original partners in the intergovernmental co-operation which is at the core of the UN system. But the idea that nation-states should have a monopoly as the only, or the main, actors on the global stage is coming under increased pressure. International civil society organizations with a global reach (such as Amnesty International, CARE, the World Wide Fund for Nature [WWF], etc.), large private foundations (such as the Bill and

Melinda Gates Foundation and George Soros's Open Society Foundations), multinational corporations, global media, large faith-based organizations or institutions, research networks, and prominent representatives from the academic community, all try to use every opportunity to influence the formal decision-making processes of member states, and they all seek more formal recognition as actors in their own right. The United Nations is working to strengthen the dialogue with these new and powerful actors on the international stage, but also in response to this the UN member states hold widely differing views, from a fairly inclusive approach to a basically exclusive approach.

In addition, a number of regional organizations are becoming much more important in the international system. These include the EU, the North Atlantic Treaty Organziation (NATO), the African Union (AU), the Association of Southeast Asian Nations (ASEAN), the Organization of American States (OAS), and the Arab League (AL), to name just some of the most significant organizations. There is also a wide range of other international organizations in which various members participate, covering larger or smaller sub-regions, communities of interest, and specific policy areas where countries seek co-operation with each other. In the field of environmental co-operation alone, there are several hundred international environmental organizations or conventions, each of which provides a framework for practical co-operation between their members. There is an ongoing debate about how to simplify this very complex system and make it better coordinated and more efficient. However, so far there is not much that points to an actual willingness to engage in more extensive reforms of the system.

The reactivation of the G20 in the autumn of 2008 was a response to the need for better policy coordination of the major economies to deal with the global financial and economic crisis. It is unlikely that the re-emergence of the G20 will in itself change the dynamics of the international system and certainly not in the short term. The participating major emerging economies have generally seemed reluctant to expand the scope of G20 coordination into to new areas and to take on larger and more forward-looking commitments within the G20 framework.

International co-operation today is complex. The interaction between global organizations such as the United Nations, of which all countries are members, and regional, interest-based or other more limited associations of countries (such as the G20) is in flux and is constantly being re-arranged. Formally organized non-state actors are knocking on the door, and at the same time there is a rapid expansion of new virtual structures that make it possible for individuals to join together in networks across national boundaries, creating new ad hoc political forces. The technical barriers to the organization of groups of individuals based on interests and ideologies are coming down with dramatic speed. Information is more widely available than ever, and people can act on it across national boundaries via electronic media.

Despite these developments and the introduction of many new actors on the global stage, nation-states have proved capable of defending their role as the key actors in the international system in general, and in the UN in particular. But it will be necessary for the UN to reach out much more systematically and much more determinedly to the new players and to create partnerships with them in order to help solve the global problems of the twenty-first century.

4 Climate Change Strategies Leading to Dramatic Changes
in the Global Economy over the Next Few Decades

The Climate Change Conference in Copenhagen in December 2009 (also known as the Conference of the Parties, or COP 15) was an eye-opener for many who saw, for the first time, how difficult it is to agree on concrete steps to reduce CO_2 emissions and thus limit future global warming. The negotiations took place under the UN Framework Convention on Climate Change (UNFCCC), which originally had a fairly narrow and technical mandate and primarily addressed issues that neither the political classes, nor the media, nor the general public saw as being very important.

When the UNFCCC entered into force almost twenty years ago, the consequences of climate change were not a high-priority political issue in most countries. Climate change was seen by many as a technical and sector-oriented issue to be addressed by climate experts, often from meteorological institutes, national environmental agencies, or environment ministries, which did not have the mandate or the competence to deal with the socio-economic and management issues of the current climate change agenda.

The scientific evidence clearly calls for a global transition to a low-carbon economy over the next few decades. This will require fundamental changes to the patterns of production, consumption, transportation, and housing in all countries. This far exceeds the purview of a single government department, and will extend over several election cycles. Quite a lot will depend on how technological innovation progresses, on what kind of research breakthroughs are made in key areas, and on how quickly new technology is disseminated. The issue of combatting climate change and limiting the increase in the global mean temperature is so important to the future of mankind that it cannot be relegated to a discussion among experts or even environment ministers in the context of a UN Climate Change Conference, at least not in its current form. It may be appropriate in the future to leave negotiations on the more technical aspects to the technicians in UNFCCC, while other UN bodies, perhaps the General Assembly or some other key UN body, could have the task of negotiating the political agreements on broader socio-economic issues which will also have to be addressed. The security aspects related to climate change are likely to become increasingly important. The Security Council has already discussed these issues in special debates in 2007, 2009, and in July 2011.

In any case, it must be expected that heads of state and government will continue to be involved in the issue of climate change. There is a strong need for a whole-of-government approach to the very complex sets of issues which have to be addressed. The United Nations will be uniquely placed to coordinate and provide political impetus to future discussions and decisions on these broader issues.

THE STRUCTURE OF THE BOOK:
PEACE AND SECURITY, FREEDOM, AND DEVELOPMENT

All books require tough editorial decisions about what to include and what to leave out. This book focuses on the three main tasks of the United Nations: peace and security, freedom and human rights, and economic and social development. The headings used here – "peace and security," "freedom," and "development" – are taken directly from then secretary-general Kofi Annan's report to the member states, setting the scene for the UN Millennium Summit in 2000, and they provide the framework for the substantive chapters (4–11) of this book.[8]

Part I: Overview

In addition to this introductory chapter, the first part of the book also contains, in chapter 2, a brief overview of the background and history of the United Nations and an equally brief presentation of the basic outline and structure of the UN system. It then examines the intergovernmental and institutional tensions that often characterize the United Nations as a negotiating forum, including the difficult relationship between the Security Council and the General Assembly. The chapter also discusses the conflicts of interest between the major groups of countries that cut across other issues and to a large extent define the framework for negotiations in the UN. The purpose of this chapter is primarily to set the stage for what follows and provide an understanding of the basic framework and rules that govern the United Nations as a negotiating forum.

Chapter 3 expands on this by focusing on the role of the secretary-general and the United Nations Secretariat. It is the member states that decide, but the Secretariat assists them in setting the agenda and in shaping the decisions. This is particularly true of the secretary-general, who is at the same time the chief executive, the chief diplomat, and the global agenda-setter of the organization – a position which has been called the most impossible job in the world. For many years the UN Secretariat and the many more or less autonomous organizations within the UN system have contributed significant and innovative ideas to move the various international processes forward. These initiatives have not always been successfully but rarely for the want of trying. Today's challenges, however, are greater than ever before, and there is a clear need to further strengthen the intellectual leadership of the United Nations and the organization's ability to prepare, launch, and implement the necessary political initiatives based on scientific data, where relevant, and on solid evidence as to what works and what does not.

Part II: Peace and Security

The second part of the book focuses on the UN's work on peace and security. This is the basic task of the UN and the very essence of the organization. The former high commissioner for human rights, Sergio Vieira de Mello, put it this way: "Security is first priority and second priority and third priority, and the fourth priority."[9]

Chapter 4 looks more closely at the UN Security Council, its mandate, and its unique right to authorize the use of force in order to maintain international peace and security. The role of the council is exemplified by its handling of the situations in Iraq in 1991, Iraq in

2003, and by its decisions regarding Libya in the spring of 2011. The composition of the Security Council still primarily reflects the world as it looked in 1945. An expansion of the membership of the council in order to better reflect the new global power structure has been debated for more than twenty years, but so far without any result. If the rise of the new global powers is not properly acknowledged by the UN membership as a whole and reflected in the composition of the Security Council, especially in relation to permanent seats, the council risks losing its political legitimacy in the long term. However, the council's effectiveness and ability to take necessary decisions are also important factors when considering its reform and expansion.

Chapter 5 focuses on the development of UN peacekeeping operations, which remain the most important instrument at the disposal of the Security Council. Over the past ten to fifteen years there has been an increase in the number of UN peacekeeping missions, and the organization now has around 125,000 soldiers, policemen, and civilians in fifteen peacekeeping missions around the world. These are primarily in Africa, especially in Sudan, South Sudan, Mali, and the Democratic Republic of the Congo. The expansion of peacekeeping activities began in the 1990s and it created a number of practical and managerial problems; the organization's track record in the Balkans in the 1990s was far from impressive. Since 2000, however, the UN has significantly strengthened the quality and effectiveness of its peacekeeping operations. These operations now have a broader spectrum, including military, police, humanitarian and political elements, with a clear focus on the protection of civilians. The UN peacekeeping mission in Liberia is a concrete example of this modern approach.

Chapter 6 deals with the challenges of the new peacebuilding agenda of the United Nations. The end of the Cold War caused a political change that made it possible for the UN to address more systematically its potential role in the early reconstruction of countries in the aftermath of conflict and civil war. The presence of the United Nations in countries before, during and after a conflict, and the many different tools that the UN has at its disposal, make it possible for the organization to develop country-specific programs which can span a conflict, through stabilization and early recovery to development. In this regard too, Liberia is used as an example of how the UN system can help a war-torn country deal with the challenges following a peace agreement and embark on a development process.

Part III: Freedom

The third part of the book deals with the work of the UN in relation to respect for human rights, individual liberties, and the prevention of atrocities in the form of genocide, war crimes, crimes against humanity, and ethnic cleansing.

Chapter 7 examines the key normative role of the UN and the establishment of the international human rights mechanisms after the Second World War on the basis of the human rights set out in the Universal Declaration of Human Rights in 1948. The relationship between civil and political rights on the one hand and economic, social and cultural rights on the other is highlighted. New and emerging issues, such as the right to gender identity, due legal process and the rights of suspected terrorists, are also analyzed. The UN's comprehensive work to combat the use of torture around the world is used as a concrete example of the practical relationship between the normative and operational work of the UN. Finally, there is a discussion of the role of human rights in the opposing stances of different value systems, including whether human rights are universal or merely Western values.

Chapter 8 focuses on the issues of genocide and war crimes and on the development of the emerging norm of the responsibility to protect (R2P), which reflects the fact that the traditional strong emphasis on national sovereignty and non-interference in other countries' domestic affairs is now on the defensive, not least because of the experiences of Somalia, Bosnia, and Rwanda in the 1990s. Recognition of the need to protect civilian populations from the threat of mass atrocities has gained considerable momentum over recent years, including in the Security Council (its decision to mandate the protection of civilians in Libya is a case in point). At the same time the establishment of the International Criminal Court (ICC) is a sign of the global resolve not to allow impunity for dictators and other political leaders who are responsible for systematic human rights violations.

Part IV: Development

The fourth part of the book addresses the work of the United Nations on economic and social development, including the impact of the Millennium Development Goals (MDGs). It also discusses the opportunities for the UN to relaunch sustainable development as the future global development paradigm.

Chapter 9 looks at the normative role of the United Nations in the context of development, and especially in the formulation of global development goals. For many years the internationally agreed official development assistance target of 0.7 per cent of gross national income (GNI) and the MDGs have been key development policy standards for member states. The MDGs have clearly helped put a stronger focus on national ownership of the goals and on the proper role of official development assistance (ODA), particularly in health and education. A number of the MDGs are well on the way to being fulfilled by 2015. Even though the fulfillment of some goals is still lagging behind, it was confirmed at the MDG Summit in 2010 that the goals could be achieved, provided that all countries intensified their efforts over the next few years. The UN General Assembly will adopt a new set of international goals to replace the MDGs no later than 2015. Some suggestions for the design of these goals are included in the analysis.

Chapter 10 covers the operational development efforts of the UN. These are predominantly funded by voluntary contributions from Organization for Economic Co-operation and Development (OECD) countries. More than thirty UN funds, programs, and specialized agencies manage a total development budget of US$22 billion per year. The big UN development organizations are the United Nations Development Programme (UNDP), World Food Programme (WFP), United Nations Children's Fund (UNICEF) and United Nations High Commissioner for Refugees (UNHCR). Most of these agencies are involved in emergency relief work as well as in development co-operation. The development efforts of the UN system are primarily focused on building institutions and developing capacities to strengthen and improve the existing systems of poorer developing countries. The UN applies a rights-based approach to development, putting the rights of individuals at the centre. Significant energy and political capital is invested in improving the coordination and delivery of the UN system in the field – the ambitious UN concept of "Delivering as One." One of the main arguments in the chapter is that the particular strengths of the UN development system lie in supporting weak and conflict-affected developing countries.

Chapter 11 deals with sustainable development. This term was coined in 1987 by the Brundtland Report and it is defined as a three-dimensional concept in which economic, social and environmental sustainability are parts of a coherent concept of development. In practice, so far the focus has primarily been on the environmental dimension of sustainable development. The international focus on climate change has reinforced the need to return to the broader sustainability concept in order to deal with the complex challenges to global sustainability. A reduction of CO_2 emissions to limit the increase in the global mean temperature to two degrees Celsius above pre-industrial levels by the end of the twenty-first century – the maximum temperature increase which the Intergovernmental Panel on Climate Change (IPCC) believes is acceptable – would require massive investments in energy, water and land management not least in developing countries. These means can only be mobilized in the form of private investment or through new and innovative forms of financing, or both. As the world approaches 2050 it will probably experience scarcity of natural resources, especially food, energy, and water. In some cases this may lead to crises and even struggles for resources, but it is more likely that it will primarily strengthen international co-operation in order to ensure the more efficient use of these scarce global resources. The road forward, therefore, is by the development of a green economy, focusing on achieving growth that is economically, socially, and environmentally sustainable. The United Nations has the potential to become the key forum for international co-operation in this regard.

Part V: Perspectives

The book ends with chapter 12, which summarizes the arguments of the preceding chapters and proposes a core agenda for the United Nations over the next ten to fifteen years. It is argued that nation-states will remain the key actors in the international system – including at the UN. Other actors, however, will join the nation-states in their decision-making processes. It is also argued that national sovereignty incurs global responsibility. All members have an obligation to adhere to the core values of the UN Charter, both in relation to the maintenance of peaceful co-existence and the management of the planet's carrying capacity. To a great extent the opportunities for the United Nations to remain a relevant, legitimate, and effective international organization will be determined by whether its member states see these opportunities and accept their share of the inherent responsibilities.

A separate argument in this book is that one should never underestimate the importance of major transformative projects which are capable of uniting the entire UN system around a common vision. European integration over the past fifty years or so would hardly have been possible without transformative projects such as the establishment of the single market and the introduction of the euro.

This book identifies three critical global issues where the UN system seems capable of playing a decisive role as initiator, sparring partner, and provider of a negotiating framework, and where the system's strength in combining normative functions – the development of global goals, norms, rules, and standards – with practical (operational) efforts to assist member states in achieving these goals or implementing these standards could come to fruition. The three transformative projects are:

- The increasingly important focus on helping fragile and conflict-affected countries build the necessary governmental, political, legal, social, and administrative institutions that can contribute immensely to greater political and economic stability in these countries and the surrounding regions, and which can also provide the needed impetus for lifting millions of people out of extreme poverty;
- The continued development and implementation of the idea of sovereignty as responsibility, strengthening respect for human rights by a broader and deeper application of the concept of the responsibility to protect and by continued efforts to prevent the perpetration of mass atrocities and gross violations of human rights; and
- A relaunch of a new sustainable development paradigm, incorporating the climate change agenda and the need to develop low-carbon growth trajectories in all countries. Such a new sustainable growth and development paradigm could help to ensure that global warming does not run out of control during the twenty-first century, keeping the increase of the global mean temperature below two degrees Celsius.

The next ten to fifteen years will show whether these three extremely important global transformative projects will be realized, and whether the United Nations and its member states have the political will and the intellectual and operational capacity to meet these challenges.

2

United Nations:
Organization and Methods of Work

Let us not fail to grasp this supreme chance to establish a world-wide rule
of reason – to create an enduring peace under the guidance of God.
US president Harry S. Truman, San Francisco 1945

FROM THE LEAGUE OF NATIONS TO THE UN

The United Nations was created as an organization which, on important points, signalled a break with the League of Nations, but which
at the same time was based on and effectively carried forward many of
the essential elements of the structure of its predecessor.

The industrialization of the nineteenth century and its inherent
technological and economic developments created the basis for more
permanent and institutionalized co-operation between nations, not
least in the practical areas such as telecommunications, postal services,
intellectual property, the standardization of weights and measures,
and international arbitration. The First World War (1914–18) involved
nearly all European countries and a number of overseas countries and
territories as well. The costs of the war were deeply felt all over
Europe; up to 10 million people died as a direct consequence of war
and millions more were wounded or psychologically traumatized.
The war also weakened populations and their natural resistance to
such a degree that the subsequent Spanish Flu pandemic had much
more serious consequences than would otherwise have been the case,
with more than 50 million dying from the disease between 1918 and
1920. The First World War ended with the economies of the belligerent countries broken and with an urgent need to overcome the effects
of war and re-establish a common belief in the future.

The Versailles Conference in 1919 drew new postwar boundaries and created new countries in Europe. Empires were dissolved and liabilities for war reparations measured out. Onerous terms were imposed on Germany resulting in hyper-inflation in the early 1920s and paving the way for Hitler's ascent to power in 1933. The main terms of the Versailles Treaty were laid down by the United States, the United Kingdom, France, and Italy, but many other countries took part in the negotiations. One of the outcomes of the Conference was the establishment of the League of Nations.[1]

The League of Nations was founded as a collective security system, which was intended to make future wars redundant through a system of sanctions, disarmament, and the peaceful settlement of conflicts. The establishment of the League of Nations was an American initiative, promoted by President Woodrow Wilson (1913–21), with the aim of ensuring that the First World War would truly be the "war to end all wars." While Wilson received the Nobel Peace Prize for his efforts, he was unable to persuade the US Senate to approve the treaty setting up the League of Nations. This meant that, despite its status as a global power following its intervention in the war on the Franco-British side in 1917, the United States never joined the League of Nations. What was intended to be a global organization was effectively reduced to being primarily a European security organization.

Given that the League of Nations was thus hobbled from the beginning, the new organization started out reasonably well. The resolution of the conflict over the Åland Islands in 1921 was a significant success, and there were other similar results. However the organization's weaknesses gradually became apparent, and in the 1930s the league failed as a security system, as the organization proved incapable of dealing with the forces that eventually plunged the world into a new and even more destructive world war in 1939. Japan's invasion of Manchuria in 1931, Italy's colonization of Ethiopia in 1935, and Hitler's annexation of Czechoslovakia in 1938 were all inscribed on the gravestone of the League of Nations as a clear statement of the Axis powers' contempt for the organization, for the values of collective security and for the peaceful settlement of disputes on which the League of Nations was based.

The organization of the League of Nations included an assembly, in which all members of the league had one vote. When the League of Nations was formed it had forty-two members, with membership peaking at fifty-eight in 1934. In addition, the league had a council that acted as a form of management committee for the assembly, with four permanent members (the United Kingdom, France, Italy, and Japan, with the addition of Germany when it joined the league in 1926), and four non-permanent members, chosen for three years at a time. The number of non-permanent members was later increased, first to six and then to nine. There was also a permanent Secretariat and a number of agencies, including the International Labour Organization (ILO). Thus the League of Nations' structure resembled that of the UN system, but, as discussed below, there are also a number of important differences.[2]

The initiative to establish the United Nations was taken as early as August 1941, during a meeting that lasted several days between US president Franklin D. Roosevelt (1933–45) and British prime minister Winston Churchill (1940–45). The meeting took place at sea off the coast of Newfoundland. Both leaders had developed an enthusiasm for naval affairs during the First World War, and Roosevelt had sailed for Newfoundland on the pretence of going on a fishing trip off the coast of Maine. His press office issued daily bulletins on the progress of the fishing tour, reporting that the president had spent a quiet day on board fishing.

The result of the negotiations on board (alternately) HMS *Prince of Wales* and the USS *Augusta* was the Atlantic Charter, a short eight-point program that sketched out the overriding political principles for the postwar world as envisaged by the Allied powers. The Charter was primarily an ideological statement providing a stark contrast to the Axis powers, not least by its general emphasis on the right to self-determination ("the right of all peoples to choose the form of government under which they will live") and the fundamental rights of individuals ("that all the men in all the lands may live out their lives in freedom from fear and want"). But it also set out a vision of a world based on international economic co-operation ("securing for all improved labor standards, economic advancement, and social security"), one where the use of force between states belonged to the past ("the abandonment of the use of force") and was to be replaced by an effective global security system ("a wider and permanent system of general security").[3]

The basic idea behind the Atlantic Charter, and subsequently the United Nations, was to create an organization which would prevent another world war in a different and much more effective way than the League of Nations. The realization of this ambition required a

break with the systemic failings which had paralyzed the league in the
1930s, and the decisive instrument for achieving this was the establishment of a new Security Council, with entirely different powers
from those of the council of the League of Nations.

It was not easy to achieve this ambition. The United States, the United Kingdom, and the Soviet Union (later joined by China) agreed on
most of the provisions of the UN Charter at a preparatory conference
at Dumbarton Oaks, Washington, DC, in the late summer of 1944.
The Americans were very much aware of the need not to fall into the
same trap as the League of Nations whose council could only take
decisions unanimously, and which had no means of enforcing its decisions. The key to solving this issue was to introduce a veto power for
all the five permanent members. This was a necessary condition for
the council to be able to function. How the veto power should be
applied, however, was not fully settled at Dumbarton Oaks.

As the preparatory conference was unable to fully resolve the question of the Security Council, it came up again at the Yalta Conference
in February 1945. Here the Soviet leader Joseph Stalin (1922–53)
accepted a compromise proposal on the Security Council whereby
the permanent members had a right of veto on substantive questions,
but not on procedural questions, and in return received what amounted to two additional votes in the General Assembly. The Soviet Union
felt under-represented in the General Assembly as compared with the
Western countries, and argued that the Soviet Republics of Ukraine
and Belarus should be given independent seats in the Assembly. Despite American scepticism, Roosevelt decided to accept this solution.
As he said to his secretary of state, Edward Stettinius, there was no
doubt that "the actual power would rest in the Security Council."

The San Francisco Conference, from April to June 1945, was also
dominated by the big three (the United States, the Soviet Union, and
the United Kingdom), whose primary interest was to maintain the
power of the veto in the Security Council. The US administration
believed that this was a necessary condition for getting the treaty
through the Senate, and thus avoiding a situation like that of the
League of Nations, with the United States unable to join the organization. It quickly became clear that a number of smaller countries,
under the informal leadership of Australia, were highly dissatisfied
with the veto provisions and wanted them watered down. Their dissatisfaction, however, did not change the final draft. What was worse
for the great powers was that it became clear during the discussions

in San Francisco that the Yalta wording on the veto was insufficiently precise, and that the five permanent members did not have the same interpretation of what had been agreed in Yalta. US-Soviet tensions over this led Roosevelt's successor, Harry S. Truman, to send one of his closest advisers to Moscow to negotiate directly with Stalin, who accepted the US position. This rescued the San Francisco Conference.[4]

THE STRUCTURE OF THE UN SYSTEM

From the very beginning, the organization established at the San Francisco Conference in June 1945 was organizationally complex, and its complexity has not diminished since, as new organizations, agencies, funds and programs have further proliferated. The graphic overview on page 271 provides the latest official organizational chart of the UN System.

The United Nations includes the following six principal organs:

- the General Assembly, consisting of all 193 member states;
- the Security Council, with 5 permanent and 10 elected members;
- the Secretariat, whose costs are covered by assessed contributions;
- the Economic and Social Council, with 54 members;
- the International Court of Justice in The Hague; and
- the Trusteeship Council, which de facto has ceased to function.

In addition to these six principal organs named in the UN Charter, there are two other categories of international organizations that are part of what is normally referred to as "the UN System":

- UN entities, funds, and programs that are independent organizations, with their own budgets funded primarily through voluntary contributions, but which are still part of the UN, and whose leaders (normally titled executive directors) are appointed by the UN secretary-general. These organizations include in particular: UNDP, UNICEF, WFP, the UN Relief and Works Agency (UNRWA), the UN Fund for Population Activities (UNFPA), and the UN Entity for Gender Equality and the Empowerment of Women (UN Women), which was formed in 2010 by the merger of four UN entities. In addition to these seven major funds and programs, there are fourteen other lesser organizations that fall into this category.

- UN specialized agencies that are almost entirely autonomous organizations, with their own statutes, budgets and funded through
reasonably secure assessed contributions from member states. In
these organizations it is the decision-making bodies which choose
the organization's director-general. The most important of these
organizations are: the ILO, the WHO, the Food and Agriculture
Organization (FAO), the International Atomic Energy Agency
(IAEA), and the UN Educational, Scientific and Cultural Organization (UNESCO). In addition to these five major specialized agencies
there are eleven smaller organizations as well as the World Bank,
the International Monetary Fund (IMF), and the World Trade
Organization (WTO) which, to a lesser extent, are formally part of
the UN system and participate in some of the UN's internal
activities.[5]

Any overview of the UN system is dominated by acronyms. Rather
than learning them by heart, it is important to focus on which intergovernmental UN bodies play the most important roles in the key
areas of UN activity.

On questions of peace and security, the Security Council is without
question the most important actor, supported in recent years by the
relatively new Peacebuilding Commission (PBC), and other UN institutions that work to maintain and consolidate peacekeeping and
peacebuilding by helping promote more rapid economic and social
development in countries affected by conflicts, their immediate goal
being to prevent these countries sliding back into conflict.

In relation to freedom, respect for human rights, and other more
value-based normative issues, it is the General Assembly and the
Human Rights Council that are the key players, supplemented by the
work of the various human rights conventions.

On economic and social co-operation, the responsibility lies partly
with the General Assembly – and formally also in part the Economic
and Social Council (ECOSOC), which does not have much of a say in
practice – and partly with the UN's mostly voluntarily funded development programs (especially the UNDP, UNICEF, WFP, UNFPA, and
UNHCR) and the technical specialized agencies, such as the ILO, WHO,
FAO, and the IAEA. The coordinating UN body, the Chief Executives
Board (CEB), which the secretary-general chairs, has twenty-eight UN
organizations and entities as members.

INTERNATIONAL NEGOTIATIONS

The United Nations is often referred to as the world organization, and the terms *organization* and *system* tend to be used interchangeably. Strictly speaking, a distinction should be made between the UN as an intergovernmental organization and the UN as a secretariat, or between what has been called "the first UN" and "the second UN."

The first UN is the United Nations as framework and meeting place. It is the place where the member states meet, negotiate, and make decisions. In this context what the UN can achieve is a direct reflection of the common aspirations and wishes of its member states and therefore depends entirely on what the 193 member states both can and will agree on.

If the member states agree on the need for coordinated international measures, for example to prevent the spread of a new infectious disease such as SARS or avian flu, the UN can quickly draw up international standards and ensure the necessary support for their implementation.

On the other hand, if member states do not agree, the UN can be paralyzed. This is most clearly seen in the Security Council when one or more of the permanent members applies a veto.

Not surprisingly, there is a considerable grey area between these two extremes. The usual situation is one in which member states agree on something, but not on everything, and where they must therefore negotiate to reach decisions on which all or most can agree.

It is not least in these frequent situations that the second UN plays an important role. The second UN is the Secretariat and the many corresponding staff members in other UN organizations who enable the first UN to meet, who help the negotiations along with analyses and proposals, and who are often responsible for implementing the decisions taken. In many negotiations the Secretariat can play an important role in building bridges between the differing views of member states, and it often also helps draft specific compromise solutions. This, of course, depends on the Secretariat being willing to take risks, exploit the political room for manoeuvre, and sometimes put forward proposals that do not, on the face of it, appear to be viable.

There is a close connection between the first and second UN. It is the member states which have the ultimate power to decide and which also control the funding of the organization. But the Secretariat

nevertheless has considerable scope for pushing ideas and for supporting member states in their efforts to find common ground if it
makes use of the possibilities for being pro-active and taking initiatives. The interaction between the Secretariat and the member states
will be further discussed in chapter 3.[6]

The focus of this chapter is on the UN as an intergovernmental
organization and as a forum for international negotiations, in other
words the first UN. This covers everything that goes on, both formally and informally, between the UN's 193 member states in connection
with discussing and deciding on the questions which are the subject
of intergovernmental negotiation, whether this concerns questions of
politics, international law, development policy, or something entirely
different.

There is no doubt that there is considerable scope for improvement
in the way intergovernmental negotiations are carried out at the UN.
Negotiations in the General Assembly and in other UN forums with
universal participation are often seen – and felt – as irrational, unfo-
cused and unproductive, and as areas where considerable efforts are
invested with very limited returns.

One need only think of the conclusion of the Climate Change Conference in Copenhagen in December 2009 (COP 15). The chaotic international negotiations at COP 15, dominated by interruptions and long
procedural discussions, were more dramatic than is the case with most
UN conferences, but they reflect the point that in recent years UN
negotiations have been more complex and more difficult than many
participants have found entirely necessary. For this reason many close
observers of negotiations in the General Assembly and in major UN
conferences have pointed to an increasingly dysfunctional negotiating system at the UN, unable to produce substantial results.

The United Nations is not short of things to do; indeed, challenges
are piling up. So why is it so difficult for member states to reach agreement in the General Assembly or at large UN conferences?

The answer is not a simple one. A major part of the explanation for
why it is so difficult to agree is obviously because different countries
have different interests. The essence of international co-operation,
whether at the UN or in other organizations, is to find compromises
between differing and sometimes even opposing interests. The basic
premise is that countries enter into negotiations with each other willing to make concessions because ultimately it is better for all to reach
an agreement than for the problem to remain unresolved. Difficult

problems often take longer to resolve, and important conflicting interests often require creative package solutions, where a broader range of interests is included in carefully calibrated solutions, reflecting the old saying (often attributed to Dwight D. Eisenhower) that if you can't solve a problem, expand it. This is no different in the UN than it is in the wto, the imf or the EU, or in national parliaments, for that matter.

However, there are a number of other factors which often make negotiations more difficult in the United Nations than elsewhere. Some of these are historical and others are the result of the way in which negotiations are organized. Six elements are identified here (not in any particular order) which can have a negative effect on negotiations in practice. Their influence can differ from case to case.

The first explanation is that the history of the UN is also the history of decolonization. As stated above, the number of member states of the UN has risen from 51 to 193, mostly as a consequence of the independence of former colonies from the end of the 1950s and up to the 1970s.

The first thing a country does when it achieves independence – and South Sudan in July 2011 is a good example – is to seek membership of the United Nations, establish a permanent mission (representation) to the UN, and appoint a UN ambassador. By doing so a new country gains admission to the circle of free and independent nations, and finds its voice, both literally and metaphorically. But a newborn nation is not like a newborn baby, without a past, and independence is not just a cause for celebration, and for introducing a new flag and a new currency. Often, independence has been hard won and only after a war of independence, which may have been long and bloody. Prior to that there may be a colonial history characterized by subjugation, economic exploitation, racism, and discrimination. The stories of India's independence in 1947, of Kenya's in 1963, and of Mozambique's in 1974 are all different, but their overall narratives share many common elements. The feeling of having been seen as and treated as second-class citizens does not disappear in one or two generations.

It is important to bear this in mind when analyzing negotiations at the UN. Even though the global economic balance is gradually shifting to the advantage of the new economies in the south and not least in the east, the oecd countries (many of them old colonial powers) are still economically dominant on a global basis. China has moved up to second place, Brazil is in seventh, and India is tenth, but the rest of the top-ten richest countries, measured in gross national product (GNP), are still the established economies such as the United States, Japan, Germany, France, the United Kingdom, Italy, and Canada. The United States and the twenty-eight members of the European Union together still control over half the world's economy.

It is not hard to understand that developing countries often view this history with considerable frustration and a desire to bring about a situation in which countries and peoples are treated more equally and where global resources are more equally shared. Many representatives of developing countries feel, doubtless rightly, that historically their countries have suffered great injustices, which the former colonial powers now have a responsibility to make good. And they do not feel much delight in former colonial powers lecturing them about breaches of human rights and about the "right" values.

This does not mean that developing countries are unwilling to listen, or that they reject international human rights standards, or dismiss the experiences of other countries with economic and development models which appear to be able to create growth and employment. But they expect at least a dialogue on equal terms and a certain acceptance of the shared responsibility of their more developed partners, and they do not accept being lectured to or treated with what they consider to be a lack of respect for where they are coming from.

A certain forgetfulness of history by representatives of the old colonial powers and a distinct political touchiness among representatives from developing countries is thus part of the reason why negotiations at the United Nations are sometimes more difficult than they should be.

The second reason is to be found in the internal group dynamic of the developing countries. It is important to realize that about 130 developing countries often still act together as a group in UN contexts. This goes back to the formation of the Non-Aligned Movement (NAM) in 1961, on the initiative of Indonesia, India, and Yugoslavia. NAM is a forum for co-operation between developing countries on more political questions. The formation of the Group of 77 (G77) in 1964 corresponds in economic and development terms.[7]

There are active regional groups in the United Nations, including those from Africa, Asia, and Latin America. Although these regional groups can play a role in certain situations, particularly on regional questions, they primarily deal with election issues – i.e., the election of member states from different regions to various UN bodies. On substantive questions the key actors remain the NAM or the G77. Both groups cover widely differing countries, from Mali to Singapore, from Brazil to the Maldives, and from Cuba to Saudi Arabia. Since these groups were formed in the early 1960s their members have moved in different directions, politically, economically, and in terms of their core political values. However, history and common bonds remain important and NAM and the G77 are not groupings which developing countries leave easily unless, like Mexico and South Korea, they are admitted to the OECD, the economic co-operation organization of the industrialized countries, and the schizophrenia becomes too evident.[8]

It ought to be almost impossible for the members of the G77 to agree on much, and it is. The solution to this problem has been not to try but instead to leave it to those countries that have a particular interest in a matter to determine the group's common position.

In practice, this has meant that relatively few countries, often with rather extreme views which are not shared by the great majority of developing countries, have been able to set the tone in the UN General Assembly on behalf of the G77 or NAM. This is particularly the case with the ALBA (Alianza Bolivariana para los Pueblos de Nuestra América) countries of Latin America, where Bolivia, Cuba, Nicaragua, and Venezuela in particular pursue a clearly stated anti-capitalist and anti-Western line in the UN, which is substantially out of line with the attitudes of most of the other developing countries. In this context, one may often see these countries using their "successes" at the UN to demonstrate to their domestic audiences how they make their weight felt on the international stage, thus translating their positions at the UN into political capital back home.

Some countries also unquestionably use the United Nations as a platform for drawing attention to themselves and their proper place in the informal hierarchy of nations, though not necessarily with the same ideological motivation. When from time to time a big developing country creates difficulties in UN negotiations, this is not only due to a calculated regard for their national interest; it can also be a reflection of a political need to be more visible, even if this merely means injecting a measure of "nuisance value" into the negotiations. It helps maintain their status in the United Nations and shows that they have certain global ambitions, such as a seat in the Security Council.

A third factor is the defensive stance, which is particularly applicable to developing countries especially in the area of human rights. The background to this is easy to understand. Virtually all governments are sensitive to criticism from international organizations with regard to their failure to comply with international human rights standards. It does not look good to their own populations, and it provides ammunition to national non-governmental organizations (NGOs) and political opponents for criticizing the government. There is already a feeling in many developing countries that much of the human rights criticism is asymmetrical, and is primarily aimed at developing countries' failures to comply with the standards while industrial countries can get away without criticism because their human rights problems are less visible than the infringements of civil and political rights which are often in focus in developing countries.

On this basis, there has been a significant reluctance in the General Assembly to deal explicitly with other than the most obviously offending countries – such as Iran, Syria, Myanmar, and North Korea. For example, the African countries see no reason to discuss the situation in Zimbabwe at the UN. This is something that the AU or the Southern African Development Community (SADC) may discuss, but it is not something with which the broader membership of the United Nations need concern itself. What is not said is that if the situation in Zimbabwe is not discussed, then there will be no cause to discuss the situation in country X or Y if the situation in X or Y were to develop in a negative direction. By not discussing country-specific situations, except for a few countries, countries in general are taking out an "insurance policy" to protect them from criticism if the worst should happen.

The fourth factor is that the resolutions of the General Assembly – contrary to those of the Security Council – are not binding but only advisory, and so are, to a large extent, a matter of sending a political signal. This tends to shift the focus from the substantive issue at hand and toward such resolutions being seen primarily as part of a tactical game. The emphasis on the tactical aspects is strengthened by the fact that the UN's agenda has grown exponentially in recent years, not least driven by the needs of member states to develop their political profiles. In the General Assembly in the autumn of 2010, member states introduced twenty-five different resolutions on various aspects of sustainable development, and the negotiations and adoption of the resolutions proceeded as a matter of routine with little focus on the content of the proposals. It all became an issue of which resolutions were introduced and supported by whom – with no real emphasis on the different substantive positions on sustainable development.

It is fairly simple: if multilateral negotiations are to lead to a result which countries seriously want to achieve, the negotiators must understand the substance and their national interests, and they must naturally have detailed discussions with, and instructions from, their own authorities. However, these conditions often do not apply in the UN context. With twenty-five resolutions on sustainable development alone the resources of the member states' permanent missions to the UN are too limited to cover the ground in full, and it is often difficult for them to obtain detailed instructions from their capitals. What happens is that tactics predominate and a diplomatic board game is set in motion, in which the pieces are moved around the board without much regard for substantive interests.

The fifth factor is the fundamental contradiction between the Security Council and the General Assembly, and how member states deal with this.

The basic contradiction is rooted in the UN Charter. As stated in chapter 1, there is a fundamental difference in approach between decision making in a co-operative (the General Assembly) and a limited company (the Security Council). The General Assembly is a forum in which there is universal participation (193 members), where each member has one vote, and where it is only possible to adopt resolutions which are not binding on member states and which are basically declarations of intent. On the other hand, the Security Council is a forum with limited participation (fifteen members), with the power concentrated in the five permanent members, and with the possibility of making decisions that are binding on all UN members.

Under the UN Charter, both the General Assembly and the Security Council are principal organs. Their mandates and tasks differ, but there are also many overlapping areas. Purely in terms of power, there is a clear tendency to see the Security Council as being dominated by the major powers and a predominantly Western organ, and the General Assembly is dominated by small states, among which the developing countries have a clear majority – a classic North-South divide.

The tensions come to the surface when the Security Council attempts to deal with a matter that, in the eyes of many member states, is not directly relevant to the issue of international peace and security. This happened in the spring of 2007, when the United Kingdom, as president of the Security Council, put on the agenda an open debate about the impact of climate change on international stability in the long term, and again in the summer of 2011 when Germany did the same. In both cases the debate started with submissions from the G77 and NAM claiming that, in principle, the Security Council was trespassing on an area which was solely a matter for the General Assembly. The argument was that the Security Council was encroaching on issues which were under the purview of the General Assembly, and that the *few* (the Security Council) thereby sought to extend their powers at the expense of the *many* (the General Assembly). This did not prevent a large number of developing countries from entering into a lively debate and agreeing that climate change did indeed threaten international peace and security.

A sixth factor can be expressed briefly as the issue of fair exchange. This reflects the fact that the overall agenda of the UN is an expression of a balancing act between important global interests. The UN started out as a collective security system after the Second World War, with the major powers firmly in the driving seat. What mattered was ensuring peace and security, both in order to avoid new wars and to support postwar growth in the same way and in parallel with the European integration project. With decolonization and the trebling of the number of member states in the 1950s and 1960s, development was included in the agenda, both because there were substantial reasons for doing so and, in the eyes of the developing countries, in order to balance the issue of peace and security. This basic "grand bargain" still applies to some extent. The various parts of the UN agenda are parts of a whole, and it is difficult to achieve results in one area (such as peace and security) without at the same time being willing to achieve results in the other area (development).

This was underlined at the UN's high-level meetings in 2000 and 2005, where on both occasions the overall result struck a balance between the results in the area of politics and international law and the results in the area of economics and development. These connections are not always put into words but they exist as an important subtext, expressing a higher sense of negotiating fairness which affects the general climate of negotiation. It is difficult to put something on one side of the scales without putting something on the other.

A TYPICAL UN NEGOTIATION

In the General Assembly and at the major United Nations conferences, tradition and culture usually require decisions to be taken by consensus (i.e., unanimously and without a formal vote). This means that it is necessary to negotiate agreement between all 193 member states. There is no doubt that unanimity and consensus has a value in itself and can help create both legitimacy for the organization and ownership of its decisions. The other side of the consensus culture is, of course, that one often ends up with the lowest common denominator, because some countries will oppose the majority point of view, or decisions are accepted with some countries distancing themselves from the outcome and thus not accepting ownership of the agreement and having no inclination to implement it.

In the Security Council, there is also a desire to achieve unanimity, but not in quite the same way as in the General Assembly. The Security Council's decision making is governed to a much greater degree by the five permanent members (P5) and agreement between the P5 is normally decisive; in this case, the other ten elected members will usually fall into line without significant problems (though no rule is without its exceptions; see chapter 4).

In a typical negotiation (only slightly exaggerated) in the General Assembly or in one of the major United Nations conferences, the G77 will put forward a proposal drawn up by the most radical of its member countries and reflecting the political thinking of North-South confrontation in its golden era of the 1980s. The proposal will be absolutely unacceptable to the United States, the European Union, and other Western members, and it will only have been accepted in the G77 because no one felt strongly enough to vehemently oppose it. Outside the meeting room and under four eyes, many developing countries will say that they do not agree with the G77 proposal, but what can you do?

The intergovernmental negotiations are typically led by two co-facilitators (one from the North and one from the South), appointed by the president of the General Assembly after informal consultations with member states. Typically negotiations will extend over a long period, and the G77 coordinator (a role which rotates between the regional group: in 2011 it was Argentina; in 2012, Algeria; and in 2013, Fiji) will always be surrounded by representatives of the ALBA countries and other like-minded member states to make sure that concessions are not given too quickly. The G77 coordinator will privately tell the co-facilitators that regrettably he or she has to defend the group's extreme position, at least for some time.

By this time most of the more moderate developing countries will have given up taking part in the negotiations, and from the other side it will primarily be the EU, the United States, Japan, and CANZ (Canada, Australia, and New Zealand) that participate actively. As the end approaches, some of the larger developing countries and representatives for the emerging economies which have hitherto kept in the background, will canvass within the G77 and encourage the idea that it is now necessary to reach a compromise. The co-facilitators, who have of course long had a compromise ready at hand, will put this proposal on the table and by and large that will be the end of it.

No doubt, the artistic impression of this kind of negotiating processes could be greatly improved. What is more problematic is that the outcomes of such processes are often of very limited value. Rather than using the negotiations to put forward realistic proposals and present substantive opportunities, the G77 start out by adopting entirely unrealistic positions which can only be met with direct dismissal from the other side. And rather than listening to the real interests of other partners, and seeking to achieve a substantive compromise which can move the issues forward, the result is often a consensus text which largely recycles agreed language from previous resolutions and which will not normally leave any trace in the outside world.

There are exceptions. There are times when the negotiating system shifts into a more productive gear and delivers results. But generally speaking the General Assembly and many other parts of the United Nations have developed a negotiating culture which is increasingly divorced from the real problems of the world and from serious attempts to solve them.

A wise colleague once said that there is too much consensus and too little compromise in the UN. What he meant was that a real compromise requires each of the parties to set out their opening positions and goals and to negotiate a compromise on this basis, with a genuine desire to reach a result. In contrast, consensus often means adopting what we adopted the last time because we have to have some outcome and because in the course of negotiations we never come close to achieving what anyone really wants.

The weakness inherent in the UN negotiating culture may be illustrated by comparing it with similar intergovernmental processes in the European Union. In the EU, a member state seldom succeeds in bluffing and claiming that it has a vital interest in some matter unless such an interest really exists. Everyone understands that national interests, whether economic, political or otherwise, must be respected and taken into account when developing a compromise solution – in so far as these proclaimed interests are real and substantial. If a negotiator tries to claim a vital national interest where none exists, he or she will not succeed; the bluff will be called. In some UN contexts, it is not merely possible to get away with claiming interests one does not have; as indicated, a country and its negotiators can also attract attention and win increased influence by being difficult, even if nothing is at stake. At the United Nations it is not only possible to bluff without negative consequences, it is even possible to gain an advantage by doing so.

REFORM OF THE NEGOTIATING CULTURE?

Over the last ten years, especially since the UN High-Level Plenary Meeting (World Summit) in 2005, there have been ongoing discussions at the United Nations with member states trying to correct some of these structural problems. This has resulted in efforts to revitalize both the General Assembly and ECOSOC as more effective negotiating and decision-making bodies. Even though several attempts have been made, the progress so far has been limited.

No major steps have been taken to make good the fundamental weaknesses of the negotiating system. One of the measures introduced has been to increase the use of thematic debates in the General Assembly, where member states have the opportunity to discuss topical issues, such as the green economy or peacebuilding, in a less formal way and without the need to make decisions or adopt resolutions. But this is a small step.

The core of the problem is the negotiating culture and the informal rules of play in the United Nations. There is a fundamental need to develop a stronger sense of responsibility among member states for the effectiveness of the global system at large.

There should, of course, be consequences if a country overplays its hand in relation to what can be realistically presented as its legitimate interests. This is easier said than done, but one of the possibilities for changing the culture is by closer dialogue at government-to-government level on items on the UN agenda, so that national authorities become more involved in the negotiations, and not only the countries' permanent missions to the UN. In such a government-to-government dialogue, most countries would probably be ready to formulate a more realistic and serious definition of their own national interests and priorities than they do at present in the bear pit of New York or Geneva.

The increased involvement of member states' technical expertise, including capital-based experts, is thus one of the measures necessary for improving the negotiating climate at the United Nations. A more realistic and distinct formulation of genuine national interests, a more strategic approach to the links between these and the identification of the possibilities for substantive compromise will also be necessary.

Furthermore, member states will have to agree to put fewer items on the UN's agenda, and to prepare better for discussions. It will require a high degree of self-discipline from all member states for the UN to streamline its agendas and work programs to better reflect the real scope for negotiation. Ultimately, what is discussed in the UN, and when, is a political question, but it is important that the capacity of the negotiating system should not be overburdened, as is the case at present.

Increased use of high-level panels of eminent persons on key global issues, with the participation of influential politicians and experts, could also help reveal substantive interests and the possibilities for broadly acceptable solutions in given areas. This applies in particular if the reports of such panels are drawn up with a view to the planned negotiating process and UN high-level meetings, and if their secretariat is staffed with people who have both professional knowledge and political acumen. In recent years there have been a number of such panels, including the High-Level Panel on Global Sustainability that presented its report in January 2012.[9]

It will also be necessary to make more use informal forums, where member states can explore issues with representatives from other groups or regions prior to the start of formal negotiations. Here it is important that the Chatham House Rule applies, i.e., that all participants can speak freely in their personal capacities, without anything said later being attributed to specific participants. The UN already makes use of the "Groups of Friends" institutions where a group of interested member states from different regions gathers to informally discuss specific issues, such as energy, the responsibility to protect or violence against children in armed conflict. This system could be further developed in more negotiation-oriented areas. There are examples of informally convened "Friends of the Chair" groups during key negotiations, but not many.

Participation in a Group of Friends does not mean that the member states in question have the same view on the issue at hand. On the contrary, the value of such groups is very often that the parties have the possibility of testing each other's positions informally and thus getting a better understanding of them. To the extent that representatives from the Secretariat also take part, Groups of Friends make it possible to hold informal yet substantive discussions which can be helpful in subsequent negotiations.

Another possibility for informal co-operation is the establishment of inter-regional groups of like-minded member states with the aim of co-operating with selected countries from other regions that are on the same wavelength on a particular issue. One of the more successful recent examples has been an inter-regional alliance for the adoption of a moratorium on the use of the death penalty. In this case, European member states deliberately kept in the background in favour of like-minded countries from Asia, Africa, and Latin America, which made it clear that the death penalty was an issue that divided member states across regions and that no regional group spoke with a single voice on this issue. This effort was successful, first in 2007 and then again in 2010 and 2012, in winning an ever larger majority in the General Assembly encouraging all countries which still had the death penalty to introduce a moratorium on executions.

Increased contact with academics, NGOs and the private sector could also improve the quality of the discussions and decisions of the United Nations. Lobbying often has a bad reputation, but most decision makers have an interest in listening to groups which have special knowledge and experience of a given subject in the preparation of national legislation, and the UN should be no different. The development of closer co-operation between the UN Secretariat and the private sector – primarily through Global Compact, established in 2000 – and the adoption of ten Global Compact principles on human rights and social and environmental aspects of employment, as well as on anti-corruption, to which the participating private companies must subscribe, has generally been successful as has the development of public-private partnerships under the auspices of the UN.[10]

Finally, some of the informal negotiating processes could also be strengthened if it were possible to develop new crosscutting forms of coalitions or alliances between interested countries, private companies, civil society institutions, NGOs, and research institutions. Such multi-stakeholder initiatives – like Every Woman, Every Child and

Sustainable Energy for All, established in 2010 and 2011 respectively
– should be able to create significant political momentum as well as
a practical bottom-up approach to implementing the formal outcomes of United Nations' negotiations.

Strengthening the negotiating process and unblocking the systemic
barriers for member states to use the United Nations' negotiating
framework more effectively is important, but ultimately it is a technical question of how to redesign the negotiating system to provide for
better outcomes.

What really matters, of course, is what the negotiation is about. The
many organizations, funds, programs and organs of the United
Nations, and their respective partners or opposite numbers in the 193
member states, deal with a very broad and comprehensive agenda.
The issues range from large all-encompassing global questions to the
very small or highly practical ones affecting the everyday lives of all of
us. If the three global transformative projects referred to in chapter 1,
or other similar projects, are to stand a chance, it will be essential to
reform the negotiating processes as they function today. This will not
happen of its own accord, or by means of some theoretical discussion
of the reform of the negotiating framework and the working methods
of the UN.

However, changes may come about as an indirect result of the
secretary-general and some member states deciding to arrange negotiations on some of the important items on the UN's agenda in a new
way.

As stated above, this will require the Secretariat to play a more
assertive role, to strengthen its proposals both analytically and politically, and take a more active part in negotiations in informal forums.
The Secretariat will also have to further engage national governments,
by the strategic use of panels of experts, and by drawing more systematically on external experts and academics in the preparatory phases.

These steps can be supplemented by supporting the formal negotiating processes through parallel initiatives in which some countries
that are willing and able to take the lead on an issue actually do so
without having to wait for those that only want to hold back, often
merely to frustrate a solution.

There is no guarantee that this will succeed, but without some
change in the way in which UN member states negotiate, especially
in the General Assembly and prior to high-level meetings and major
UN conferences, it is difficult to envisage the United Nations in a new

and strengthened position and as the place where global agreements can be reached over the coming years, providing both direction and common actions to deal with the most important issues on the global agenda.

The 193 member states are the basis on which the United Nations decision-making processes are built. Negotiating groups like the NAM or the G77 play an important role in negotiations and have done so for almost half a century. A strongly integrated regional organization like the European Union, however, is a fairly new feature in the United Nations and it has been difficult to gain understanding of such an organization as an integral part of the UN negotiation system. Regional groups are well known at the UN, primarily as loosely organized coordinating groups for election issues, but an organization such as the EU with its own identity, representing both its member states and itself has been difficult to reconcile with the UN's fundamental characteristics as an organization for the conduct of relations between sovereign states.

With the Lisbon Treaty and the establishment of a High Representative of the Union for Foreign Affairs and Security Policy and of a European External Action Service (a parallel to a Foreign Ministry at EU level) the EU has created a new kind of representation, to a high degree replacing the former six-monthly rotation of the presidency as the face of the European Union at the UN with a permanent representative office, the EU delegation, responsible for both internal coordination and external representation. The European Union as such remains an observer at the UN, as the Union cannot, of itself, be a member of the UN; that status is reserved for sovereign states.

However, in 2011 the EU achieved an enhanced observer status, making it possible for the EU delegation to take part in UN meetings and to represent the EU member states to the extent they want such representation. This was not easy both because, as stated, the EU's structure can be difficult to understand unless one is accustomed to it, and because many developing countries wanted to send a clear signal to the EU delegation that it should not become yet another member state from Europe or try to reach some de facto status as a member state. Other countries, including some Western countries, were concerned that enhanced observer status for the EU would be followed by similar demands from other regional organizations which did not mirror the EU's level of political integration.[11]

There are areas of UN policy where the EU member states do not have a common position and where there is no common EU participation in the work of the UN. For example, this includes the reform of the Security Council on which the EU member states have very different opinions. It also applies to participation in the work of the executive boards of UN funds and programs, where coordination takes place at the level of the Western European and Others Group (WEOG) and not through the European Union. On top of that, there are a number of technical areas where the EU member states maintain their sovereign national competences (in the area of taxation, for example).

In most of the other areas there is ongoing EU coordination in the UN. The EU is a significant actor in intergovernmental negotiations, whether it is represented by the EU delegation or by one of the EU member states acting as a so-called burden-sharer as can be necessary for practical or staffing reasons. Either the EU presidency or one of the other member states can take on this coordinating function, but naturally with a mandate from the other EU member states.

3

The Secretariat

The Secretary-General ... must embody the principles and ideals of the
Charter to which the Organization seeks to give effect.

United Nations preparatory papers 1945

SECRETARY OR GENERAL?

In April 1953 when the first secretary-general of the United Nations,
Trygve Lie of Norway, received his successor, Dag Hammarskjöld, at
New York's Idlewild Airport, he explicitly referred to his position as
the "most impossible job on this earth." Subsequent secretaries-general
have surely felt the same from time to time.

Hammarskjöld is still the standard against which UN secretaries-
general are measured. He was a virtually unknown Swedish diplomat,
extremely creative, with an ability to find the right words in any given
situation and with a philosophical turn of mind – in short, precisely
the man needed for his time and for the challenges which confronted
the still very young global organization. The aura which still sur-
rounds the memory of Hammarskjöld is also due to the fact that he
died in office when his aircraft crashed during a mission to
the Congo on 17 September 1961. Hammarskjöld's legacy, like John
F. Kennedy's two years later, was thus one of the many unfulfilled
dreams and hopes of the 1960s.

There is nevertheless a reality behind the myth. Hammarskjöld clearly saw the political potential in the secretary-general's job, and he introduced a number of new instruments which subsequent secretaries-
general have refined. The original concept of UN peacekeeping operations was designed by Hammarskjöld and his closest colleagues in
connection with the Suez crisis in 1956. Also the secretary-general's

personal good offices with regard to the prevention and mediation of conflicts were developed by Hammarskjöld, originally in 1954 as the basis for his pendulum diplomacy between the United States and China in order to seek the release of thirteen American military and civilian personnel whose aircraft had been shot down while they were on a spying mission over China, and ultimately in connection with the peacekeeping operation in Congo, which cost him his life.[1]

The United Nations has had eight secretaries-general since 1945: Trygve Lie (Norway, 1945–53), Dag Hammarskjöld (Sweden, 1953–61), U Thant (Burma, 1961–71), Kurt Waldheim (Austria, 1972–81), Javier Peréz de Cuéllar (Peru, 1982–91), Boutros Boutros-Ghali (Egypt, 1991–96), Kofi Annan (Ghana, 1997–2006), and Ban Ki-moon (Republic of Korea, since 1 January 2007). Of these eight, only Annan had deeper prior experience of the UN from the inside. His career in the United Nations started as a very young budget officer with WHO in Geneva in 1962, and he had been a staff member ever since, with the exception of a few years back in Ghana in the mid-1970s. Prior to his appointment as secretary-general, Annan served as assistant secretary-general dealing with personnel and budget issues, and as under-secretary-general for peacekeeping.[2]

The UN secretary-general has three basic tasks, each of which could easily keep the job-holder fully occupied. First, he (or she – so far all secretaries-general have been men) is the world's chief diplomat, and as such is actively involved in dealing with and solving crises and conflicts around the world. Second, he is the chairman of the board of a multinational conglomerate which includes a large number of organizations, funds, and programs, with thousands of employees all over the world. Third, he has the opportunity to set a global political agenda with the aim of influencing political leaders and public opinion around the world on the basis of the UN's values, and thereby to put pressure on the political decision makers in the UN member states. The secretary-general has unique access to speak to truly global audiences and to argue his case before global public opinion. Adapting Marshall McLuhan's famous epigram, one could say that "the man is the message." In the light of this, it is probably not stretching the point too far to say that the secretary-general personifies the moral authority and legitimacy of the United Nations. When he speaks, people listen.

The secretary-general's political role is based on Article 99 of the UN Charter, which states: "The Secretary-General may bring to the attention of the Security Council any matter which in his opinion may threaten the maintenance of international peace and security." Formal references to Article 99 are seldom made, but it is this article which gives the secretary-general the authority to refer matters to the Security Council.

It is his role as the world's chief diplomat that takes up most of the secretary-general's time. He must always consider how to place the UN in the right context in any international crisis or conflict, and when to use the instruments at his disposal so as to make the best possible use of the organization's potential for helping prevent and resolve conflicts.

As discussed in chapter 4, in crisis situations the political power is clearly rooted in the Security Council, without whose mandate the UN is prevented from taking action which is binding on all 193 member states. The secretary-general must always tread carefully to hold the balance between the five permanent members of the council and assess where the balance between them lies, and he must be clear about his aims and those of the Secretariat and about what is possible in the given situation. In some cases one or more of the permanent members will have clear interests at stake, which the secretary-general has to take into account: China's interests in Myanmar and the Sudan; Russia's interests in Serbia, Kosovo, and Syria; the United States' interests in the Middle East; France's interests in West Africa; and the United Kingdom's interests in Zimbabwe. This is only one aspect of the political reality with which the United Nations and the secretary-general have to work.

In 2006–07, first Kofi Annan and subsequently Ban Ki-moon closely followed the situation in Darfur with a view to obtaining a mandate from the Security Council to establish a United Nations peace operation to reduce the conflict in that part of Sudan. The conflict was developing into a situation with mass killings and atrocities, and into what the United States termed the genocide of the non-Arab settlers in Darfur. The interests of the United States and China were far from the same, and the Sudanese government, which supported the Janjaweed militia that was behind most of the attacks in Darfur, did what it could to prevent the Security Council from giving a strong mandate for a UN operation in the area. Moreover, the AU needed to develop concrete measures to prevent conflict in a way which could help strengthen pan-African co-operation for peace and security. The political solution emerged in the form of a joint UN-AU operation (UNAMID), which proved difficult to manage and not the most effective operation one

could imagine, but it was what was possible given the dynamics of the
five permanent members of the Security Council.[3]

In contrast, Secretary-General Ban Ki-moon was much more to the
fore when the situation in Côte d'Ivoire deteriorated following the
presidential election in November 2010. The incumbent president,
Laurent Gbagbo, refused to leave office even though he had lost the
election. Ban Ki-moon decided to draw a line in the sand and to make
Côte d'Ivoire the decisive test of the clearly expressed resistance to
military coups emanating from the regional organization for West
Africa (the Economic Community of West African States – ECOWAS)
and from the AU, both stressing the need to respect the outcomes of
free and fair elections all over the continent. The secretary-general
required Gbagbo to accept his election defeat and to hand over power
in the country to his rival and long-standing opponent Alassane Ouattara. The secretary-general made it clear that in Côte d'Ivoire he did
not see any possibility for a government of national unity including
both the winner and the loser of the election, along the lines which
the UN had helped broker in previous years after elections in both
Zimbabwe and Kenya. In many ways this was a high-risk strategy for
the secretary-general, and it was not equally valued by all the members of the Security Council. But Ban Ki-moon succeeded in holding
the line, even though it took some time before Gbagbo relinquished
power in early April 2011 (see chapter 4).

These two situations in Darfur and Cote d'Ivoire demonstrate the
extent of the secretary-general's political room for manoeuvring.
Sometimes the way forward will be entirely blocked. Sometimes there
may be possibilities that can be exploited to resolve crises and conflicts and to do so in a way that strengthens the values and norms on
which the United Nations is based. In these situations the secretary-
general must have both a strong and viable political vision and a clear
understanding of the way in which the wind is blowing, not least with
regard to decoding the various opinions of the permanent members
of the Security Council and other key actors. This calls for wide diplomatic experience and the ability to draw from a pool of diplomatic
creativity in order to provide leadership. In summary, he must be
much more than a clever secretary, but certainly not a four-star general, as any decisions on the use of military force clearly rests with the
Security Council.

These restrictions on the secretary-general with regard to his capacity to take political initiatives primarily apply to issues of peace and

security which are matters for the Security Council. In relation to the United Nations' mandate in the area of economic co-operation and development, and in relation to political and human rights issues dealt with by the General Assembly, the secretary-general has much greater latitude, though here too there are certain limits.

In relation to the General Assembly and its 193 member states, the power of secretary-general is based on his – and the Secretariat's – possibility of putting forward proposals to member states and thus determining the political agenda. To use these possibilities the secretary-general needs to work diligently with both member states and global public opinion, using his "bully pulpit" to promote his proposals and convince others to act accordingly. Much also depends on his ability to catch the zeitgeist and to use the windows of opportunity that sometimes open up to enable new international initiatives to be taken. An example of this was Kofi Annan's efforts to make governments responsible for atrocities against their own peoples, which were important factors in developing the concept of the responsibility to protect and its later inclusion in the Declaration of the World Summit in 2005 (see chapter 8).

Another example, also from Annan's time as secretary-general, is the establishment of the Global Fund to Fight AIDS, Tuberculosis and Malaria (GFATM) in 2002. The HIV/AIDS pandemic exploded around the turn of the millennium, and there was great willingness in donor countries and among private philanthropic foundations and companies to make additional funds available for combatting this new disease, but not necessarily within the framework of the United Nations. In 2001, Annan took the initiative by suggesting setting up a special fund to mobilize new means, including from the private sector, to combat HIV/AIDS, tuberculosis, and malaria. The proposal was well received at the special General Assembly on AIDS in June 2001.

The new Global Fund was established in record time and began to make grants to support specific projects as early as the spring of 2002. Since then the GFATM has raised over US$25 billion and supported more than 1,000 projects for prevention, treatment and care in 151 countries. The Fund estimates that it has succeeded in offering AIDS treatment (antiretroviral therapy) to 4.2 million people, anti-tuberculosis treatment to 9.7 million people and that it has disseminated more than 310 million mosquito nets, effectively combatting malaria across the globe. Thanks not least to the Global Fund, it is now no longer a utopian dream that all those infected should be able to receive HIV/AIDS treatment by 2015. The fact that it was possible to establish the fund so quickly and to develop a model also making it attractive for private funds to contribute must be ascribed largely to Kofi Annan's ability to seize the moment, and, together with leading civil society actors, to mobilize the necessary popular and political support for the initiative.[4]

Sir Brian Urquhart, who joined the United Nations Secretariat in 1945 and rose to become under-secretary-general for political affairs, still willingly shares his experiences. He has recently characterized the job of the secretary-general as one of the best examples of responsibility without power, meaning that power in the United Nations lies with the member states, both in the Security Council and in the General Assembly. The secretary-general is allowed by the member states to do many things: to negotiate, mediate, declare ceasefires, bring the parties to the negotiating table, make proposals. Sometimes he can use the opportunities to act, or create such opportunities, but he is not really entitled to take action entirely on his own and has few resources at his personal disposal. The secretary-general's ability to lead depends entirely on whether the member states accept his leadership, and it only extends as far as they are willing to follow. For Urquhart this means that the most important requirement for a secretary-general is that he should provide "restrained but charismatic leadership, a highly developed analytical intellect, and controlled but determined strength of character and vision." Where can one find such a person?[5]

THE APPOINTMENT OF THE SECRETARY-GENERAL

The secretary-general is appointed by the General Assembly upon the recommendation of the Security Council. This is the brief wording in Article 97 of the UN Charter. The words are not chosen by chance. The General Assembly appoints; it does not elect. That power lies with the Security Council. When the Security Council makes its decision and passes its recommendation to the General Assembly, the routine is then for the assembly to show unanimous support for the new secretary-general and quickly formalize the appointment.

As for the recommendation of the Security Council, this comes in the form of a resolution, which means that all five permanent members have a right of veto. In addition, over the years a rotation between regional groups has gradually developed so that by the autumn of

2006, on the last occasion when the post had to be filled, it was fairly clear that it was the turn for a candidate from an Asian country to be appointed. Only some members of the Eastern European group objected to this, pointing out that a secretary-general had never been appointed from their group (as vassal states of the Soviet Union, Eastern European candidates had de facto been excluded from getting the job during the Cold War).

The unwritten rules also indicate that the secretary-general cannot come from one of the five permanent members, as they would presumably all block each other. Secretaries-general have usually been recruited from relatively small countries that are not too dominant in their respective regions. In 2006, there were six Asian candidates (from Afghanistan, India, Jordan, South Korea, Sri Lanka, and Thailand) and one Eastern European candidate (Latvia's president Vaira Vīke-Freiberga). The various candidates conducted active campaigns, and visited the countries that were members of the Security Council in order to introduce themselves and discuss their visions and specific ideas.

The election process took the form of straw polls, where for each candidate the fifteen members of the Security Council stated whether they would encourage the candidacy, discourage it, or whether they were neutral. Thus each member of the Security Council could encourage or discourage several candidates. The first straw poll in July 2006 showed that Ban Ki-moon (then the Republic of Korea's minister for foreign affairs) and the Indian candidate, Under-Secretary-General Shashi Tharoor, were in the lead, but none of the candidates had only positive support. Subsequent votes in September and October showed the same picture. The first three straw polls were conducted with identical ballot papers, so it was not possible to distinguish between the votes of the permanent members with a veto and the elected members.

In the fourth round of voting, ballot papers were issued with different colours for the permanent members and the elected members. This vote showed that Ban Ki-moon was the only candidate whom all the five permanent members agreed not to oppose. For all the other candidates, there were negative votes from one or more permanent members, and thus an indication of a possible veto. The outcome of the vote could not be misunderstood, and the Chinese ambassador to the UN was quick to draw this conclusion in his comments to the press. The other candidates withdrew their candidacies, so that Ban

Ki-moon was the only candidate and could be unanimously recommended by the Security Council. This took place on 9 October and
the General Assembly appointed him the new secretary-general on 13
October 2006.[6]

What would have happened if it appeared that all the candidates
would have been vetoed? There could have been a formal vote, to see
if any of the permanent members changed their position. This was
the case in 1971 when Kurt Waldheim was selected after having been
subjected to fourteen veto votes along the way. However, in this case
it is more likely that new candidates would have been put forward, as
happened when Pérez de Cuéllar was selected in 1981, after China
had vetoed a third term of office for Waldheim thirteen times and
either the United States or the Soviet Union had vetoed the other two
candidates. Peru's former UN ambassador and then under-secretary-
general for political affairs was a natural compromise candidate.

The secretary-general's term of office is five years. A more or less
fixed practice has developed for a secretary-general to be reappointed
for a second period and thus to hold office for ten years in all. The present secretary-general, Ban Ki-moon, was reappointed for a second
term in June 2011 and his term of office therefore will extend until
the end of 2016. This reappointment for a second term naturally
requires that all five permanent members agree. This was not the case
in 1996 when in the Clinton administration decided to veto a second
term for Boutros Boutros-Ghali, both because of dissatisfaction over
his policies in Bosnia and the Middle East, but equally because in the
summer and autumn of 1996 Boutros-Ghali had become a point of
contention in Bill Clinton's re-election campaign against the Republican candidate, Bob Dole.[7]

Which regional group is in line to provide the next secretary-general?
The claims of the Eastern European group have been referred to, and
the Western European group could also state its claim as Europe has
not provided a secretary-general since Waldheim. Some people will
presumably argue that Europe has had its turn, with three of eight
secretaries-general so far, and that the pendulum should naturally
swing again toward the emerging economies of Latin America. Even
though the regional rotation for the appointment of the secretary-
general is reasonably well established, it is not written down. This
means that the practice need not be followed if the Security Council
decides not to do so.

Thus, here too it is ultimately the five permanent members of the Security Council which outline the rules and decide the result. On the next occasion there will undoubtedly be a number of strong candidates and arguments will be made for and against regional rotation and about what this means in practice. Given the way of the world, the frontrunner will probably be the candidate on whom the United States and China can agree – and to whom Russia does not object.

He – or she – will be the UN's next secretary-general.

THE UN SECRETARIAT

The Secretariat is referred to in Article 7 of the Charter as one of the principal organs of the United Nations, on the same footing as the General Assembly and the Security Council. As leader of the Secretariat, the secretary-general is described as "the chief administrative officer of the Organization." This made sense when the Secretariat was of such a size that, when he was appointed, Dag Hammarskjöld promised all the staff that he would come round and visit each of them in their offices, and did so in the first six weeks.[8] However, it makes less sense today when the UN Secretariat has grown enormously and when the whole UN system, of which the secretary-general is the formal leader, now consists of a score of more or less autonomous organizations, funds, programs and bodies spread throughout most of the world. And it makes even less sense in a situation where the secretary-general's leadership and decision-making powers are considerably less than if he were the chief executive of a multinational company or a government minister.

In fact, the secretary-general does not decide on very much when it comes to how his Secretariat (the second UN) is organized and how its staff resources are allocated. Put simply, he cannot move a key staff position from one office to another without referring the issue to the member states.

The UN's budget and staffing levels are determined in detail by the General Assembly's budget committee (the Fifth Committee), which traditionally makes its decisions unanimously. The tradition for unanimity is in everyone's interests, otherwise a majority of small countries, which together only pay a very modest portion of the UN budget, could vote for cost increases which would have to be overwhelmingly paid for by the Western countries (for historical reasons the EU members states together pay nearly 40 per cent and the United States 22 per cent of the UN's budget). But the tradition for unanimity also means that budget decisions are usually bundled together in large compromise packages in which everyone has to get something and the balance is therefore carefully calibrated. This makes it difficult to change specific decisions without re-opening the whole package.

In practice this means that the Secretariat's organization reflects the global priorities of last year, or ten years ago, and that staff resources are not allocated optimally. The Secretariat's work is determined by the tasks which the member states ask it to carry out, whether this involves the organization of a peacekeeping operation, holding a conference, drawing up a report on the basis of discussions between the members, or something entirely different. It is easier to initiate tasks than to terminate them.

The Secretariat performs many useful, sensible and much-needed tasks, but a lot of resources are also used in performing tasks which may once have been useful but which are no longer needed. These tasks are like the Flying Dutchman, sailing the seven seas without ever coming into port. The lack of political will among member states to terminate mandates, close down offices and shift resources with sufficient determination means that adjustments are too long delayed and the overall output from the Secretariat is less important, and less relevant, than it should be.

An example of this is the secretary-general's request, made in 2008, for the establishment of several new posts and involving additional staff in the Secretariat's Department of Political Affairs (DPA) with a view to strengthening the UN's capacity for conflict prevention and mediation, and enabling the establishment of regional political offices in some of the most critical regions (West Africa, Central Asia, etc.). This proposal was received favourably by most countries, primarily because putting extra resources into this area would presumably help prevent conflicts or the resurgence of conflicts, in which the human and financial costs would be much higher than the investment in prevention.

However, as this was seen as a Western priority, a number of developing countries reacted by demanding that the Secretariat's Department of Economic and Social Affairs (DESA) should be expanded by at least the same number of new staff members. Not because there was a pressing need for it but in order to create a political balance between what was regarded as a Western priority and a priority of developing countries. The result was, as it nearly always is, a compromise in which everyone gave and everyone received and where consequently DESA was given a number of new posts for which there was no real case and no real need.

This inherent politicization of the budget and staffing decisions means that the secretary-general is normally very reluctant to ask for new resources for any issue – and they are many – which can be taken hostage in a political debate. An example was the preparation for the UN Climate Change Conference in Copenhagen in 2009, where Secretary-General Ban Ki-moon avoided requesting additional staff, by asking instead a number of UN organizations to second staff members to his office, and by asking a number of donor countries, including Denmark, Norway and the United Kingdom, for cash contributions to enable the establishment of a special climate change team which could advise him on climate change issues.

It may seem strange that in new high-priority areas, such as climate change, the secretary-general has to approach selected member states and ask for voluntary contributions, just because it is impossible to move some of the many thousands of staff positions in the Secretariat. It is not rational for the secretary-general to be bound hand and foot in this way, and not to be able to decide how resources within the Secretariat should be allocated to deal most effectively with the tasks which member states have requested the UN to undertake. Moreover, it is difficult to see that it is in the interests of developing countries to give the traditional donor countries the additional influence which comes from their financing these kinds of initiatives, and thereby entering into a close political dialogue with the Secretariat in this regard.

The UN Secretariat has about 35,000 staff. Most of these, roughly 20,000, are civil staff in peacekeeping missions (see chapter 5). The other roughly 15,000 Secretariat staff mainly work in the UN's headquarters in New York, Geneva, Vienna, and Nairobi, or in the five regional economic commissions.[9]

The UN's development and emergency funds and programs are autonomous in many respects and not formally part of the UN Secretariat, even though to a large extent they follow the Secretariat's rules. This applies, among others, to UNICEF with about 11,000 staff (7 per cent are in New York and the rest in 160 locations around the world), to the UNDP with about 8,000, and to the UNFPA, with about

2,000 staff. It is these organizations that provide the UN's global presence.

If one includes the many special agencies, there are more than 150,000 civilian staff in total working for the United Nations, of whom about one-quarter are international civil servants, and about three-quarters are employed locally by the various UN offices, at regional, national, or local levels. It is the international staff members who are generally regarded as being UN officials and who serve in various posts around the world.

Working for the United Nations is not without its perils. A large number of those who are sent abroad by the UN are not permitted to take their families along, especially with peacekeeping missions and emergency aid missions (non-family duty stations). In 2009, forty-five UN staff lost their lives as a consequence of "security-related incidents," as they are called in UN terminology, primarily terrorist attacks. In the 2010 Haiti earthquake, more than one hundred UN personnel died.[10]

In principle, all staff in the Secretariat and in the funds and programs, but not in the special agencies, answer to the secretary-general. The staff members have a duty to disregard their national interests and positions and to serve only the UN. Under Article 100 of the UN Charter the member states on their side undertake not to seek to influence UN staff in the discharge of their responsibilities. Also according to the Charter, the paramount consideration in the employment of the UN staff is "the necessity of securing the highest standards of efficiency, competence, and integrity." At the same time, there must be due regard to the importance of recruiting the staff on as wide a geographical basis as possible (Article 101[3] of the UN Charter).

The idea of an international civil service, whose members' loyalty is due not to their countries of origin but to the international organization they serve, is part of the inheritance from the League of Nations. Dag Hammarskjöld made it clear, in a speech in Oxford in May 1961, that an international civil service was a necessary condition for the United Nations being able to operate in accordance with the intentions of the UN Charter. The idea was that UN staff "must remain wholly uninfluenced by national or group interests or ideologies [and] ... guided solely by the common aims and rules, laid down for, and by the Organization he serves." Hammarskjöld concluded that this is ultimately a question of personal integrity.[11]

The requirements for professional qualifications and integrity and the requirement for geographical diversity are naturally not contradictory. A global organization must clearly be global in its recruitment and personnel policies in order to develop and maintain a true global perspective. It is only when the requirement for staff diversity becomes a requirement for a geographical monopoly on certain positions or when member states put undue pressure on the secretary-general to appoint candidates who are not fully qualified that the requirements are not entirely compatible. And this is what happens.

This applies in particular to some of the more senior posts in the organization, such as the under-secretary-general (USG) and the slightly lower level of assistant secretary-general (ASG) in the Secretariat, and corresponding posts such as executive director and deputy executive director in UN funds and programs or as heads of major peacekeeping missions. These posts are categorized as political, with appointment for a fixed period, and where the normal UN retirement age of sixty-two does not apply.

A special kind of USG/ASG post is the position as head of a peace-keeping mission as special representative of the secretary-general (SRSG – see chapters 4 and 5). SRSGs are appointed by the secretary-general after consultation with the Security Council and the selection process is often fairly obscure. It can perhaps best be described as a diplomatic-political process from which a decision emerges by interaction between the secretary-general and in particular the five permanent members of the council. In some cases the choice falls on high profile politicians, in other cases it falls on experienced UN diplomats. Sometimes it is an advantage for the SRSG to have his or her own roots in the region in question, and in other cases it is not. The requirements and expectations have developed over time and according to the specificities of the situation.

The political nature of these senior posts is emphasized by the fact that all USGs and ASGs submit their resignations when a new secretary-general is appointed, and the secretary-general is under no obligation to reappoint them. Over the years the most important USG positions in the UN Secretariat have increasingly been reserved for candidates from the five permanent members of the Security Council, and there is often a considerable power struggle between regional groups and countries about the right to occupy certain leading positions. This often tends to overshadow the question of the candidate's personal and professional qualifications.

Even though the United Nations is still by and large able to recruit many skilled and competent staff members for leading positions, the increasing tendency to emphasize geographical and political considerations when making appointments is naturally of great concern. In the long run, both the secretary-general and member states should have a shared interest in avoiding the issue of recruitment for senior positions becoming an Achilles heel for the organization. Another problem for the UN is that the salary level is generally below that of corresponding positions in other international organizations. This naturally also influences the base for recruitment.

As with many other international organizations, the United Nations is influenced by many different administrative cultures, which have created a unique example of cross-fertilization. Unsurprisingly, the result is a thoroughly bureaucratic international administrative culture. Recent scandals such as the Iraq Oil-for-Food program (1996 to 2003) led to a tightening up of administrative procedures, which was implemented with the very best of intentions, but has made the administrative system even slower and more bureaucratic. As a result the workings of the system are becoming steadily more complex and opaque. At the same time, the size of the UN system and its division into more or less autonomous entities limits its cohesion. In some cases it has led to the creation of various fiefdoms within the UN, almost self-governing organizations or entities, in constant conflict with one another over the political lines to take and the allocation of responsibilities.

Some critics have even gone so far as to refer to the United Nations as an administratively dysfunctional organization. Many attempts have been made to strengthen the system's cohesion and coordination, especially in the area of development by the establishment of the CEB and the UN Development Group (UNDG), in which all UN development organizations participate and in which general administrative questions are discussed. In the political area the secretary-general regularly meets his key advisers in the Policy Committee. Coordination has been much improved in recent years, but it is still something the UN system definitely needs to work on.[12]

The rationalization and simplification of the UN's procedures are matters of constant debate. Essentially, they must be based on the transfer of decision-making power from the delegates to the Fifth Committee to the secretary-general and the UN's Department of Management, but it will be difficult to get such a proposal adopted.

An initiative by four member states (Chile, South Africa, Thailand, and Sweden) put forward a broad reform package for the area of management, including proposals for a new budgetary procedure, increased transparency, and improved human resource administration. Even though the package was well received, it soon struck the reef of the General Assembly.[13]

INNOVATIVE POLITICAL THINKING

One of the most important tasks of the UN Secretariat, and of the many other organizations, funds, and programs that are responsible for similar tasks in the UN system is to provide classic secretarial support for negotiations between member states. This applies to meetings in the General Assembly, the Security Council, the UNDP/UNFPA Executive Board, the UN Climate Change Conference, or any other intergovernmental body within the UN. This work consists of standard Secretariat tasks: arranging meetings, preparing drafts to serve as the basis for discussions, organizing specific negotiations and ensuring interpretation in all six of the UN's official languages (Arabic, Chinese, English, French, Russian, and Spanish), assisting various chairpersons in their direction of negotiations, interpreting the Rules of Procedure, drafting the conclusions, writing minutes, et cetera.

The UN Secretariat and the staff of other UN organizations have considerable scope for feeding new ideas into the negotiating processes and for influencing decisions, as well as for implementing them in such a way as to introduce innovative approaches and ideas in the area in question. All this makes the Secretariat a key actor in the political manoeuvring around intergovernmental decisions and their implementation. It has been said that the member states may control and direct the organization, but that the Secretariat and the UN's thousands of staff *are* the United Nations.[14]

As stated previously, one of the greatest strengths of the secretary-general's job is that he has the opportunity to use the rostrum of the UN as a global platform to lay out his proposals and initiatives. This bully pulpit of the secretary-general also makes it possible for him and UN system to challenge member states – within limits of course, as a balance always has to be struck. The secretary-general's task is to lead and to show member states the way forward, but it is no good running so far ahead that the member states lose sight of him. It is only leadership if the secretary-general succeeds in pressuring or persuading member states to follow and act on his proposals; otherwise he will just be a brilliant orator or a charismatic celebrity.

Since 1945, the UN's international civil service has developed many new ideas and proposals which have been incorporated in international decision making. Some of these proposals have been realized, others have not. Some have been developed within the system, and others have resulted from fruitful co-operation with academics, NGOs, consultants, lobby groups, and others with whom the UN and UN staff have an ongoing dialogue. The most important of these ideas and proposals are discussed in the other chapters of this book, in their appropriate context.[15]

In the area of peace and security, the United Nations has played a constructive and highly pragmatic role over time in resolving specific conflicts, naturally subject to the Security Council's mandates. The guiding principle has been that the resolution of conflicts should be moved from the battlefield to the negotiating table and should be based on right rather than on might alone. This guiding principle has had its ups and downs over the years, but the overall development has been in a generally positive direction. The secretary-general's good offices and the possibility of entering into preventive diplomacy and offering political solutions to problems have, in many cases, helped to prevent conflicts or the escalation of conflicts. And concepts such as peacekeeping missions, political missions, human rights observers, et cetera, which do not have a basis in the UN Charter but which the secretary-general and the Secretariat have developed over time, have played a decisive and global role in supporting the peaceful settlement of conflicts.

Another notable development in the Secretariat's thinking has been the increasing attention paid to the protection of individuals, not only in the classic human rights terminology but also as the protection of civilians in connection with conflicts. The Secretariat has definitely taken advantage of the fact that the issue of state sovereignty is now open for discussion and that what takes place inside a state can also be of concern to other countries and to the international community at large. Domestic affairs are not what they used to be. As will be discussed in chapter 8, the UN's development of the responsibility to protect doctrine, the Rome Statute of the International Criminal Court, and the actual establishment of the Court itself, has linked human rights and peace and security in an entirely new way.

Not all the UN's proposals for strengthened measures to ensure the peaceful settlement of conflicts have been equally positively received by all member states. Countries that have had significant political or material interests in the continuation or escalation of conflicts have opposed attempts to settle them. Countries which have a problematic human rights situation, and whose governments either cannot or will not ensure respect for their citizens' human rights have actively tried to prevent these questions being addressed by the UN. The Secretariat has been mandated to examine such questions in more detail. However, successive secretaries-general have held fast and step by step have exploited such possibilities as have come their way.

DEVELOPMENT POLICY

In the area of economic and development policy there have been substantial differences between the Secretariat's thinking in different parts of the UN system, and there have been significant policy differences between major groups of member states, particularly between the industrialized countries in Europe and North America (the OECD countries) and the developing countries (G77).

The UN's funds and programs, especially in leading organizations such as the UNDP and UNICEF, have always predominantly based their work on their actual experiences as development actors at country level. They have focused on approaches and practical measures which have been shown to work well in the real world, and which might therefore be scaled up or replicated to create economic development and contribute to the necessary social changes in other countries. These organizations have been fully financed by voluntary contributions from donor countries and their senior management is to a large extent recruited from donor countries. As is made clear in other parts of this book, over the years the UNDP, UNICEF, and the UNFPA have been key to significant advances in development thinking. Meanwhile the approach of these funds and programs has always been to focus on incremental development and on the art of the possible.

It was in the context of UN development activities that ideas about the significance of gender in the development process came to prominence in the 1970s, when the role of women as actors in development was first put on the agenda. Most recently in 2010, this has led to the establishment of UN Women bringing together four smaller programs with the aim of reinforcing the UN's broad efforts in the area of gender equality and women's empowerment, both in combatting violence against women, and promoting women's participation in politics and their economic rights and opportunities.[16]

It was also in the context of the UN that the concept of sustainable development was first developed (see chapter 11). And it was likewise in the UN context that the term *human development* (people-centred development) was first coined and placed on the international agenda when, in 1990, the UNDP began to issue its annual *Human Development Report*. The UNDP developed the Human Development Index (HDI), showing what people-centred development really means. The many tables in the HDI underline that development is not merely a question of income but that it includes factors such as health and education. The Index was created by weighing together various factors: average income per capita, income disparities, average life expectancy, average educational level, and gender differences, so that overall these factors reflect the most important conditions for allowing individuals to realize their potential.

In principle, the HDI covers all countries, but it has only been possible to obtain reliable data for 186 countries. Unsurprisingly, the Western industrial countries score highest. The 2013 index was topped by Norway, followed by Australia, the United States, the Netherlands, Germany and New Zealand. Niger is last, but the situation is not much better in the Democratic Republic of the Congo (DRC), Mozambique or Chad, which also lie at the bottom of the list.[17]

In contrast to the more practical development of ideas and approaches in the UN's funds and programs, the UN Secretariat has traditionally represented a more ideological approach, from time to time also influenced by ideas of global economic planning. The UN Secretariat has often stood rather alone in the UN system, and its proposals for more sweeping global regulatory mechanisms and more comprehensive structural measures have not had their feet on the ground, politically.

However, in some areas the Secretariat has made significant contributions, in particular in the DESA in New York, the United Nations Conference on Trade and Development (UNCTAD) Secretariat in Geneva, and the regional economic commissions, especially the Economic Commission for Latin America and the Caribbean (ECLAC) in Santiago. The work of ECLAC, and later UNCTAD and to some extent DESA, on international trade issues was important in analyzing the negative effect for developing countries of the postwar trade system, and this contributed significantly to the formulation of a more assertive agenda for the developing countries in international negotiations on trade and commodities.

Even though these negotiations may have taken place in other forums, especially in the WTO (formerly the General Agreement on Tariffs and Trade, or GATT), the UN Secretariat has clearly contributed to the development of the ideas of developing countries, paving the way for ensuring better access for developing countries to the markets of the industrialized countries. This struggle has included tackling many of the industrialized countries' protectionist measures and domestic support programs aimed at maintaining production which is no longer internationally competitive (especially the use of agricultural subsidies in the United States and in the European Union).

DESA and UNCTAD have also supported the right of developing countries to protect their own nascent industries against foreign competition in order to enable more local processing of commodities. Such protectionist measures, it is argued, will help these countries overcome the structurally conditioned fall in commodity prices over time and thereby improve their economic situation.[18]

There is little doubt that the intellectual and analytical support which the UNCTAD Secretariat in particular has given developing countries over the years has strengthened these countries' negotiating positions and thus partially made up for the imbalance of capacities which has historically existed in international negotiations between North and South. It is particularly the smaller and economically weak developing countries that have limited analytical and negotiating capacities and often have difficulty in making sufficient resources available to follow the often highly technical and long drawn out international trade negotiations. Many donor countries have also actively supported the building up of such technical capacities in low-income countries, in order to strengthen their ability to fend for themselves and ensure a better functioning international trade system.

The Secretariat's problem has never been a lack of ideas. The problem – and especially DESA's problem – has primarily been an inability to hit the ground running, i.e., to formulate ideas in such a way that they are taken seriously by industrialized countries. It has not always been a question of the ideas themselves. In many situations it has been a question of how and in what context they have been presented, and a lack of openness and consultation with external experts in the design process.

The UN Secretariat – and this also applies to DESA – has a considerable analytical capacity. However, there has been a tendency for this capacity primarily being used for drafting the many routine reports which the Secretariat is required to prepare pursuant to decisions of the General Assembly, ECOSOC or one of the other UN bodies.

The clear political stance by the Secretariat in favour of the political agenda of (some) developing countries has led to a certain scepticism among the industrialized countries with regard to the Secretariat's economic analyses and flagship reports. From an OECD perspective these reports are often seen as painting too pessimistic a picture of the situation and having a certain bias in their proposals. Thus, the UN Secretariat has never succeeded in making its annual *World Economic Situation and Prospects* or other important flagship reports international "must reads" (at least among those in the know) in the same way as the corresponding reports by the OECD and the World Bank. This is probably not entirely justified. Economics is not an exact science, and differing analytical approaches can very well supplement each other and provide important nuances. Among other things, DESA warned about the coming economic and financial crisis in 2008 at an earlier stage than others.[19]

HOW TO STRENGTHEN THE UN SECRETARIAT?

The UN Secretariat's staff and the staff of the other UN organizations, funds, and programs are thus actors in their own right in the international system. The organizations and their staff make the system work in practice, but they clearly also have a role to play in suggesting ideas and making proposals to the member states.

Formally, the authority of the Secretariat to take concrete initiatives vis-à-vis member states is based on the secretary-general's political mandate in the UN Charter. It is the secretary-general who sets the tone and defines the level of the UN's ambitions. In some situations the secretary-general's and the organization's room for manoeuvre is fairly limited. In other circumstances possibilities may arise, and then it is a matter of making the best of these opportunities. These openings may arise because the member states do not really know what to do, or because the decision-making processes are blocked by disagreements so that everybody is looking for a creative way out and it may be up to the UN Secretariat to find the right solution.

In this situation, UN organizations and their staff often find themselves in the eye of the storm. They are subject to considerable pressure from the member states. Some countries will bring pressure to bear on the Secretariat to be less critical when reporting on their compliance with international norms and standards, particularly in the area of human rights. Other countries will try to give the Secretariat good advice about which policies should be followed and which line the UN ought to adopt. In principle, this can very well be a positive contribution to the ongoing dialogue and exchange of ideas, but it can also take a more pressurized form. Yet other countries, or even the same countries, will seek to put pressure for the Secretariat on the appointment of senior staff of the "right" nationality.

The Secretariat is well aware that ultimately the power lies with the member states. The secretary-general also knows that he cannot fight on all fronts at the same time. But few secretaries-general have not, at one time or another, been in strong disagreement with one or more of the permanent members of the Security Council. When he died in 1961, Dag Hammarskjöld was not in great favour in Paris or in Moscow because of his policies in the Congo. Kofi Annan's attitude to the Iraq War in 2003 was not welcomed in Washington. And Ban Ki-moon's position on Kosovo in 2009–10 was far from popular in Moscow. In some cases this has been at the cost of not being reappointed. Trygve Lie resigned in protest in 1952 and Boutros Boutros-Ghali's reappointment in 1996 was blocked by an American veto, even though he had the active support of the other fourteen members of the Security Council.

Even if power ultimately lies with the member states, there is scope for strengthening the UN Secretariat and the staff of the other UN organizations. The starting point would be to strengthen the UN's intellectual leadership – for want of a better term. This means improving the possibilities for the UN to attract the best leaders and the best analytical minds that the world has to offer in specific areas.

This would probably require the organizations' structures to become more flexible and dynamic so that staff resources can be moved quickly and expediently to where there is a particular need for them. There is also a need to reinforce the UN's research capabilities and strengthen co-operation with universities and other research institutions around the world with a view to extending the system's knowledge base and analytical capacity and to ensure that policies and proposals are based on up-to-date research results and analyses. Of course, it is also necessary to do something about the overly bureaucratic administrative system and the time-consuming power struggles between different entities and fiefdoms, which sometimes markedly reduce the system's effectiveness and frustrate its staff.

The UN's staff *is* the UN. A strong and effective secretary-general can lift the spirit of the organization, and the same goes for skilful senior managers in the individual entities within the system. The UN brand opens a lot of doors and creates political openings in a way that is second to none in international organizations. The UN is a large system and it is difficult to master. Those who understand how to make use of the opportunities can achieve a lot.

PART II

Peace and Security

By 8 January 2009, with the fighting in Gaza that had been going on since 27 December, Israeli forces had moved into densely populated Palestinian areas in Gaza City. The news media had only limited possibilities for following developments on the ground, but it appeared that there had been considerable civilian losses among the Palestinians. A number of Arab foreign ministers were in New York, effectively camping out around the Security Council, demanding an immediate ceasefire.

The Arab foreign ministers were all present in the Security Council chamber. France was president of the council for the month of January, and the French foreign minister, Bernard Kouchner, had suspended the public meeting for some hours while negotiations took place behind closed doors. Barack Obama had been elected US president in November, but was only to take office in two weeks' time. It was the outgoing American secretary of state, Condoleezza Rice, who flew up from Washington to take part in the Security Council meeting.

The chamber was filled to the rafters. The fifteen members of the Security Council were there, of course, as were many others – ambassadors, diplomatic observers and news media. The US ambassador to the UN, the Afghan-born Zalman Khalilzad, did not conceal from his colleagues that he had recommended to Washington that the United States should vote in favour of the resolution which demanded an immediate cessation of hostilities and full Israeli withdrawal from Gaza. But he was uncertain whether the Bush administration would accept his recommendation. The president himself would decide, and Rice was waiting for an answer directly from the White House.

Suddenly there was a stir in the room. The Americans were ready; Rice came in and went straight to her chair at the horseshoe-shaped table around which the Security Council meets. Kouchner opened the session and Resolution 1860 was put to the vote. When asked who voted in favour of the Resolution, fourteen hands went up. None voted against. There was one abstention as Rice put up her hand. The Resolution had been adopted, but the United States had distanced itself from what could have been a clear and unambiguous message from the Security Council to Israel.

It took another ten days before Israel declared a unilateral cease-fire and ended its military action.

4

The Security Council

The Security Council shall determine the existence of any threat to the peace, breach of the peace, or act of aggression and shall make recommendations, or decide what measures shall be taken.

Article 39 of the UN Charter

THE UN SECURITY COUNCIL

Ask anyone how they visualize the UN and most people will probably have two images in mind. The first will most certainly be the speaker's rostrum in the General Assembly Hall, which is undoubtedly the most famous podium in the world, and the place from which virtually every statesman and head of state or government has addressed the world at the opening of the annual sessions of the assembly in September – from John F. Kennedy and Nelson Mandela to Robert Mugabe and Muammar Gaddafi. The second image will almost as certainly be of the Security Council's horseshoe-shaped table, at which representatives of the fifteen members raise their hands to vote on a decision that is intended to put a stop to some belligerent action, as during the Six Days War in the Middle East in 1967, or to authorize the use of force, as in Iraq in 1990 or Libya in 2011.

These two images encapsulate the United Nations both as a forum for the exchange of global visions and ideas, for better or for worse, and as a forum for action on behalf of the member states.

The image of the Security Council will normally be linked to one or more specific occasions. Historically, the council's most famous meeting was held on 25 October 1962, when the United States demanded that the council be convened to discuss the Soviet Union's installation of nuclear-armed missiles in Cuba, which would be able to reach the United States within minutes. This was unacceptable to the United States, and President Kennedy contacted Soviet leader Nikita Khrushchev demanding that they be removed. At the same time the Kennedy administration initiated a widespread campaign to win over both American and world opinion in favour of this stance, into which the Security Council was naturally drawn. During the "thirteen days in October" the world stood on the brink of nuclear war, and the Cuban missile crisis was unquestionably the most dangerous situation between the great powers during the Cold War.

In the Security Council, it came to a showdown between the US ambassador to the UN, Adlai Stevenson, and his Soviet counterpart, Valerian Zorin, who was also the president of the Security Council for that month. Zorin tried to evade the question of the presence of Soviet nuclear missiles in Cuba, and accused the United States of presenting false evidence. Stevenson asked Zorin directly whether he would deny that there were medium-range missiles in Cuba. "Don't wait for the translation. Yes or no?" Zorin answered: "I am not in an American courtroom," to which Stevenson responded, "You are in the courtroom of world opinion right now and you can answer yes or no ... I am prepared to wait for my answer until hell freezes over, if that's your decision," Stevenson then had the evidence brought into the Security Council chamber and set about sharing it with international news media and everybody else watching. The exchange between Zorin and Stevenson has been repeated countless times in accounts and films on the Cuban missile crisis, and it shows the Security Council acting as a battleground during the Cold War, enabling one of the parties to demand an answer from their counterpart here and now.[1]

The UN Security Council is the world's most exclusive club. It originally consisted of eleven members: five permanent and six others who were elected for two years at a time and who could not be immediately re-elected. In 1965, the number of elected members was increased to ten, so that today the council consists of fifteen members.

However, the power in the Security Council has always been in the hands of the five permanent members, in other words the five victors in the Second World War: China (represented by Taiwan until 1971, but since then by the People's Republic of China), France, the Russian Federation (originally the Soviet Union), the United Kingdom, and the United States. This is mainly because under Article 27(3) of the UN Charter, the five permanent members have a right of veto, so that any of them can at any time block a decision or resolution by voting against it. While this happens from time to time, the possibility of a veto can in itself impact negotiations in the Security Council, which is highly focused on the interaction between the P5, the five permanent members. The five permanent members represent nearly 30 per cent of the world's population and over 40 per cent of the world's economy. Together they have 26,000 nuclear weapons, amounting to 99 per cent of all existing nuclear weapons, and collectively they have 5.5 million people under arms. The P5 are therefore still the world's military great powers.[2]

As distinct from the P5, the ten elected members (often called the E10) are divided among five regional groups: Western Europe and others (WEOG), Eastern Europe, Asia, Africa, and Latin America. It is considered very important – and prestigious – to serve as an elected member of the Security Council. In some regional groups the seats on the council are distributed through fixed geographical rotation within the group (especially among the African countries), but in most groups, and especially in the WEOG and in the Eastern European group, there is often a contested election for the seats on the council, i.e., there are more candidates than seats available.

The veto power means that in controversial political questions the ten elected members are mostly just bystanders. However, on issues on which the permanent members are generally on the same political wavelength, and which are thus not perceived as controversial or divisive, the elected members have greater possibilities for influencing decisions.

Among other things, the elected members can obtain influence by chairing Security Council committees, by entering actively into the drafting of the council's resolutions and, when they serve as president of the council (the presidency rotates each month), by setting the agenda and taking up various themes, such as the protection of civilians, climate change, or peace and security in various other contexts. Also, one should not underestimate the power which comes from the political desire of the permanent members that as many decisions as possible should have the unanimous support of the Security Council. This gives the elected members the opportunity of influencing the content of council resolutions, especially if they act together.

The Security Council has a unique mandate and legitimacy. Under the UN Charter, the international use of force (i.e., where one or more states use force in relation to another state) is only lawful in the case of self-defence (Article 51) or if it is authorized by the council.

In contrast to the General Assembly and other UN organs, the Security Council can adopt legally binding decisions. This means that the fifteen council members can decide on behalf of the 193 member states of the United Nations in matters concerning threats to international peace and security. The council can authorize the use of force, whether in the form of sanctions against states or persons, such as trade restrictions (prohibitions of exports and imports), freezing of financial assets, inspections of ships, prohibition of aircraft landings, and travel restrictions on individuals. The use of force can naturally also take the form of military action. The council can authorize the use of armed force and thus give authorization under international law for the United Nations itself or for member states to intervene militarily in other countries.[3]

Thus the Security Council has a unique position in global decision making. This is one of the reasons why, after Iraq's military occupation of Kuwait in August 1990, US president George H.W. Bush went to the UN Security Council, first with a demand for economic sanctions against Iraq and then, on 29 November 1990, put forward Security Council Resolution 678, giving Iraq a deadline of 15 January 1991 to withdraw its troops from Kuwait. If it did not do so, the Resolution authorized member states "to use all necessary means" to force Iraq to leave Kuwait.

Security Council Resolution 678 was adopted by a vote of twelve to two (Cuba and Yemen). What was more important was that China, which could have imposed a veto, chose to abstain. There was no doubt about the choice of words: "All necessary means" means the use of military force. During the autumn of 1990 the United States had established a broad international coalition behind military operations against the Iraqi dictator Saddam Hussein, and obtained agreement to use Saudi Arabia as the main hub for the military operations. But the Security Council authorization was important. Resolution 678 legitimated the military action, both under international law and in the eyes of global public opinion.

The same did not apply in 2003 when the United States, under President George W. Bush (son of President George H.W. Bush) once again decided to use military force against Iraq. Iraq's failure to comply with a long list of Security Council resolutions had resulted in an increasingly tense confrontation between Iraq and the international community. On 8 November 2002, after extended negotiations between the governments of the P5, the council unanimously passed Resolution 1441 which authorized the UN weapons inspectors to return to Iraq to try to uncover the extent to which Iraq was in possession of weapons of mass destruction.

Resolution 1441 emphasized that by its failure to co-operate with the UN, Iraq was in material breach of its obligations under the 1991 cease-fire, but in contrast to Resolution 678 in 1990, Resolution 1441 did not authorize military intervention against Iraq. The American and British efforts in February 2003 to get agreement on a second resolution giving a clear mandate for the use of force against Iraq led to French and Russian indications that they would veto such a resolution.[4]

In this situation the US administration sought to create a new "Adlai Stevenson moment," by going to the Security Council and presenting the evidence showing that Iraq did indeed have weapons of mass destruction and that these weapons had been kept hidden from the UN weapons inspectors who had returned to Iraq following the adoption of Resolution 1441. Secretary of State Colin Powell was given the task of presenting the evidence to the Security Council at its meeting on 5 February 2003, with the director of the CIA, George Tenet, sitting right behind him to emphasize the credibility of the intelligence.

Powell's presentation included enlarged satellite photographs shown on video screens, and clips of internal Iraqi conversations. However, the evidence presented was much more circumstantial and much less convincing than Stevenson's had been in 1962, and it did not shift public opinion or any votes in the council. There was a good reason for this; as time would show, Saddam Hussein had no weapons of mass destruction at his disposal by 2003.[5]

When it became clear that, regardless of the French and Russian vetoes, the Bush administration probably would not even get the nine votes required for a majority for a resolution in the Security Council, the United States chose not to put a resolution to the vote, but to continue the buildup for military intervention in Iraq in March 2003 without a clear Security Council mandate. The lack of a council mandate, and the lack of global legitimacy which this involved, fundamentally put in question the lawfulness of the intervention under international law. In September 2004, the UN's then secretary-general Kofi Annan told the BBC that, in his view, the second Iraq War had been illegal under the UN Charter.[6]

The two Iraqi wars are contrasted here in order to emphasize that the Security Council's decisions can be significant. The council can decide to adopt sanctions which all UN members are required to comply with or ultimately to authorize the use of armed force against a country which, in the view of the Security Council, constitutes a threat to international peace and security. In doing so it is interpreting how to define a "threat to the peace" or "breach of the peace," which are the terms used in the UN Charter.

There has clearly been some development in the understanding of these terms. In 1945 a breach of the peace was seen as being a country's attempt to change its situation by the use of force. This understanding has gradually developed so that a breach of the peace now also encompasses circumstances within a country which constitute a threat to mankind, not least in relation to gross human rights violations such as under the apartheid regime in South Africa or Sudan's treatment of some of the tribal groups and peoples in the Darfur region. International law and the view of what constitute a threat to the peace is a living concept which the Security Council and especially the P5 have a high degree of responsibility for protecting and enabling to develop (see also chapter 8).

As is the case in many other parts of the UN system, the Security Council is restricted in what it can and cannot do by what its members, and especially the five permanent members, will agree to. During the Cold War, the council had very limited scope. The United States and the Soviet Union held each other in check, and if one of them saw an advantage in using the Security Council as a forum for taking up a specific political issue, one could be quite sure that the other would do everything to prevent it.

At the start of the Korean War in June 1950, the United States received authorization from the Security Council to help South Korea defend itself against an attack from the North. This only happened because the Soviet Union boycotted the council in protest against the fact that the People's Republic of China was still not allowed to take China's place in the Security Council (as said, this first happened in 1971). This was a mistake which the Soviet Union did not repeat. Neither the Soviet Union's suppression of the popular uprising in Hungary in 1956 nor the invasion of Czechoslovakia in 1968 left their marks in the form of a Security Council resolution. However, this did not prevent the Western members from using the Security Council as a platform for the ideological contest and criticism of the Soviet Union during the Cold War. During the invasion of Czechoslovakia in August 1968, the Czech foreign minister was brought to New York

and in the Security Council he expressed Czechoslovakia's unwillingness to receive the Soviet "fraternal support," which was how the Soviet Union described its military occupation. The US ambassador to the
UN, George Ball, noted that the Soviet veto of a Security Council resolution condemning the occupation of Czechoslovakia was the 105th
veto by the Soviet Union since the Security Council had been established.[7]

The United States has been particularly concerned not to have the
Security Council becoming too substantially engaged in political
issues in the Middle East, and especially the Israel-Palestine conflict,
as this might question the US role as the main actor and mediator in
the region. This does not mean that over the years the council has not
discussed developments and adopted resolutions on the Middle East.
On the contrary, the council regularly discusses the Middle East, not
least in connection with armed conflicts, of which there have been
many, most recently in the Gaza territory in 2008–09.

Unquestionably the Security Council's most important resolution
on the Middle East has been Resolution 242 in November 1967,
adopted following the Six Days War in June 1967. It continues to be
the political fulcrum for Israeli-Palestinian negotiations on an enduring settlement of the conflict. The resolution defines the principles
for a settlement in very clear terms. Israel should withdraw its armed
forces from the occupied territories in return for respect for Israel's
sovereignty, territorial integrity, and the right to live in peace within
secure and recognized borders. This quid pro quo is normally summarized under the heading of "land for peace."

The role of the Security Council in relation to the Middle East
is normally limited to confirming what has been agreed in other
forums, in particular in recent years within the framework of the Middle East Quartet (the EU, Russia, the UN, and the United States). As
already stated, the council regularly discusses developments in the
Middle East, now in the form of routine monthly meetings, but the
United States' clear and unmistakable desire to play a leading role, and
the Israelis' and Palestinians' equally clear acceptance of this American leadership, has created a situation in which the role of the Security Council is effectively fairly limited.

If, from time to time, anyone has not fully understood this, the
United States has always been ready to impose the necessary veto. For
example, this happened on 18 February 2011, in the vote on a proposed Palestinian resolution, formally submitted by Lebanon as the

Arab member of the council, which characterized the Israeli settlements in the occupied Palestinian territories as *illegal* under international law (pursuant to the Fourth Geneva Convention, which prohibits the colonization of occupied territory). However, this is not the term used by the United States. In US terms the Israeli settlements are only *illegitimate*, not *illegal*, and this difference was enough to make the United States impose a veto.

The Middle East has generally been an equally difficult subject for the EU member states to deal with in the Security Council. Despite more than thirty years of efforts to coordinate the EU member states' policies on the Middle East, since the Venice Declaration in 1980, there are still considerable differences between European countries on the subject of the Israeli-Palestinian conflict. This means that the EU, as an observer, normally restricts its dealings with the council to carefully negotiated submissions during the debates.

In the spring of 2011, the Security Council demonstrated a considerable, and for many an unexpected, ability to act on two questions. The first concerned Côte d'Ivoire, where the council maintained a very broad mandate for the UN peacekeeping mission and supported the UN forces when in March, together with French forces, they intervened decisively in a situation which appeared to be developing into a civil war and succeeded in putting a stop to the emerging conflict. The background to this was that the opposition candidate, Alassane Ouattara, had defeated the sitting president Laurent Gbagbo in Côte d'Ivoire's presidential elections in November 2010. President Gbagbo, however, refused to leave office and resisted increasing pressure from the UN, the Economic Community of West African States (ECOWAS), and the African Union (AU). The UN peacekeeping force took an increasingly military role in the dispute between Ouattara and Gbagbo, and ultimately helped arrest Gbagbo so that Ouattara could move into the presidential residence in Abidjan.

The Security Council also demonstrated its ability to act in relation to the situation in Libya in 2011. After the Arab Spring had spread from Tunisia and Egypt to Libya, opposition forces had taken control of the eastern part of the country and Libya's long-serving dictator, Muammar Gaddafi, threatened to use his military forces to make reprisals. There was a real fear of a full-scale bloodbath in Benghazi and in other towns which were controlled by the opposition. Therefore, in February 2011 the council unanimously imposed an arms embargo on Libya, froze Libyan assets in foreign banks, and requested the International Criminal Court to assess whether there had been serious crimes in connection with the conflict. The aim was to put pressure on Gaddafi and to halt his military progress against the towns controlled by the opposition.[8]

This resolution did not succeed in its aim and a few weeks later, on 17 March 2011, in Resolution 1973 the Security Council therefore authorized the use of "all necessary measures to protect civilians and civilian populated areas under threat of attack in the Libyan Arab Jamahiriya, including Benghazi, while excluding a foreign occupation force of any form on any part of Libyan territory." This decision was taken in close co-operation with the twenty-two member states of the Arab League, but not without some concerns on the part of some members of the Security Council. The Resolution was adopted with ten votes in favour (one more than the majority required), and five abstentions including two permanent members, China and Russia. The African members (Gabon, South Africa, and Nigeria) provided the decisive votes in favour of the Resolution, while Brazil, India, and Germany abstained together with China and Russia. The fact that neither China nor Russia blocked the Resolution by using their veto was presumably out of concern for what Gaddafi might do to the civilian population in the area controlled by the opposition. Neither Beijing nor Moscow wanted to take responsibility for that.

The Security Council's mandate to take all necessary measures gave a green light to an international coalition of the United States and European and Middle Eastern countries to initiate an air offensive to halt Gaddafi's progress toward the eastern part of the country. Together with the almost contemporaneous offensive in the Côte d'Ivoire, the Libyan decision seemed to herald a more active role for the council in the protection of civilians.

While in the spring of 2011 the Security Council appeared in a more active role in relation to Côte d'Ivoire and Libya, it afterwards proved impossible for the council to reach agreement on a response to the Syrian government's brutal suppression of its own people. As in other countries in the region, the Arab Spring led to tens of thousands of young Syrians taking to the streets of Damascus, Homs, and Aleppo, spontaneously raising demands for freedom and democracy after decades of brutal suppression by Bashar al-Assad's regime. Russia and China in particular opposed the imposition of sanctions on Syria and on a number of occasions (in October 2011, February 2012, and July 2012) as the situation in Syria deteriorated both countries vetoed resolutions which were supported by the other permanent members and the majority of elected members. The Russian position was undoubtedly influenced by geopolitical considerations, trying to maintain a foothold in the region, but in retrospect it also seems that the bold decisions on Libya could be interpreted as a deviation from, and thus a de facto undermining of, the principle of non-intervention in the domestic affairs of other countries, to which Russia and China attach great importance (see chapter 8).

ENLARGEMENT OF THE SECURITY COUNCIL?

As stated above, the Security Council is the primary UN body dealing with international peace and security. The UN member states have an obligation to comply with the council's binding decisions and ultimately the council can enforce its decisions by sanctions and by authorizing the use of force. However, the United Nations has no army of its own, so it is dependent on countries being willing to take the lead in military actions, as the United States did in the First Gulf War in 1991, and as France, the United Kingdom, and the United States did in Libya in 2011. If no member state is willing to take on such tasks, the Security Council has no means for enforcing its decisions.

In the real world, its strength and its ability to enforce its decisions depends to a great extent on the Security Council's legitimacy. This legitimacy is a reflection of the council's role in international law, but also of historical and political developments. Key concerns in this regard are the council's moral authority and credibility, and its representativeness. A Security Council that is united sends out a much stronger signal to the international community than a Security Council that is divided. The fact that all council members agree on a decision, regardless of whether they are Asian, African, or European, and regardless of whether they are permanent or elected members, strengthens the political legitimacy of the decision and the credibility of the council. This is why in practice so much effort is put into getting everyone on board and to have as many decisions as possible adopted unanimously.

The composition of the Security Council has not changed since it was enlarged to fifteen members in 1965. The permanent members (China, France, Russia, the United Kingdom, and the United States) have five seats. The Western countries (Western Europe plus Canada,

Australia, and New Zealand) have two elected seats, and the Eastern European countries have one seat. This allocation goes back to the days of the Cold War. This means that today there are EU member states (such as Germany and Spain) that are members of the Western group, and EU member states (such as Poland and Estonia) that are members of the Eastern European group. The UN election system is one of the last places in the world where the Cold War regions still exist.[9]

Latin America and the Caribbean countries have two elected seats in the Security Council, while Africa and Asia form one group which elects members to five seats. The reason that Africa and Asia form a single group is to take account of the "Arab swing seat." There is an informal agreement that one of the five seats for Africa and Asia will always be taken by an Arab country, alternately in Africa (North Africa) and in Asia (Jordan, Saudi Arabia, the Gulf states, and so on, which are members of the Asian regional group). Of the remaining four seats, two go to Africa (minus North Africa) and two go to Asia (minus the Arab states). Thus the African-Asian group effectively covers three groups of countries.

Asia contains more than half the world's population, and given global demographics, the number of countries, and the economic strengths of the different regions, there is no doubt that Europe is over-represented in the Security Council. Europe has two permanent members with veto rights (France and the United Kingdom), and up to three elected members (for example in 2011 it had Germany, Portugal, and Bosnia and Herzegovina as European members). This gave Europe five votes, or a third of the total votes in the council.

It has been clear for many years that the Security Council is not representative of the United Nations' membership as a whole, and this view is generally not challenged. Most countries agree that there is a need to reform the council's composition to make it more representative of the member states, and thus more legitimate. But that is where the agreement ends.

The question of enlarging the Security Council has been on the UN agenda since 1992. For the first sixteen years, the issue was discussed by a working group, where it was a condition that decisions could only be taken unanimously. This was much the same as saying that no decisions should be taken at all. However, since 2008 the matter has been discussed in the General Assembly, where it is possible to put the issue to the vote. This has given the process a new negotiating dynamic and the question of Security Council reform – primarily enlargement of the council in both categories, that is permanent and elected members – is now back on the international agenda. But member states are still eyeing each other up, and so far progress has been going at a snail's pace.

One of the challenges is that the Security Council's legitimacy is not only secured by its representativeness, it also depends on its ability to act. Ideally the legitimacy of the (preferably unanimous) decisions of the Security Council should be supported by the council being geographically and preferably also politically representative of member states as a whole. But if such an ideal council is not able to act quickly and effectively in a crisis, it will lose some of its moral authority. One need only think of how the council lost a great deal of credibility by its inaction in relation to the genocide in Rwanda in 1994.

The challenge thus lies in balancing the representativeness of the council and its ability to act. An enlargement of the Security Council must strike the right balance between these two aspects and ensure that both considerations are taken into account in the best possible manner. If enlargement happens, it will have to encompass both permanent and non-permanent members. There has always been a majority of elected members, so that if, for example, the number of permanent members were to be increased from four to six, it would be logical to increase the number of elected members from at least one to three in order to retain a majority of non-permanent members.

The driving force behind enlarging the Security Council is the so-called G4 collaboration between Brazil, Germany, India, and Japan. These four countries have taken a "musketeer's oath" – one for all and all for one – under which they all seek permanent membership of the council. Regard for the council's effectiveness means it would be politically impossible (at least for the time being) for them to have a veto power in the same way as the existing P5 countries, but that is not an insurmountable problem for these four countries. It has been many years since France or the United Kingdom last used their vetoes, though as indicated above, France threatened to do so in relation to the proposed Iraq resolution in 2003.

In order to ensure representativeness, the G4 have proposed that there should also be two new permanent members from Africa. This would result in an allocation of permanent seats in the council, apart from China, Russia, and the United States, with one to Latin America

(Brazil), three to Europe (France, Germany, and the United Kingdom), two to Asia (India and Japan), and two to Africa. The additional one to three non-permanent seats should go to the regions which have the fewest seats in relation to the number of member states (that is Asia, Africa and Eastern Europe).

Any change to the composition of the Security Council would require an amendment to the UN Charter. Any revision of the Charter requires a two-thirds majority in the General Assembly and ratification of the amendment by two-thirds of the member states, including all five permanent members of the Security Council. The P5 thus have a veto with regard to amendments to the UN Charter. When the council was last enlarged, France and the Soviet Union voted against, the United Kingdom and the United States abstained, and only China (at that time Taiwan) voted in favour. However, subsequently all five permanent members chose to ratify the amendment to the Charter and the enlargement of the council entered into force on 1 January 1966.

Unsurprisingly, the strongest opposition to the G4 proposal comes from those countries which see themselves as being excluded from obtaining a permanent seat if the proposal were accepted, regardless of how realistic or unrealistic such expectations may be. It follows that neither Italy nor Spain think it is a good idea that Germany should be given a permanent seat, which would only serve to reinforce the idea of an EU Directorate consisting of the "big three" EU member states (France, Germany, and the United Kingdom). Pakistan's enthusiasm for India's permanent membership of the Security Council is fairly muted, as is that of Mexico and Argentina in relation to Brazil's ambitions. These countries have therefore become the leaders of a group called Uniting for Consensus, which is primarily united in opposition to the G4 proposal and in encouraging a continued search for broad agreement on the enlargement of the council.

However, what is really delaying any decision is the African position. The African countries have agreed to stand together on this issue, and there is a high-level decision of the AU on this; however, what they have agreed to stand together on is less clear. There most probably will not be more than two permanent seats for Africa, and one of the problems is how to deal with the Arabian seat, which is a general problem in relation to permanent seats on the council. Should one of the two permanent African seats go to a North African/ Arabian country, or should they both go to sub-Saharan Africa? Which countries are possible candidates: Egypt, Nigeria, South Africa? What are the implied expectations for the political and economic stability of a country with permanent-member status on the Security Council? How can permanent seats be reconciled with the usual allocation of seats in the UN's organs between the African sub-regions, and between anglophone and francophone Africa?

These questions are not easy to answer, and in the absence of an answer the African countries have asked for the impossible: two permanent seats with full veto power, and for Africa alone to decide which countries should fill these seats. The explicit call for veto powers in itself puts a stop to further discussion, and the African countries know this. Their negotiating tactic is to put down a marker with an unrealistic opening gambit which they have maintained for some time. With fifty-three votes, the African group has more than a quarter of the UN's members and thus a substantial portion of the minority required to block the two-thirds majority required to amend the Charter. The trouble for the African group is that some of the countries which could become permanent members of the Security Council, in particular South Africa, increasingly appear to feel that putting down this marker leaves them out in the cold, which is not as comfortable as being invited to come inside and have a place at the table.

This gridlock has intensified efforts to find a solution which, in line with established diplomatic practice, is not entirely clear but perhaps for this reason may be better able to build a bridge between the two opposing negotiating sides (G4 and Uniting for Consensus). This would be a bridge over which the African group could walk, as it has been expressed.

The proposed solution essentially expresses an ambition to solve the issue in a way which will make it possible to describe the glass as being either half full or half empty, depending on the perspective. And in this case the glass is an intermediate solution.

The idea would be to institute a new category of Security Council members, which would be neither permanent nor elected for the usual two years at a time but rather elected for periods of perhaps four to ten years. For those countries that aspire to permanent membership, such a solution can be presented as a first step toward permanent membership, especially if the period is long enough and if the arrangement is reviewed at the end of the first period so that at that point it will be possible to demand that the arrangement be amended and be turned into permanent membership. For those countries that are opposed to at least certain new permanent members, such an arrangement can be a lesser evil, especially if the period is shorter and if it is possible to propose opposing candidates to a country in the new category, making such new arrangement more like the existing arrangement with elected members. In this context the decisive question is whether a country could be elected to membership of the council for a new period immediately after the expiry of an existing period. The UN Charter does not presently allow this.

The negotiations on the enlargement of the Security Council are ongoing, and will probably continue for some years to come. The United States has doubts about the ability of the council to act if it were enlarged with more than a few members, but it is also aware that, in the long run, the council's composition must be more representative in order to justify its unique powers. The United States rightly emphasizes that the council's legitimacy has not so far been questioned.

As described above, the G4 proposal would increase the number of permanent members by at least six, i.e., enlarging the council from fifteen to at least twenty-one members, but in reality further increasing it by at least an additional one to three elected members, both out of regard for balance in the council and to make it attractive for a broad group of member states to support the enlargement. The more elected members there are on the Security Council, the greater the chances of smaller countries becoming members of the council from time to time. The United Nations has more than one hundred member states with populations of fewer than 10 million people, and there are still many countries that have never been council members.

REGIONAL REPRESENTATION

The Security Council's legitimacy is unlikely to be questioned in the medium term. It is also clear that a larger council would be less able to act and be less effective in a crisis. In the real world, it is primarily the P5, and especially the US Senate, which must be persuaded that enlargement with new members would be the best way to secure the council's future.

Enlarging the Security Council will not occur spontaneously, but the pressure for it exists. In the long run, the council can only maintain its legitimacy if its composition becomes more representative. This not only applies to geographical representation, it should also reflect balances of power at regional and sub-regional levels. Nigeria is a major power in West Africa and the leading country in ECOWAS. If there is a regional conflict in West Africa, the international community would expect Nigeria to engage in finding a political solution and by contributing troops to any UN military operation.

In the light of this, it is difficult to argue that Nigeria does not to some extent outweigh Benin or Mali. Likewise, it would expected that Brazil would be an important actor if problems were to arise in Latin America, and Brazil is also in important contributor of troops to the UN peacekeeping mission in Haiti. South Africa plays a key role both in the AU and in the Southern African regional organization SADC, even though South Africa has been very hesitant about putting its weight behind the demands made on Zimbabwe by the international community.

One important part of the emerging thinking on integrated conflict resolution is expanded co-operation between the Security Council and the regional organizations. Political and economic instruments generally play an increasingly important role, alongside military solutions and peacebuilding initiatives. In practice, this requires the leading regional powers to be drawn more into the political processes of the Security Council. This applies not only in respect of their capacities as (potential) troop contributors to UN operations, but also to their political influence in their regions and their scope for supporting threats of sanctions which have been effective instruments, in particular in West Africa, in putting a cap on spiralling military coups.

There is no doubt that the votes of Turkey and Brazil, in the spring of 2010, against stricter sanctions on Iran gave pause for reflection. After many months of negotiations, the P5 countries had reached agreement on tightening up the sanctions regime because of Iran's non-compliance with the demands of the International Atomic Energy Agency (IAEA). The P5 clearly expected the ten elected council members to fall into line and vote in favour of what the P5 proposed. However, both Turkey and Brazil voted against, arguing that the scope for negotiation had not been exhausted. Resolution 1929 of 9 June 2010 was nevertheless adopted with twelve votes in favour and two against, with Lebanon abstaining. This meant that the resolution did not have the legitimacy which a unanimous Security Council would have given it, and thus in most Western eyes it did not have the impact on Iran that was hoped for.

The five permanent members may now be able to assess how new permanent members of the Security Council would act. The council's composition in 2010–11 could very well serve as laboratory for an enlarged council, as some of the most likely candidates for a permanent seat were members during this period. This applies to Brazil (2010–11), Germany (2011–12), India (2011–12), Japan (2009–10), Mexico (2009–10), Nigeria (2010–11), South Africa (2011–12) and Turkey (2009–10). Not least because of the formally established IBSA co-operation (comprising India, Brazil, and South Africa) there were some expectations with regard to these three countries' simultaneous membership of the council. Many Western countries hoped that democracies such as India, Brazil, and South Africa would have overlapping interests with Western members in relation to protection democratic rules, and taking action against undemocratic regimes' violent repression of their own people.

What conclusions can be drawn from the prospective permanent members' participation in the Security Council's work in 2010–11? There is no doubt that the IBSA countries in particular were hesitant about the council being too active in specific crises and generally displayed a non-interventionist attitude. This was most notable with the adoption of sanctions against Iran in the summer of 2010, to which Brazil and Turkey voted against while Russia and China voted in favour, and in the context of the Libya decision in March 2011 when Brazil, India, and Germany abstained along with Russia and China.

The Libya resolution, and the way it was interpreted by the coalition taking charge of the military intervention, resulted in much closer co-operation in the council between the IBSA countries, Russia, and China. This alignment was apparent in the vote on Syria in October 2011, when both Russia and China imposed a veto and the IBSA countries all abstained. It also applied to Côte d'Ivoire, where it probably was only the very clear position of Nigeria and ECOWAS that made it possible to ensure respect for the democratic process, despite Russian opposition and lack of co-operation from South Africa. And at the end of 2011 it proved difficult for the council to send a clear message to Sudan, because of Russian and Chinese reluctance to criticize the regime in Khartoum, again to some degree backed by the three IBSA countries.

It is not difficult to understand the background to this. For India the conflict in Kashmir and its insistence of non-interference in that conflict probably very much affects New Delhi's perspective. And although South Africa's experiences from the struggle against apartheid should lead to human rights considerations being very high on its agenda, ultimately it might be more politically tempting to encourage the loyalty of other African rulers, whatever their misdeeds (Zimbabwe's Robert Mugabe comes to mind). And finding Brazil in this camp, a country and a government that is otherwise strongly associated with the defence of human rights, might be a reflection of a long history in which Brazil has never actually fought a war.

However, seen from Washington, London, and Paris, the immediate conclusion could easily be that emerging global actors such as India, Brazil, South Africa, and Turkey would only reinforce the traditional Russo-Chinese resistance to "interference" in countries' internal affairs. They could very well divert the Security Council from the emphasis on the protection of civilians and embryonic application of the concept of the responsibility to protect. It becomes harder to put pressure on Russia and China if they have the backing of IBSA and are able to hide behind the regional leadership and democratic legitimacy of India, Brazil, and South Africa.

This analysis could cast doubt on whether the ongoing efforts to reform and enlarge the Security Council will succeed. Maintaining the council with its present composition, however, will not prevent the council from being confronted with a more non-interventionist group of countries formed around Russia, China, and a number of the emerging powers. There are indications that a number of the emerging powers will seek election to the Security Council at increasingly shorter intervals. That means that India, Brazil, South Africa, and Turkey will continue to seek membership with the same frequency as Japan and Germany (i.e., every third or fourth two-year term). That might lead to even more competitive elections for seats in the council, and it will probably also put a further damper on the political activism of these countries. It is probably easier for an emerging power to achieve the necessary two-thirds of the votes of the General Assembly if it has a more cautious profile in international relations and does not align itself too closely with Western positions.

For the time being the smaller countries look on from the sidelines. The scenario described above will make it more difficult for smaller countries to win a seat on the council. At the same time it is clear that the larger countries have more to contribute, both politically and with regard to the practical implementation of Security Council decisions. This means that their participation often helps strengthen the council's legitimacy. On balance, this means that smaller countries may become council members at ever greater intervals in the future – but also that this might be a price worth paying.

If at some point the General Assembly decides to enlarge the Security Council, this can be done in one of three ways. It can take form of an increase in the number of permanent members in the traditional form (but without veto powers), as well as in the number of elected members. It can be by introducing a new category of members, elected for a longer period and with the possibility of being re-elected. Or it can be done by merely increasing the number of elected members, combined with allowing members to seek immediate re-election. All three solutions will require an amendment of the UN Charter.

If the first solution is chosen, the lack of a veto power for the new permanent members would, of course, make them less full members than the existing P5, but this is probably a less important difference than might appear. It is not difficult to imagine that the veto will be less used in future, and that, for example, India as a permanent member of the Security Council without a veto would come to hold more power than its former colonial power, the United Kingdom, despite its ability to cast a veto.

There are already movements underway to get the existing permanent members to declare that they will refrain from using their vetoes in cases involving genocide. The P5 countries do not, in principle, make such declarations, but if there were a repetition of the genocide in Rwanda in 1994, the use of a veto would presumably have such political consequences around the world that a permanent member would be extremely careful in using it. The world has changed. International relations, including in the Security Council, is now conducted openly before the world, and sailing against the stream of media images and global opinion has its costs. The council's handling of the situation in Libya in the spring of 2011, and the Chinese and Russian acceptance of military intervention partly reflects this change.

The expected global bipolarity, with China and the United States at opposite poles, will probably affect the Security Council in the future. Russia will still be a major power, but its sphere of interest will probably be more limited, with its focus on its more immediate neighbouring regions, where it has important political and commercial interests (the Balkans, Georgia, Iran, the Middle East, and North Africa). The interests of the United States are global and have been so for decades. What is new is that China also has growing global interests to protect, not least in relation to security of its supplies of energy and other raw materials and the protection of its investments in other developing countries. This makes China an important new player in the Middle East and Africa.

It will be essential for the Security Council that the United States and China establish a functional working relationship for dealing with threats to international peace and security. China's basic stance is to be cautious and to adhere to the principle of non-intervention in the domestic affairs of other countries (Article 2[7] of the UN Charter), but it will come under increasing pressure to accept sanctions, as in recent years in relation to Sudan, North Korea, and Iran. Better dialogue in the council with major regional powers such as Brazil, India, and South Africa, and their expected leadership on threats and difficult political situations in their own backyard, will not make it easier for China to adopt a stance which is at odds with global public opinion.

Thus, the debate about the effectiveness of an enlarged Security Council goes both ways. Having more members, and especially having more permanent members, means there will be more parties in the inner circle where the decisions are taken, and this means that the decision-making process will be more complex. But it will also lead to a broader acceptance of the decisions, especially if the major regional powers are involved in promoting the decisions in their own regions. And it will also make it easier to implement decisions if the major economic powers, countries with significant regional influence and some of the biggest contributors of troops to UN peacekeeping operations are also sitting at the table where the decisions are taken.

What is important is that enlarging the Security Council should help maintain and even reinforce the council's legitimacy. If an enlargement of the council with the addition of more permanent members and more elected members were at the same time to ensure both the council's legitimacy and its ability to act, this would clearly be the best deal possible.

It would presumably help strengthen both the legitimacy and the effectiveness of the Security Council if countries such as Brazil, Egypt, Germany, India, Indonesia, Italy, Japan, Mexico, Nigeria, Pakistan, South Africa, Spain, and Turkey were to be elected more frequently than in the past. This would, however, be at the expense of the participation of smaller countries in the work of the council, creating a situation where the majority of UN member states – the more than one hundred countries with populations of less than 10 million each – will be even further distanced from the work of the Security Council. It will be difficult to strengthen the representativeness and the effectiveness of the Security Council without a downside.

5

Peacekeeping Operations

UN peacekeeping operations are now increasingly complex and multi-dimensional, going beyond monitoring a ceasefire to actually bringing failed States back to life, often after decades of conflict.

Secretary-General Kofi Annan

FROM RALPH BUNCHE TO LAKHDAR BRAHIMI

United Nations peacekeeping operations originated as a response to ceasefires or temporary peace agreements between two countries, where the UN, with the consent of the parties to the conflict, placed a lightly armed UN force in an area on both sides of the border between the parties. These are the well-known blue helmets, which are the most recognized symbol of UN troops. Such a UN peacekeeping force would give the temporary agreement between the parties its basic international legitimacy and would in principle be regarded by both parties as being impartial. The most important task of the UN force would be to ensure compliance with the agreement while negotiations continued on the terms for a final peace settlement.

However, this concept is no longer typical for the UN's peacekeeping operations. Today peacekeeping operations have become much more militarily challenging and they are conducted with a much greater emphasis on the active protection of weak and threatened parts of the population.

International institutions are often created with a view to what has gone before, much as generals often seem to be fighting their previous war. There is not a word about peacekeeping operations or peacekeepers in the UN Charter. The key provision in the Charter is in Chapter VI and in Chapter VII, Article 42, which mandates the

Security Council to take such action by air, sea, or land forces as may be necessary to maintain or restore international peace and security.

The Charter provisions are linked to the United Nations' role as a collective security system. As stated previously, the United Nations took on this role in connection with the Korean War in 1950, when the Security Council authorized US-led operations to counter North Korea's invasion of South Korea. The circumstances surrounding this decision, primarily the absence of the Soviet Union from the council, were unusual and the Korean intervention is the only example of peace enforcement under UN auspices during the Cold War.

However, already in 1948, prior to the Korean War, in an effort to find a solution to the conflict between the Israelis and the Palestinians after the formation of the state of Israel, the UN sent peace negotiators to the Middle East. The first of these was the Swedish diplomat Folke Bernadotte, and following his assassination by the militant Israeli Stern group, the American UN diplomat Ralph Bunche negotiated a ceasefire in the area in 1949. The United Nations Truce Supervision Organization (UNTSO) was set up to monitor this ceasefire; it still exists and is thus the oldest functioning United Nations peacekeeping operation.

A few months later a second UN monitoring mission was established in Kashmir, on the borders between India and Pakistan. This group, the United Nations Military Observer Group in India and Pakistan (UNMOGIP), is also still an active peace operation.

The real breakthrough for what became the classic model of UN peacekeeping came with the Suez crisis in 1956. This conflict was provoked by Egypt's nationalization of the Suez Canal in July 1956. The canal had hitherto been owned jointly by France and the United Kingdom. The nationalization led to military intervention by France, the United Kingdom, and Israel against the wishes of the United States. After the ceasefire between Egypt and Israel, in November 1956, the Security Council voted to set up a United Nations Emergency Force (UNEF) to monitor the agreement.

It was in connection with this decision that the United Nations developed its fundamental principles for peacekeeping operations: acceptance by the parties, impartiality of the UN force, and the minimal use of force. The original UNEF peacekeeping force was mobilized very quickly, with the active involvement of Secretary-General Dag Hammarskjöld. Military contributions were made by countries that were far removed from the conflict and which were considered acceptable by all, including Brazil, Canada, India, and the Scandinavian countries. Altogether 6,000 troops were deployed, mostly in the Sinai Peninsula, and the operation continued until 1967 when the Egyptians demanded that the troops be withdrawn shortly before the start of the Six Days War in June 1967.[1]

The scope for the United Nations to establish a peacekeeping (military) operation with the aim of contributing to the resolution of armed conflicts, regardless of the nature of the conflict (i.e., both conflicts between states and conflicts within states) depends on the Security Council deciding on a specific mandate for such an operation. For many decades the Cold War and competition between the Soviet Union and the United States strictly limited the role which the United Nations was allowed to play in various international conflicts. However, in a number of situations there was some scope for an active role for the UN.

In the Middle East, the UN's active engagement and the maintenance of UNEF in the period 1956–67 created the basis for a number of subsequent UN peacekeeping missions: UNEF II in the Sinai from 1974–79 (up to the Camp David Accords), the UN Disengagement Observer Force (UNDOF) in the Golan since 1974, and the UN Interim Force in Lebanon (UNIFIL) in Lebanon after 1978. But the Middle East has been the exception, not the rule.

Other than in the Middle East there were very few actual UN peacekeeping operations up until 1989. By far the most important were the UN Operation in the Congo (ONUC) in 1960–64, and the UN Peacekeeping Force in Cyprus (UNFICYP) since 1964. In addition there were briefer missions in Western New Guinea (part of Indonesia), Yemen, and the Dominican Republic in the mid-1960s.[2]

When the United Nations was established in 1945, experience showed that the great majority of conflicts in the first four decades of the twentieth century had been conflicts *between* states. This naturally influenced the thinking in relation to the future UN role collective security. However, soon after 1945 the opposite was shown to be the case. Even though there have still been wars between states (Suez 1956 is an example), the great majority of conflicts in the world since the end of the Second World War have been within the territory of a single state, with parties from within that state – though often with the active support of other countries for some of the parties in the conflict.

The fall of the Berlin Wall in 1989 and the end of the Cold War changed this situation dramatically. The five permanent members of the Security Council (China, France, Russia, the United Kingdom, and the United States) naturally still had their different interests to promote and defend, but they were no longer engaged in a bitter ideological struggle with each other. This created new possibilities for the UN in the area of peacekeeping in the 1990s.

This decade became crucial for the development of UN peacekeeping. The new Russian Federation had to find its feet in international politics, and China was in the process of making a dramatic change in its domestic economic policies and still only cautiously engaged in issues outside its immediate neighbourhood. Because of this the United States had the windfall opportunity to play a very dominant role in shaping international relations. The many internal conflicts in Africa were no longer pawns in an ideological confrontation between the Soviet Union and the United States, where either one or the other of these powers blocked any kind of UN intervention. At the same time, the breakup of Yugoslavia and the Balkan wars of the 1990s created a political and diplomatic space in which it was expected that the United Nations could and would play a role. In both contexts, the main emphasis quickly moved from the classic focus on wars between states to a new focus on civil wars and armed conflicts within states. This change, which became very clear in the course of the 1990s, created a whole new field for the further development of UN peacekeeping concepts.

It was like shaking a ketchup bottle: "First none'll come, and then a lot'll." New international conditions created a renewed demand for peacekeeping operations under the auspices of the UN, but it took some time for this potential to materialize.

The start was modest. In 1997, the total strength of UN peacekeeping forces was only about 15,000, but over the next decade this was multiplied by eight times to about 120,000. Only the United States has more troops actively involved in international military operations. While, during the Cold War, the main emphasis of the UN's peacekeeping operations had been in the Middle East, the rapid expansion since the late 1990s has mainly taken place in Africa.

The first new peacekeeping experiences after the end of Cold War were difficult for the United Nations. The theory was fine, but the reality was markedly different. The UN struggled with what to do and when to do it, and the organization basically felt its way forward for most of the 1990s.

Many mistakes were made, often leading to tragedies. Not least the genocide in Rwanda in 1994, when an estimated 800,000 people were killed in the course of three or four months while the UN and the Security Council pondered what to do, clearly showed that the UN often did not make a proper prior evaluation of the situation and often deployed its forces in hopeless situations. The same applied to the Srebrenica massacre in Bosnia in July 1995, where 400 Dutch soldiers, in what was inappropriately called the United Nations Protection Force (UNPROFOR), did not have a mandate to intervene to prevent the killing of thousands of Bosnians.

The problem was that the United Nations, and especially the Security Council, had not thought through how the organization should deal with situations where one or more of the parties to a conflict simply pulled the carpet from under the UN operations and to some extent breached the agreements and understandings under the eyes of the UN troops. This new reality made it clear that UN peacekeeping operations often had insufficiently clear rules of engagement, unclear lines of command, poor intelligence, and limited analytical capacity, coupled with the problems of moulding together forces composed of troops from many different countries so as to function effectively. The political will was there, but the capacity on the ground was lacking.

The turning point for the UN's peacekeeping operations came with the publication of the Brahimi Report in 2000, drawn up by an international panel headed by the former Algerian foreign minister, Lakhdar Brahimi. The Brahimi Report emphasized the necessity of the United Nations having a coherent and thoroughly considered approach to peacekeeping activities. Thus the report underlined the importance of the civilian aspects of peacekeeping operations and of the initiation of peacebuilding measures as early as possible. The report emphasized that the establishment of effective policing was essential, as was the building up of local political systems and judicial systems and measures to reinforce respect for human rights and the rule of law. However, the key message was the need to create integrated missions in which military, police, and civilian efforts could support each other, underpinned by sufficient and sufficiently qualified resources.

It was stressed that, in connection with UN peacekeeping operations, all these elements had to be put in place quickly and that planning for a coherent and integrated UN mission therefore had to start even before the Security Council had given a mandate for the operation. UN forces should have the necessary authority to carry out their duties professionally, and they should be able to defend themselves and their mandates if one of the parties to the conflict seeks to undermine or threaten the operation.

UN forces should therefore have militarily robust rules of engagement which were able to ensure the necessary respect for the concerted efforts of the UN forces. According to the Brahimi Report, this meant that UN forces should be larger in numbers and better trained. This would, of course, make the operations more costly, but it would also result in operations that were able to fulfill their goals and have the necessary credibility and military authority on the ground.[3]

There are a number of different forms of peacekeeping operations under the auspices of the UN, as different situations require different kinds of measures. Today the United Nations carries out peacekeeping operations of the classic kind, securing a ceasefire between two consenting parties and not much more, based on Chapter VI of the UN Charter. This is the case in Cyprus, for example, where the UN has maintained a peacekeeping force (today of about 900 troops) since 1964 on the border between the Greek and the Turkish Cypriots. In contrast, new peacekeeping operations are much more complex and involve many different elements. Modern peacekeeping operations are multi-dimensional, requiring a much higher degree of coordination between military and civilian operations than was previously the case, and they seek to develop exit strategies early on, through early planning for subsequent peacebuilding measures. The catchphrase is that "peacekeepers are the first peacebuilders."

Since 2000, UN peacekeeping operations have been planned on the basis of the Brahimi Report, and they are thus much more concerned with the broad spectrum of military, humanitarian, political, and civil measures in order to stabilize a situation, consolidate a political peace agreement, and create incentives for the parties to the conflict to continue to work for peace and not be tempted to resort to armed conflict again. This means that modern peacekeeping operations are often more political and diplomatic than military in character, and the fact that they are sometimes also closely linked with emergency situations means that there are sometimes humanitarian operations as well.

Other important elements of modern peacekeeping operations include undertaking political reforms, organizing judicial systems, improving prison facilities, demobilizing soldiers, disarming and re-integrating former combatants into civilian life, and mine clearance. At the same time, purely military mandates have been strengthened, as mentioned above. UN troops have always been entitled to use military means in self-defence, but beyond this the earlier mandates for using military force were very limited. In recent years there has been a strengthening and clarification of mandates in relation to the protection of civilians, particularly women and children, and the military capabilities and ability to react have also been improved, among other things by the use of armoured vehicles and attack helicopters which are among the heavier weapons in the UN's military arsenal.

The difference between the former peacekeeping operations and today's the more complex operations reflects the fact that armed conflicts are now predominantly internal rather than between countries. To a large degree, classic peacekeeping operations depend on the consent of the parties, which means that there are limited demands on the military capabilities of UN forces. In more complex operations, where the parties are not states but warring parties within a state, getting the consent of the parties is often more problematic. In many cases, one or more of the warring parties does not accept the Security Council's mandate for the UN forces, or the parties may be very loosely structured movements or militias which do not have the ability to find internal agreement and are unable to comply with agreements with other parties or with the UN.

This makes new and different demands on the mandates for UN forces and on the UN troops who act under the mandates. The mandates are usually robust and they require robust implementation. The mandates define the limits set by the UN and what UN forces will accept on the part of the warring parties. If one or more of the parties to a conflict seeks to challenge the UN, the UN troops can and must react, if necessary by using arms.

This has an effect on the requirements for the training, armaments and equipment of UN soldiers, and also affects expectations as to their attitudes and value systems. The individual officer or soldier must be able and willing to use such means as are necessary for fulfilling the mandate for the operation. As stated, most of today's UN peace operations are carried on the basis of Chapter VII of the UN Charter, which permits the Security Council to take such action as may be necessary to maintain or restore international peace and security. This means that mandates are usually tailor-made to the specific situation and they are often changed in line with developments in the area of operations.

Peacekeeping missions are normally led by a senior civilian UN official, the special representative of the secretary-general (SRSG), who has overall leadership of the operation, both its military and civilian components. This underlines the fact that a UN peacekeeping operation is not merely a military operation.

A number of issues and challenges, of course, continue to exist with regard to the specific political mandates, the size of troop contingents, their training, equipment or general ability to fulfill the key protection tasks. But serious efforts are being made to solve these problems and to continue to improve the quality of peacekeeping operations.

CHALLENGES FACING UN PEACEKEEPING

The Security Council provides the framework for the UN's peacekeeping operations. Thus, in order to establish a peacekeeping mission the council must have the political will to act on the conflict in question. In the first instance this will often be in the form of an attempt to calm the conflict at an early stage by diplomatic means, and to the extent that this succeeds, to ensure the cessation of hostilities. A decision to deploy a UN peacekeeping force will normally only be made later, and often only after a ceasefire or temporary peace agreement.

As a starting point, there must be a peace to keep, in other words an acceptance by the parties that the United Nations has a role to play in relation to the implementation of a ceasefire or peace agreement, and that UN forces will be able to help consolidate such an agreement. This applies equally to internal conflicts and agreements between local hostile parties, though as noted before it can sometimes be difficult to get a proper acceptance of the UN's role from all the parties to a conflict.

In addition, the establishment of a UN peacekeeping operation and the deployment of soldiers and police officers must be thoroughly prepared politically, financially, and logistically. It is also important to create a reasonable degree of coherence between the mandate (understood as the Security Council's formulation of the aims of the operation) and the resources which can reasonably be expected from the UN member states for carrying out the task. This was also an important conclusion of the Brahimi Report.[4]

Here it is necessary to distinguish between the UN operations (normally under the title "UN Mission to ...") which are what this part of the book primarily deals with, and operations with a UN mandate. A

UN-mandated operation refers to often very comprehensive international operations carried out under a mandate from the Security Council but not under the control of or financed by the UN. The most well-known recent example of this is the international operations in Iraq when in August 2003, nearly half a year after the US-led intervention, a unanimous Security Council agreed to give a UN mandate to the international coalition under the leadership of the United States. But it applies equally to the international operations in Afghanistan since 2001, where NATO has been at the forefront of the International Security Assistance Force (ISAF) operation, which is financed by the participating NATO countries and their allies.

The UN peace operation in Darfur (African Union UN Hybrid operation in Darfur, UNAMID) is jointly led. The operation in Somalia (African Union Mission in Somalia, AMISOM) is another kind of hybrid. It is led by the AU under a mandate from the UN, and with the EU as the foremost financial contributor. In 2008 the UN secretary-general sought backing for a UN mission in Somalia, and contacted about fifty member states to make troops available. No country gave a positive response and instead AMISOM was established as an AU mission, mainly operating around the capital Mogadishu.

In early 2013, the UN had fourteen of its own peacekeeping operations, meaning military missions with a mandate from the Security Council, carried out under the leadership of the UN, organizationally based in the UN Secretariat's Department of Peacekeeping Operations (DPKO), and financed out of the UN's peacekeeping budget. The actual number changes from time to time. Sometimes missions are brought to an end, sometimes they are divided, and sometimes new missions are established by decision of the council.[5]

Altogether about 113,000 personnel are deployed on these operations, of whom about 82,000 are military. The biggest and most difficult operations are in Sudan where the mission to Darfur (with UNAMID's nearly 25,000 personnel) and two new missions in South Sudan (with together about 13,000 personnel) together account for around 35 per cent of the UN's total peacekeeping budget. Other large UN missions are the UN Organization Stabilization Mission in the Democratic Republic of the Congo (MONUSCO) with about 23,000 personnel, including military, police, and civilian; the UN Mission in Liberia (UNMIL) with about 9,500 personnel; and UNIFIL in Lebanon with about 12,000 personnel.[6]

The basic principle for the United Nations' peacekeeping activities, and for the work of the UN in general, is not neutrality but impartiality. This means that the United Nations should not just find the midpoint between the opposing parties and treat them in the same way, but that the UN's position to a conflict, its causes and its consequences, should reflect the values on which the organization is based. If one of the parties to a conflict is closer to applying these values than the other parties, impartiality means that the UN will have to take that into account in the various demands which it makes on the parties. Impartiality therefore means that the United Nations may very well find itself in a situation where it has to treat the parties to a conflict differently.

As already pointed out, in recent years there has been increased attention on the issue of peacekeeping forces and the effective protection to civilians. A number of important mandates have been adopted by the Security Council on women, peace and security (Resolution 1325 in 2000), on children in armed conflicts (Resolution 1625 in 2005), the protection of civilians in general (Resolution 1674 in 2006), and on the use of sexual violence in armed conflicts (Resolution 1888 in 2009).

Resolution 1325 not only concerns women as victims in conflicts but also as important partners in the political resolution of conflicts and as necessary actors in peacekeeping operations. Resolution 1674 reflects the clear focus in recent years on reinforcing the provisions on effective protection for civilian populations.

The protection of civilians is now a consistent part of Security Council mandates for peacekeeping missions and one of the essential tasks for all UN peacekeeping operations. However, there is often some uncertainty about how the mandate and the instructions to UN troops should be implemented in practice.

The degree to which UN troops have the authority to intervene when civilians are threatened is not always clear. This involves the abilities of the troops in question, their attitudes and morale, and not least leadership at all levels of UN operations. It is naturally the job of the military leadership to turn Security Council mandates into operational instructions which are fully comprehensible to the individual soldier, so as to leave no doubt about where the thresholds for action lie.

The increased focus on the protection of civilians has led to the development of an approach that focuses on three different levels of intervention. First, there is protection by means of political processes in order to reduce the level of violence, which is by far the most effective. Second, there is the direct protection of threatened groups of people, which is the classic form of protection of civilians and makes great demands on the numbers, mobility, and training of UN forces. And finally, there is the creation of a protective environment by building up a country's own institutions, particularly its police force, which are linked to the more long-term reconstruction and peace-building agenda.[7]

Considerable attention has rightly been paid to the issue of sexual violence in armed conflicts. In 2010, the secretary-general appointed the first special representative (SRSG) on Sexual Violence in Conflict, Margot Wahlström, who was formerly an EU commissioner and who reported directly to the Security Council on this issue. The focus has been particularly on the situation in the eastern part of DR Congo, which is the most problematic area in what was already one of the world's most fragile societies with the lowest level of institutional reach. Prosecutors in DR Congo regularly point to the repeated, planned, and deliberate use of sexual violence, including mass rape by armed groups, usually rebel fighters but sometimes also government soldiers.

There have been severe criticisms of the failure of the UN forces in DR Congo (MONUSCO) to intervene. While, by virtue of its major civilian and military presence in DR Congo, the UN has the possibility of reacting more directly in relation to government soldiers who commit assaults (for example, by depriving them of UN food rations and logistical support), it is more difficult to take effective measures against rebel troops. The problems are not made any easier when, despite a very clearly stated zero tolerance for sexual assaults, there are reports that UN troops themselves have committed such assaults on the civilian population.

Such conduct is extremely damaging for the credibility of the UN's peacekeeping operations. The UN has pointed to the limited number of military forces available in the areas in question, and the lack of information-gathering capacity and mobility (primarily helicopters) which would make it possible to quickly transfer MONUSCO troops to areas where there are reports of mass rape or other atrocities. For this reason, steps have been taken to provide UN forces with more effective means of communication and to strengthen co-operation with intelligence services which know the area.[8]

At the same time, attempts have been made to obtain more helicopters, particularly for MONUSCO in the DRC, and for the missions in

Sudan and South Sudan. Demand for helicopters naturally changes over time and varies from mission to mission. This being said, there seems to be an almost permanent shortage of helicopters in the UN peacekeeping operations, which seriously hampers the mobility of the missions and their ability to move troops quickly to areas where they are needed. The effect of this shortage is that the missions in general have to rely more heavily on patrolling by vehicles, which is far less effective than using helicopters.

A UN peacekeeping mission has many tasks: the protection of civilians, reform of the security sector, disarming and re-integrating ex-combatants, mine clearance, logistical assistance in the conduct of elections and human rights monitoring are key elements of many mandates.

At one time, the UN mission to DR Congo had forty-one different mandates, each based on a specific Security Council resolution, but the various mandates had not at any time been prioritized. Not surprisingly, there are so many mandates that the individual operations almost collapse beneath their weight, and most of the mandates are only half implemented.

This situation is further complicated by the fact that it is difficult for the United Nations to recruit sufficient and sufficiently well-qualified civilian staff for its many peacekeeping missions. It is not always easy to get civilian staff to serve under the very difficult conditions in an area of conflict and with a security situation which means that they usually cannot bring their families. Ultimately it is necessary to make difficult choices and to acknowledge that it is impossible to do everything at once, which will inevitably disappoint some local expectations.

There is considerable risk associated with trying to go too far, too fast, and in believing that in a few years it is possible to patch up what are, more often than not, likely to be long-lasting, deep, and fundamental conflicts in a society. There is no doubt that the mandates for the largest UN peacekeeping missions, as in DR Congo and the Sudan, are very exacting and cover large geographical areas, with only a modest number of UN troops per square mile. The lack of helicopters and the limited mobility of UN forces do not make it any easier.

THE EXAMPLE OF LIBERIA

The UN Mission in Liberia is more geographically limited, which may be one of the reasons why it appears to be on the road to success.

At the same time it reflects the development from a more traditional peacekeeping operation to a more modern multi-dimensional one.[9]

Fourteen years of civil war in Liberia were brought to an end in 2003, with a peace agreement between the opposing parties. The civil war had caused between 200,000 and 250,000 deaths, and more than 1 million people (one-quarter of the population) lived either as internally displaced persons or as refugees in neighbouring countries. As part of the peace agreement the country's former dictator, Charles Taylor, was exiled to Nigeria. When in 2006 Nigeria made it clear that Taylor would be handed over to international prosecutors in order to face charges for war crimes and crimes against humanity, he fled again, and was arrested in northern Nigeria before being handed over to Liberia. From there he was immediately handed over to the Special Court for Sierra Leone in The Hague. In April 2012, Taylor was convicted on all eleven charges against him and sentenced to fifty years in prison.

The peace agreement contained a request to the United Nations to deploy a peacekeeping mission in Liberia with a view to stabilizing the fragile peace and supporting the interim government. The Security Council decided to send a force of up to 15,000, which has been there since then, primarily in the capital Monrovia, with detachments in other parts of the country, in order for the UN forces to control the whole of Liberia. UNMIL has succeeded in keeping the peace in Liberia since 2003, but the focus of the mission has changed considerably along the way. First, the UN forces have been reduced as the political stability in the country has improved and the risk of the civil war flaring up again has diminished. UNMIL now consists of about 7,000 soldiers, and the number of local detachments has also been reduced. Next, the recruitment and training of the Liberian police force has intensified, and the judicial system, the prison service, and border controls have also been strengthened to some extent. Finally, the United States has taken on the building up and training an entirely new Liberian army which will be able take over responsibility for the country's security in a few years. Liberian-US relations have always been close. Liberia was founded by freed American slaves in the first half of the nineteenth century, and the descendants of those slaves held power in Monrovia up until 1980.[10]

The United Nations has also paid greater attention to stimulating economic growth in Liberia (see also chapter 6). In recent years, there has been significant economic growth in the country (over 7 per cent

growth per year since 2005), though of course from a very low base. It
will take many years before the Liberian economy is fully restored,
even to its pre-conflict level. The economy was almost ground down
to nothing by the fourteen years of civil war, and the task of economic reconstruction and development has been, and remains, massive.

The expectations are that UNMIL will continue to be reduced in
numbers as the political and security situation in the country becomes
more stable and resilient. But the regional situation also plays an
important role. In 2011, the conflict in Côte d'Ivoire caused a large
flow of refugees into Liberia, and a number of Liberian rebels who
had settled in Côte d'Ivoire have presumably returned among the
refugees. In the longer term this can threaten the positive political
process and the reconciliation that has taken place in recent years, and
raises doubt about how soon the UN forces can be phased out. It is
essential that the Liberian police force should be able to maintain law
and order in the country. It may thus be necessary to phase out UNMIL's
police component more slowly than the military part of the operation,
to match the buildup of the country's own police force.

The presence of UN forces influences the country in many ways.
The troops are visible on the streets, not least in critical situations
where they perform important logistical tasks, including in connection with elections. They are also an economic factor in the country.
UN operations in Liberia have a total annual budget of about US$520
million, which is around the same size as Liberia's total annual state
budget for 2011–12 of about US$516 million. However, it is assumed
that only 5 to 10 per cent of the peacekeeping expenses are spent in
Liberia. Most of the money is used for salaries which are paid to soldiers in their own countries and on equipment for the operation, pro-
cured from outside the country. Nevertheless, a number of Liberians
work for UNMIL, which gives them useful training and work experience that they will hopefully be able to use elsewhere in the country
when the UN mission is eventually phased out.

THE FUTURE OF PEACEKEEPING

In 2012–13, the total budget for the UN's peacekeeping operations
was US$7.3 billion, of which around 35 per cent was spent on opera-
tions in Sudan.

The biggest expenditures are salaries, equipment, and logistics, but
even so the UN's peacekeeping operations can generally be regarded

as shoestring operations, i.e., they are generally fairly simple and low cost. UN operations are much less expensive than the high-technology military operations which countries such as the United States have engaged in recent years in both Afghanistan and Iraq. The cost of keeping each American soldier in Afghanistan is about US$1 million per year, while the cost of a typical soldier in a UN peacekeeping operation is about one-tenth of that. This, of course, reflects the fact that UN peacekeeping missions generally do not have very advanced equipment or much firepower at their disposal.

Even where a Security Council mandate is very robust, it is usually directed at dealing with rebel forces and militias with limited availability of advanced weapons. In principle, the UN can ask the member states to make more advanced equipment available for UN missions, but experience shows that it is difficult to persuade them to do so.

Peacekeeping operations are financed by the member states, each of which pays an assessed contribution determined by the General Assembly on the basis of a specific scale of assessment for peacekeeping. This is slightly different from the usual UN scale of assessment, as the permanent members of the Security Council all pay a mark-up compared to the regular budget. The United States is the largest contributor, paying 27.1 per cent of the total; Japan comes next, paying 12.5 per cent, and the United Kingdom pays 8.1 per cent. The share of most of the poorest developing countries is 0.001 per cent.[11]

About 114 of the United Nations' 193 member states make troops available for UN peacekeeping operations, but the great majority of the soldiers and police officers who serve in these operations come from just a few Asian countries. Bangladesh (with nearly 9,000), Pakistan (with nearly 8,000), and India (also with nearly 8,000) are the biggest contributors of troops for UN operations, and have been so for some years.

These countries generally have large numbers of troops available, and participation in United Nations operations is a chance for them to show their material support for the UN by engaging so visibly in peacekeeping activities. Countries that make troops available to the UN are compensated for it on the basis of politically negotiated average costs. Countries with relatively high cost levels, such as most Western countries, receive less than full coverage of their actual expenditures for providing troops and equipment, while for countries with lower salary and cost levels, contributing troops for UN operations is unquestionably more financially rewarding.

The five permanent members of the Security Council only provide a limited number of troops for UN peacekeeping operations. However, the United Kingdom provides troops for the Cyprus operation, China has provided military engineers for the Darfur operations and overall contributes almost 2,000 troops and France is a major contributor of troops to UNIFIL. The United States has only contributed around one hundred military observers and police officers since the United States does not, as a matter of principle, place American troops under "foreign" command. On the other hand, the United States often contributes significant amounts of logistical support for the various operations. This was the case in the very rapid and effective American support for the United Nations Stabilization Mission in Haiti (MINUSTAH), when Port-au-Prince was hit by a major earthquake in January 2010 in which UN headquarters and offices were destroyed and more than one hundred UN staff members died.

Recently, European countries have provided more troops for UN operations, primarily in the Balkans and the Middle East. For example in Lebanon, UNIFIL is an operation with notable participation of European countries, especially by France and Italy. Most European countries, however, are cautious about getting too deeply involved in African operations, and only 2 per cent of the UN forces in Africa are provided by European countries.

This is due to the difficult and unknown circumstances surrounding peacekeeping in Africa, both in terms of logistics and security and with regard to the risk of contracting tropical diseases. However, it is also due to the ambition of the African states themselves to provide more troops for operations in Africa, under the heading African solutions to African problems. Where this solution is not possible, host countries often prefer Asian troops to troops from former colonial powers.

The EU made a significant contribution to the start of operations in Chad in 2008 when, under a mandate from the United Nations, twenty-three European countries established European Union Force Chad (EUFOR) with 3,700 personnel to protect civilians and provide emergency aid until March 2009 when the UN was in a position to take over responsibility for these tasks with the establishment of the United Nations Mission in the Central African Republic and Chad (MINURCAT).

Recently, the Security Council has again picked up the thread of the Brahimi Report from 2000, with a view to making the deployment of

UN peacekeeping missions even more effective. The background to this is both the significant growth in this area since 2000, and the assumption that it will not be possible for member states to increase their troop contributions at the same rate in future, as defence bud-gets around the world are generally facing cuts. The discussions are taking place under the heading of the New Horizon Initiative, driven mostly by the UN Secretariat. One of the most important questions is how to ensure better coordination between the Security Council's formulations of the specific mandates for individual operations on the one hand, and the capacities, ambitions, and demands of the troop-contributing countries on the other.

It is important for the council to have its feet on the ground and to secure the backing of troop-contributing countries (TCCs), so there will be no great delay in mobilizing UN forces when these are need-ed. The key to coping with this challenge is to ensure, as far as possi-ble, that there is an alignment between what is desirable in a given situation and what is realistic to expect.

Another key issue is the need to ensure that UN missions have suf-ficient capabilities to carry out their tasks. As stated above, the nature of United Nations peacekeeping operations has become ever more complex, calling for increasingly specialized skills from troop con-tributors. There is still a need for infantry soldiers with blue helmets and rifles, but less so today than previously. The most urgent need today is for helicopters and other mobile units that can move troops around quickly and give added firepower when needed.

There are also issues concerning the sharing of intelligence infor-mation, including satellite monitoring, which can be essential for planning and implementing specific field operations. And finally there is the question of whether there is the suitable military-planning capacity for the operation, and whether the troops, and the police officers and civilian staff which are increasingly involved in peace-keeping operations, have the necessary training in the special tasks which more complex and multi-dimensional peacekeeping operations involve.

The question of the training and preparation of the UN troops, and thus the capacities of the TCCs, is central to the discussions. Building up military capabilities in TCCs is not a task for the United Nations. If such efforts are needed, they must be carried out by countries which have the economic resources to do so, in close co-operation with the relevant regional actors. For example, the United States has put a lot of effort into the training of African troops so they can be deployed in the AU-UN mission in Darfur, and many other partners are working on assisting African military forces to develop the capabilities necessary for them to gradually take over the manning of a greater part of peacekeeping operations in Africa. The ambitions of the AU and its decision to create a standing African force are an important background to these efforts.

When the parties to a conflict are urged or persuaded by the Security Council to cease hostilities and start peace negotiations, and when as part of a peace agreement they often request the council to establish a UN mission to help them keep the peace, this is primarily because of the council's unique status and legitimacy as the UN institution dealing with international conflicts and threats to international peace and security (see chapter 4).

The fact that the United Nations is normally able to deploy the desired forces in the course of a few months and is capable of providing the necessary financial means to maintain the mission as long as the mandate is in force reinforces the council's status. The legitimacy of the Security Council and its proven ability to act – when not blocked by any of the permanent members – are important parameters in any consideration of whether, for example, to seek a corresponding regional solution through the AU.

It is difficult to predict developments in peacekeeping over the next decade. What will happen will depend on many factors, including the extent to which the world makes progress in the prevention of conflicts and in the more effective use of political mediation at an earlier phase of a conflict, before the parties to a conflict actually resort to arms. The UN's Department of Political Affairs (DPA) is seeking to develop its capacities in this area, and the same applies to a number of regional or sub-regional organizations.

With the main focus of the UN's peacekeeping operations in only three countries (the three operations in Sudan and South Sudan and the operation in DR Congo), the developments in these countries alone could be decisive for the overall size of UN peacekeeping operations. DR Congo's president Joseph Kabila does not hide the fact that he would like to see the UN's mission in Congo restricted to the eastern part of the country around Kivu and Ituri, and thereafter wound up. This is primarily based on the argument (which is not widely shared internationally) that the Congolese authorities and armed forces are now able to deal with the problems in the country.

The situation in Sudan is, if possible, even more fluid. The division of the country in July 2011, and the establishment of the new state of South Sudan, has not solved the border problems or the outstanding issue of sharing the oil revenue, and the risk of conflict between Sudan and South Sudan remains high. At the same time, there is nothing to indicate that the situation in Darfur is getting any closer to a solution.

The UN's work on peace and security, and its deployment of peace-keeping troops in specific situations, is characterized by a considerable degree of uncertainty and change. The prevailing circumstances are constantly shifting, and however skilled one may be at picking up warning signals, one will always be surprised how quickly some situations can reach a political meltdown. Events across Africa in recent years have demonstrated how inflammable a situation can be after an election, especially if the result goes against the ruling party. The tense situations and disturbances in Kenya in December 2007, in Zimbabwe in May–June 2008, and in Côte d'Ivoire after the elections in November 2010 are all examples of this and underline the need for the United Nations to closely monitor the political climate before, during, and after such elections. Peaceful transitions from government to opposition after elections are seen, with Ghana as probably the best example, but it is not a given in Africa as a whole.

It normally takes some months to establish a UN peacekeeping mission. The preparatory work includes review missions to formulate the force specifications and requirements and then the troops required must be found. This is normally done by a force-generation process in which the UN invites the member states to put forward their offers for specific capacities. The DPKO then reviews the various offers, appoints the force commander and leading officers, and seeks to assemble a well-functioning military operation.

It is easier to attract troop contributions for some peacekeeping operations than for others. Sometimes member states almost compete to be allowed to contribute. On other occasions the United Nations has to search long and hard for troops as well as for civilian personnel. It is also important to ensure that the overall mission is functional, and that the different contributions of specific force components can actually work together. All this takes time.

This is why, from time to time, it has been proposed to establish a standing UN force, which could be deployed rapidly in urgent situations. This was also the idea behind the international brigade, the

Multinational Standby High Readiness Brigade for United Nations Operations (SHIRBRIG), which was set up in 1996, in which sixteen countries eventually took part. However, the SHIRBRIG force was only used sporadically, and primarily in the planning of individual operations in Africa. In view of this, the SHIRBRIG co-operation was gradually reduced and finally wound up in 2009. The issue of standing forces is now primarily a matter for discussion in regional organizations. This is particularly the case with the AU, where several countries in the region are working on the establishment of an African standby force.

As stated above, the majority of the UN's member states contribute militarily to the implementation of the UN's peacekeeping activities, some only with individual military observers and some with thousands of soldiers, others again with logistical support. The many different contributions, the varying skills levels, the different military traditions of different countries, and the limited budgets do not always make it easy for UN military operations to function optimally.

Unlike the ISAF forces in Afghanistan or the international coalition assembled around the intervention in Libya in 2011, which operated on the basis of a UN mandate but not under UN command and control, the United Nations' own peacekeeping operations are not fully capable of conducting modern warfare. This may be changing as the Security Council in its Resolution 2098 of 28 March 2013 decided to establish an Intervention Brigade as part of MONUSCO in order to better address the issue of armed groups in the Eastern part of DR Congo. UN forces have significant legitimacy, and local populations do not normally ascribe to them motives of power-grabbing or neo-imperialism, as might be the case with American forces in Iraq or Afghanistan or French forces in West Africa.

The United Nations' peacekeeping activities have developed significantly since the failures in Rwanda and the Balkans in the mid-1990s. It is not easy to say what new challenges will arise in the future, as this will depend on the dynamics of the Security Council as well as in conflict-affected countries. But it is reasonable to assume that the council will still want to establish and maintain UN peacekeeping operations as one of the key United Nations instruments for maintaining international peace and security, especially in Africa and in the Middle East.

These operations will presumably be even more complex in the future and they will also increasingly include peacebuilding measures (see chapter 6). The leadership challenges of getting civilian and military components to work effectively together will continue to be fairly complex. In some cases, the Security Council's more robust mandates will mean that UN peacekeeping will take on more of the character of peace enforcement, possibly increasing the risk of participation and the number of fatalities.[12]

In this case this will call for improved co-operation between national force contributions, improved information-gathering, increased mobility, and ensuring that forces in general have available to them the means for implementing more militarily challenging tasks. In other situations one must expect that the emphasis will shift from peacekeeping to peacebuilding. The present mission in Liberia is a good example of this.

It seems likely that the UN will increasingly implement its peacekeeping mandates in co-operation with regional organizations, such as the African Union; today Darfur and Somalia are examples of this. The relationships with the European Union and with NATO are less clear. Both organizations have military capabilities which could be used positively, but for historical and political reasons it is not always easy for the UN to make use of these capabilities.

Finally, one can expect some obfuscation of the traditional distinction between peacekeeping and the buildup of national or regional military capacities to resolve such problems as currently fall under the UN mandates. The buildup of military and police capacities will become more important as part of exit strategies from peacekeeping operations, whereby the scope and time span of UN operations can be reduced and responsibilities passed to regional or national authorities.

United Nations peacekeeping operations are not static. Political elements must be included in mandates and exit strategies must be included in the planning from the very beginning. Wars are seldom won on the battlefield, and future peacekeeping operations will only be successful if they are closely woven together with national reconciliation and political processes and reforms of the security sectors (military and police), so that the country's authorities can in due course take on the responsibility for security, active peacebuilding measures, and ensuring economic and social progress.

It is of utmost importance that peacekeeping and peacebuilding should be seen as a continuum, and as a positive and mutually reinforcing circle of events. The omens for any operation may be determined at the very beginning soon after a peace agreement, from the early impressions of former combatants as to whether they are likely to gain more by taking part in the peaceful development of their society than by resorting to arms once more. The first weeks and months after the end of conflict – when expectations are usually unreasonably high and disappointment lurks just beneath the surface – must therefore be carefully managed in order to set in motion a positive train of events. Early investments to ensure this will give a very high rate of return.

Careful long-term planning is, and will remain, the key challenge for UN peacekeeping, as will better coordination of peacekeeping and peacebuilding measures.

6

Peacebuilding

One of the most difficult and important tasks facing the United Nations is to ensure that nations emerging from devastating conflicts are not allowed to slide back into violence.

Secretary-General Ban Ki-moon

FROM CONFLICT AND CRISIS
TO STABILITY AND DEVELOPMENT

Over the last decade the United Nations system has clearly sharpened its political focus on – and prioritized its operational activities in – conflict-affected developing countries. Previously the UN operated with three more or less separate circles of issues and sets of operations at country level: peacekeeping operations, which were subject to Security Council decisions and managed by the DPKO in the Secretariat; humanitarian operations, which were the coordinated by the Office for the Coordination of Humanitarian Affairs (OCHA); and development activities which, on the part of the UN, were undertaken by the UN's funds, programs and specialized agencies under the leadership of the Resident Coordinator (see chapter 10). Today the United Nations operate in a much more strategic and integrated fashion, combining all three sets of operations at country level, often under the overall heading of peacebuilding.

The recognition of the need for a more holistic approach to UN operations in countries affected by armed conflict or emerging from years of civil war and internal strife has grown naturally out of the ever more complex peacekeeping operations described in chapter 5. In recent years, most of the UN's peacekeeping missions have developed into operations of a distinctly more civilian character. The number of civilian staff has increased, and there has been more focus on institution and capacity building, not least with regard to government institutions, political processes, and judicial systems.

This is primarily due to better planning and especially to the inclusion of exit planning at an early stage of preparation for the implementation of peacekeeping operations. The Security Council has repeatedly seen the difficulty which the UN faces when it wants to reduce its military presence, let alone withdraw all its troops, before local institutions are able to take over responsibilities for the security system and development activities in a conflict-affected country. In Timor-Leste, where the UN established a peace mission in 1999 and phased it out when the country gained independence from Indonesia in 2002, it became necessary to return with a new UN peacekeeping force from 2006 to 2012. If a mission is to succeed, there is a clear need to plan for transition and local takeover from the very early stages of a peacekeeping mission.

This need for joint and system-wide planning applies not only to the relatively few countries where the UN has deployed peacekeeping missions. There is a wider group of developing countries which have been affected by violent internal conflict or civil war and where the warring parties have entered into a peace agreement, but where after some time the countries nevertheless still run the risk of sliding back into conflict, very often because the so-called peace dividend only appears too late and remains too limited.

Among others this happened in Liberia in the mid-1990s, when the country's first civil war was temporarily halted by an international intervention led by ECOWAS with UN participation. However, the intervention failed to secure and consolidate the peace and a few years later Charles Taylor was elected president and a new phase of civil war began. This is one of the many examples of how a peace agreement and the way it has been implemented and supported by the international community, has not been able to form the basis for an enduring peace and the start of a recovery process which could ultimately turn a country aside from the path of recurrent conflict.[1]

A few years after the end of the Cold War in 1989, the United Nations, the World Bank and many donor countries were actively involved in efforts to help countries out of conflict situations. These supporting measures, which went under various headings, such as early recovery, state building, nation building, or peacebuilding, were of very different kinds, ranging from assisting the parties to a conflict to reach a negotiated political settlement, to increased humanitarian aid, to the reconstruction of infrastructure and the implementation of much-needed political and economic reforms, and even to the taking over of responsibility for the entire government, as the United Nations did in 1999 in both Timor-Leste and Kosovo.

In the period from 1989 to 2006, the Security Council adopted binding resolutions on a total of twenty-seven civil wars. "Civil war" is defined here as internal armed conflict over governmental power or territory, with two or more parties (government or rebel movement), and where the war causes at least 500 fatalities per year. Most of these civil wars took place in Africa (Angola, Burundi, DR Congo, Côte d'Ivoire, Guinea-Bissau, Liberia, Mozambique, Rwanda, Sierra Leone, Somalia, Sudan, and Uganda), but there have also been internal conflicts in Latin America (El Salvador, Guatemala, Haiti, and Nicaragua), Asia (Afghanistan, Cambodia, Iraq, and Yemen) and in Europe and its border territories (Azerbaijan, Bosnia and Herzegovina, Croatia, Georgia, Serbia and Montenegro, and Tajikistan).

In the great majority of these conflict-affected countries it has been possible, over time and often with pressure from the Security Council and active negotiations initiated or supported by the UN secretary-general and the Secretariat, to get the opposing parties to enter into an agreement and cease hostilities. In some of these countries it has been necessary to deploy UN peacekeeping forces in order to secure the peace, but in most cases it has been up to the country itself, with international support, to keep the previously warring parties at peace and to ensure implementation of the peace agreement.[2]

The years around 2000 were watershed years for the United Nations. As stated in chapter 5, toward the end of the 1990s the international community finally found a formula to improve peacekeeping operations in such a way that the scope of mandates and the means of implementation would correspond. Humanitarian operations had also been improved through a much clearer allocation of tasks between organizations and by the strengthening of centralized coordination of humanitarian activities by an empowered OCHA. Rapid progress was also being made in the area of development in improving internal coordination and developing a clearer focus on the UN's comparative advantages in developing institutional capacities. But there was still a lack of coherence between the different kinds of operations, signalling the need for better coordination and joint planning of the various measures and for adopting a unified UN approach before, during and after a conflict.

With this in mind, then secretary-general Kofi Annan appointed, in 2003, an independent international panel to look at new threats, challenges and changes to the international system, and to answer the question of why it had not been possible to hold the parties to peace agreements to their word and avoid relapses back into renewed conflict. The panel presented its report in December 2004, and its answer was that the UN system, and the international community at large, was not sufficiently well organized to deal with the special challenges emerging from the end of armed conflicts.

Once a peace agreement had been signed and once the international news media had moved on to their next story, there was a clear tendency for a post-conflict situation to disappear from the international radar. The conflict had been solved, the killings had stopped, what more could we ask for? More often than not, conflict-affected countries were left to their own devices. Economic assistance from the international donor community to implement peace agreements often falls significantly, and the same applies to the political support and advice for dealing with the political tensions and problems which the peace agreement may have created. However, without continued economic support and continued political engagement from the international community, it can be difficult to deal with the problems which any peace agreement will encounter. These different factors all help explain why there are such frequent relapses into conflict.[3]

The UN panel proposed the establishment up of a Peacebuilding Commission to fill the institutional vacuum that existed between peacekeeping and development. This Commission should deal with the transition from conflicts to peace agreements, and from there to the start of recovery after conflict. It should also focus on improved and integrated planning for this entire transition process and on how to secure continued support from the international community for these transformational changes, both economic and political.

THE PEACEBUILDING COMMISSION

At the World Summit in September 2005, agreement was reached in principle on the establishment of a Peacebuilding Commission (PBC) in the UN, and the specific modalities for the new body were negotiated during the following months. It was agreed that the PBC should advise both the Security Council and the General Assembly and that it should deal with peacebuilding in general as well as with the situation in specific countries. An Organizational Committee of thirty-one members was set up to plan the work of the PBC and its more detailed procedures. The main emphasis, however, was on the country-specific configurations, one configuration for each country which asked to be included on the PBC's agenda. Other countries in the region in question, relevant donor countries that had been involved by providing emergency or other assistance, and countries which had supported the political processes, as well as relevant regional and international institutions were all to be invited to participate in the country-specific configurations.

Quite simply, all international actors which were interested in a particular conflict-affected country should have the opportunity to sit around one big table and, together with the authorities of that country, discuss the country's problems in relation to its post-conflict and peacebuilding strategies, its longer-term development plans, and its prospects for financing the various strategies and plans. In addition to the discussions in the country-specific configurations at the UN Headquarters in New York, it was also envisaged that there would be discussions at local level in the country in question, and that there would be close contact between the New York level and the national level.[4]

Thus, from the very beginning, the PBC has been envisaged as an intergovernmental advisory body looking at a comprehensive agenda and working with a broad spectrum of development partners in country-specific configurations. The composition of the Organizational Committee is deliberately more innovative and democratic than that of most other UN organs, with members appointed by the Security Council, the General Assembly, and ECOSOC, as well as from the major donor countries (i.e., Western countries) and the major troop contributors (primarily developing countries). But it is still a forum operating on the basis of the standard UN procedures and in practice acts solely on the basis of consensus. This of course often limits how far the commission can go in its recommendations.

Simultaneously with the establishment of the PBC, the secretary-general established a Peacebuilding Fund (PBF) to ensure that means would be available for the rapid financing of important peacebuilding operations and to avoid processes being derailed by the lack of funds for catalytic measures. The PBF is intended to contribute to countries which are on the PBC's agenda as well as other countries which need support for peacebuilding activities. Decisions on grants from the fund are taken by the secretary-general (i.e., the Secretariat) rather than by the PBC.

There has been very broad political and economic support for the PBF which received a total of US$499 million in the period from 2006 to the end of 2012, mainly but not solely from Western countries. Today the fund has a broad base of almost fifty donors, including China, India, and Russia, even though these countries still only provide limited contributions (US$4–8 million). The aim is to make grants of up to US$100 million per year for strategic and quickly implemented peacebuilding projects in conflict-affected countries. In the wider context, taking into account the number of conflict-affected countries and the severity of their problems, the PBF is a fairly modest fund, but it has been praised for focusing on critical operations and for its quick decision making.[5]

Retaining the engagement and economic support of the outside world after the television cameras have packed up and the international news media have moved on was an important reason for the establishment of the PBC. For developing countries which have to decide whether or not to come under the Commission's purview there was another key question.

For Burundi and Sierra Leone, which were the first two countries to accept being part of the PBC's agenda, there is no doubt that, in addition to the hope of getting access to funds from the PBF, there was a genuine desire not to be forgotten. Both countries had been through ruinous civil wars which had resulted in the deployment of UN peacekeeping missions. In both cases, peace had been secured and the UN missions had been phased out to be replaced by small UN political missions. International attention was soon diverted elsewhere and part of the assistance for early recovery and reconstruction after the conflicts, which had been promised while the television cameras were still rolling, seemed to have vanished into thin air. Not all donor countries live up to the promises they make when political and media attention is at its height.

For both Burundi and Sierra Leone the establishment of country-specific configurations in the PBC sent the signal that their continued struggle to regain their footing after conflict and their continued need for economic and political support was acknowledged. Later Guinea-Bissau, Guinea, and the Central African Republic have been added to the number of country-specific configurations and with basically the same motives as Burundi and Sierra Leone – a desire for easier access to funds from the PBF and an express statement of the need for continued political and economic support from the international community. All five countries are forgotten conflict-affected countries, i.e., countries that are struggling with critical problems, but which, for one reason or another, are never among the developing countries with which most major donor countries have established more comprehensive co-operation (often called "donor darlings" in contrast to the "donor orphans" that are the countries most relevant to the PBC's agenda).

It was first in the autumn of 2010, after nearly five years of existence, that the PBC finally got to deal with a country situation – Liberia – which involved an existing major UN peacekeeping operation and was thus required to focus properly on the original proposition for the PBC: how to ensure better cohesion between the phasing out of a peacekeeping operation and the phasing in of peacebuilding and development assistance.

The reason why it took so long, also in the case of Liberia, was the considerable caution of the governments of the countries hosting UN peacekeeping missions. These countries primarily feared that the active promotion of the concept of peacebuilding could advance the winding up of the peacekeeping mission too soon and before the country was ready for it (with the example of Timor-Leste in 2002 in mind).

Conflict-affected countries hosting a UN peacekeeping mission clearly feared that they risked losing more in relation to the political attention of the Security Council, the stability and security provided by the UN forces, and the funds which the peacekeeping missions brought to the country, whether directly or indirectly, than they stood to gain in the form of attention from the PBC and the economic support which they would be able to obtain from the PBF or in some other form of donor assistance related to the peacebuilding agenda. In other words, to be on the agenda of the Security Council was more attractive than to be on the agenda of the PBC, and the Security Council's financing of peacekeeping operations through assessed contributions looked more secure than the voluntary financing of peacebuilding assistance.

This explains why the PBC did not become an instant success in 2006. It also took time for it to agree on the composition of the Organizational Committee and for the members of that committee to acknowledge that it was what its name said – a committee to take care

of practical and procedural matters and not a super-committee direct-
ing the work of the country-specific configurations. The declaration
from the World Summit had been unclear on these points and had
only laid down the overall principles.

As is often the case, the composition of the Organizational Committee became highly political. Most of the member states that were
candidates for permanent or frequent membership of the Security
Council also wanted to be members of the PBC, if for nothing else
than to show their active support for a broader concept of security
including peacebuilding.

In 2010, a review was carried out of the whole peacebuilding architecture after the establishment of the PBC in 2006. The overriding conclusion was that experiences had been rather mixed. The same conclusion appeared in relation to the individual countries that were on
the PBC's agenda. For example, in relation to Burundi, where the
discussions in New York had been unusually difficult and time-
consuming, it was clear from the review that there had been very limited coordination between the strategic discussions in New York and
the practical and operational discussions of relevant partners in
Burundi's capital Bujumbura. On the other hand, it had been possible
to raise US$35 million for Burundi from the PBF, and as far as could
be assessed the PBC discussions had actually helped mobilize new
funding for peacebuilding in Burundi from a number of donor countries. The PBC (and especially the first chairman of the Burundi country-specific configuration, the Norwegian Ambassador to the UN,
Johan Løvald) had also played an important role in solving concrete
problems between Burundi and the IMF.[6]

After a somewhat slow and uncertain start, the PBC is now finding
its feet. The politicking in the Organizational Committee has calmed
down, and the PBC's focus is now clearly on the country-specific configurations and on the added value which these should be able to generate in the form of increased awareness, mobilization of additional
resources, and better coordination of peacebuilding in the individual
countries. In this connection it is in particular the discussion on
Liberia that will be able to point to the way ahead.

At the same time, it is clear that neither the Peacebuilding Commission nor the Peacebuilding Support Office (PBSO) in the UN Secretariat, which has the task of coordinating the work of the PBC and
serving as Secretariat for the PBF, has the capacity to deal with more
than a handful of countries at any given time. Given that there is a

long list of conflict-affected countries in the world, the PBC will only be able to tackle part of the overall peacebuilding agenda. However, the experiences gained, especially in the country-specific configurations, will also be applicable in other contexts and will thus be able to contribute to the continued development of UN peacebuilding, both as a political concept and a practical strategy. This is the case not least in relation to Liberia, and there are thus good reasons for looking more closely at that country.

LIBERIA

As described in chapter 5, for fourteen years up to 2003 Liberia experienced a bloody civil war in several phases, costing between 200,000 and 250,000 lives. In addition, about one-quarter of the population fled their homes, seeking shelter either elsewhere in the country or in neighbouring countries. Since the peace agreement in 2003 there has been considerable progress in Liberia. As described in relation to peacekeeping, the security situation has improved significantly and it has been possible to reduce the peacekeeping mission (UNMIL) to about 7,000 soldiers (to which should be added about 3,000 police officers and civilian staff).

The Liberian economy has grown by more than 7 per cent per year since 2005, though from a very low base. Before the civil war the average annual income in Liberia was more than US$1,200 per capita (1980); after the civil war it was a little over US$200. There is a long way to go before the people of Liberia will be back at the same living standard they had thirty years ago.

The Liberian government is aware of the risk of taking peace and stability for granted prematurely. Many wounds must first be healed. Nearly all Liberians have friends or family who were killed or maimed in the civil war, and they often know where the perpetrators can be found. There are many emotional wounds that will take a long time to heal, if ever. And there are many who have suffered trauma because of the war, which is still part of many Liberians' everyday lives. After the civil war ended in 2003, a truth-and-reconciliation process was initiated, based on the model used in South Africa, but this process rapidly became a pawn in the political power struggle in Liberia, and so did not contribute much to the necessary reconciliation and healing. The ghosts of the past are still there, and the time will probably come when it will be necessary to address head-on the issues of guilt and responsibility during the civil war. However, such a process will not be without risks for political stability.

Liberia held presidential elections in November 2011, re-electing Ellen Johnson Sirleaf as its president. The elections were by and large conducted peacefully and without major problems, and with significant logistical support from UNMIL. The elections were an important milestone in the country's stabilization process, but there are also concerns about long-term regional stability. In order to assess the perspectives for a reduction or phasing out of UNMIL, one should look at the five essential parameters for development: security, the social sectors, employment, the political situation, and the administrative apparatus.

1 Security

There are still a couple of thousand armed Liberian combatants in neighbouring Côte d'Ivoire. These could create problems if they were to return or if they were driven back by new conflicts in Côte d'Ivoire. The situation in Guinea, one of Liberia's other neighbours, is fragile and preparations have been made in Liberia to receive refugees from there. In other words, the regional situation holds considerable risks. However, in recent years the Economic Community of West African States (ECOWAS) has shown itself to be a robust organization, able to deal with crises in the region effectively and in a way that has clearly reduced regional tensions and increased security. Within the country there is anxiety that there can be some hidden militia units ("sleepers") left over from the civil war, and that these could be a real threat to security if they were mobilized.

2 Social Sectors

The state budgets and institutions are short of funds and are dependent on aid in order to cover running costs and the necessary investments. This applies particularly in the educational and health sectors, though it has been possible to increase markedly the number of children in primary schools and to raise the level of health care.

3 Growth and Employment

There are high levels of unemployment and underemployment in the country, perhaps up to 85 per cent. The number of unemployed and underemployed young people constitutes a political risk in itself. At the same time, there is a great lack of well-trained workers, and thus a great need to develop vocational training and skills. Like other African countries, Liberia has been hit by the consequences of the global financial crisis. Continued strong economic growth will depend on whether Liberia succeeds in exploiting the country's great potential, both in agriculture (rubber and tropical products) and minerals (iron, gold, and oil). The extractive industries may provide revenue, but they are not likely to generate a lot of jobs. The potential for job creation lies primarily in the agricultural sector. There is a great need for foreign direct investments and new and improved mineral concessions could give a boost to state revenues. Apart from the lack of well-trained workers, the inadequate infrastructure is also a bottleneck for economic development. In particular, the lack of good roads is a significant problem, as large parts of the road network cannot be used in the rainy season.

4 Political Situation

Several of the local warlords who, together with the former president Charles Taylor, were the main actors in the civil war, are members of the Liberian Parliament and are thus part of the political system. From time to time there is a rattling of sabres, but most observers do not believe there is a risk of renewed civil war. However, the traces of the civil war are all too clear, and the wounds of the people are still open. There is a clear need for a national reconciliation process. People's nerves are still raw and it does not take much to trigger episodes that can quickly spread and lead to widespread unrest. This situation is not made any easier by the fact that one-third of the population live in the capital Monrovia which, in a crisis, could easily become a flashpoint.

5 Administrative Capacity

The public administration below the level of permanent secretary or under-secretary is characterized by having very limited administrative skills and experience. At the same time, there are significant problems of corruption in the public sector. The possibility of drawing on the large diaspora of well-educated Liberians is lessened by the traditional animosity toward those who return home as a new upper class (often from the United States). The court system has significant capacity problems, with extensive corruption and administrative bottlenecks blocking cases coming forward.

The picture, thus, is fairly mixed. Solid results have been achieved and the outlook is promising. But significant risks remain and development could still be derailed.

A reduction and subsequent phasing out of UNMIL is conditional on responsibility for security in the country being passed from the UN to the Liberian security forces. Liberia is ready for this but at the same time there are fears of a too-rapid reduction of the UNMIL forces. There is a widespread view that it is better to play safe, given the obvious risks.

The size of the army has been set at 2,000 soldiers (two battalions). The army only has a function in relation to external threats (and natural disasters). The police are solely responsible for dealing with internal disturbances. The total number of Liberian police is around 4,000, but it will take several years before the police force is fully operational, especially outside Monrovia. Altogether, there are good reasons for keeping a UN police mission in Liberia for some time to come.

Thorough reforms of the army and of the police are needed in order to re-establish popular confidence in these institutions and to ensure the continued peaceful development of Liberia. There is a need for new leadership of the army and the police and political control of these institutions, as well as training and the establishment of new standards and new institutional cultures. However, security reforms are necessary but not sufficient; there is also a need for economic growth and development.

The attention of the United Nations and of the international community is now clearly focused on the the country's economic reconstruction. The UN is working to create a coherent program in Liberia with a view to supporting the peacebuilding task which the Liberian government is to embark on and which is formulated in the government's development strategy.

Liberia is actively seeking to increase the number of bilateral donors and will undoubtedly try to use the Liberian country-specific configuration to persuade new donor countries to provide assistance to Liberia.

Is the current international development assistance sufficient to calm the political tensions which still exist after fourteen years of civil war, and to compensate for the very limited economic capacity in the country? The total development assistance for Liberia in financial year 2009–10 was about US$450 million, of which, because of its historical links, the United States provided half. Liberia was founded by freed American slaves and there has traditionally been a strong and close connection between Monrovia and Washington. The World Bank, the African Development Bank, and the EU together stood for a little over one-quarter of the aid, and bilateral donors and the UN system together were responsible for the rest. But it is typical that, as in other post-conflict situations, the UN organizations are responsible for a relatively large part of the total assistance.

It is also part of the picture that, in addition to their regular resources (i.e., the organizations' core budgets), the UN organizations also administer some of the other donor funds. The UNDP's operations in Liberia have an annual cost of about US$50 million, of which only one-third comes from the core budget, and UNICEF's operations amount to about US$30 million per year, with likewise one-third coming from the core budget.

The UNDP's Liberia office has 280 staff, of which 35 are international staff and the rest are local Liberians. UNICEF's local office has 74 staff, of which 18 are international staff. The number of workers reflects the organizations' focus on developing capacities and training, and in helping public authorities with advice and practical assistance. This applies particularly to the UNDP, which has established a special department in its headquarters in New York called the Bureau for Crisis Prevention and Recovery (BCPR), which is tasked with helping countries affected by conflicts or natural disasters, and is one of the UNDP's most important departments. In relation to operations in Liberia, its very weak administrative capacities has led the UNDP to execute large parts of the aid program itself, which is something that may give results, but which is not necessarily as effective in building up the long-term administrative skills of the various government departments.[7]

The UN organizations are generally considered as being good at planning and at ensuring that the activities carried out are in line with a government's political priorities; however, they are often less focused at the practical implementation of programs. From the perspective of national governments, the UN often wants to do too much in too little time. Internal coordination between different UN organizations is still being developed and the will to coordinate is clear. The need to do so will not be any less as UNMIL is reduced and some of its civilian tasks are transferred to other UN organizations. At the same time, in Liberia, as in other places, there are a number of internal financing and incentive structures which make it difficult to achieve optimal coordination (see chapter 10).

In line with normal practice, the UN peacekeeping mission in Liberia is led by an SRSG, assisted by a force commander and a police commander, and two deputies with responsibilities for civilian recovery and reconstruction (usually someone from one of the UN's development organizations) and for reforms of the justice system respectively.

There is no doubt that the job of the SRSG, as head of the overall operations in countries like Liberia, Haiti, or Timor-Leste, is essential for dealing with the very broad-spectrum function of the United Nations in these situations. There is also no doubt that people matter in this context. Sergio Vieira de Mellos's work in Timor-Leste and then in Iraq, prior to his death in the terrorist bombing of the UN's headquarters in Baghdad in August 2003, is an example of this. The work of Haile Menkerios in Sudan in connection with the referendum and the subsequent division of the country in 2011 is another example. It is therefore important that the right people should be appointed to these leading positions, and that the selection process should aim at identifying the best-qualified candidate.[8]

THE FUTURE OF PEACEBUILDING

Liberia is a positive example of a UN operation's gradual shift from peacekeeping to peacebuilding. However, the UN mission to Haiti (MINUSTAH) is a less positive example. The operation in Haiti is still affected by the huge earthquake on 12 January 2010, in which about 220,000 people were killed, including more than one hundred UN staff.

The reconstruction efforts in Haiti, following years of conflict, have been plagued by difficulties. Haiti's government has insisted that it will itself lead the reconstruction process. There has been considerable international assistance, but the results have not been equal to the efforts. National ownership, political decision making and administrative capacities have not been sufficient to get the job done, and MINUSTAH has not had the same privileged role as a sparring partner for the government as UNMIL has had in Liberia. There has not been a clear strategy for reconstruction in Haiti, and progress in different areas have not sufficiently supported each other and created the synergies necessary.

Paradoxically, in some countries a major natural disaster in a fragile society and massive international aid in response to the disaster have been used as a political game changer. Unfortunately this has not been the case in Haiti. But in the Aceh province in Indonesia, which was one of the areas hardest hit by the tsunami in December 2004, the devastation of the area led to a political process which, with international mediation by the former president of Finland, Martti Ahtisaari, led to the resolution of the long-lasting deep conflict between the Free Aceh Movement (Gerakin Aceh Merdeka, or GAM) and the Indonesian government.

It is one of the organizational strengths of the UN system that, in one form or another, the UN will virtually always be present before, during, and after a conflict. The global presence of the United Nations also means that in principle the organization has an office in almost all developing countries and has a representative in place. Likewise, the major UN development funds and programs all have ongoing activities in the great majority of these countries.

Naturally, a more serious internal conflict in a country will require a very different UN operation and it will often be difficult to continue the usual development activities. A conflict will focus the UN's attention on coordination of humanitarian assistance and on providing active support to the UN secretary-general and others who may try to act as mediators in the conflict and to resolve the political problems that lie behind it.

A peace agreement again changes the situation and very often leads to new tasks for the UN and new demands for the skills which the UN system must have at country level.

The most important challenge for the United Nations after the settlement of a conflict will typically be to quickly introduce strong and experienced leaders who have the necessary qualities for carrying out the task of peacebuilding and to mobilize the necessary economic resources and professional skills to assist the government in drawing up a plan for the first post-conflict priorities.

In these situations the countries will quite often have a new and untested government, with a weak administrative system behind it, and therefore in need of considerable professional help. The United Nations must also help ensure the plan is implemented and help the government convince other actors (such as bilateral donors, the EU, the World Bank, et cetera) to follow the plan. Only by this means is it possible to create a reasonable degree of coherence in the overall external operations in the critical phase immediately following a peace agreement or an end to conflict.

An important aspect is to help governments manage their populations' expectations especially among the formerly warring groups. There are usually unrealistic expectations as to how quickly a ceasefire or peace agreement will be able to lead to economic growth and development. Only few are aware that a conflict typically breaks down the government and the administrative system which usually deliver the social services and benefits to the people at large and that it takes time to reassemble the system.

The idea that assistance to a country can help reinforce a peace agreement and create a virtuous circle of development requires setting aside the concept of a linear succession of humanitarian, peacekeeping, and peacebuilding operations. All experience shows that development takes time, and that development from a complex starting point takes a long time. Experience also shows the necessity of including peacebuilding activities right from the start of a crisis, and constantly to have peacebuilding in mind when planning humanitarian and peacekeeping operations.

Peacebuilding activities must be initiated as early as possible in a conflict situation. The concept calls for the UN system to create synergies between different streams of UN activities, which remain one of its most significant comparative advantages in post-conflict situations.

What is important in this context is the speedy establishment of a coherent framework for all the UN's many different activities – the UN's coordination of humanitarian aid; the emergency operations of the UN's humanitarian organizations (especially UNICEF, WFP, and UNHCR); the UN's peacekeeping operations; the unique legitimacy of the UN in initiating peace negotiations and contributing to political solutions; and the clear focus of most of the UN's development agencies, funds, and programs on capacity building in the public sector, democratic government, and development based on rule of law.

In recent years, there have been intense international discussions on the future of peacebuilding and these discussions have been closely linked with the deliberations on the special challenges faced by conflict-affected and fragile states. However, not all conflict-affected countries are fragile. The World Bank defines *fragility* as: "lack of capacity, accountability, or legitimacy to mediate relations between citizen groups and between citizens and the state, making them vulnerable to violence," and thus as a question of the sustainability of public sector institutions and their ability to resolve conflicts between citizens. A civil war leads to a breakdown of these institutions, and one of the key tasks of peacebuilding is to re-establish and renew these institutions.[9]

Sometimes the breakdown of institutions occurs in the wake of a major natural disaster. But most often it is caused by the vicious cycle of violence, conflicts, and fragile institutions, and the challenge is to break the vicious cycle and to establish an alternative route which takes the country out of the crisis and to create the basic conditions which make it possible to initiate and maintain a sustainable development process.[10]

In general, poverty and the risk of conflict are closely linked. Statistically, a low-income country has a 14 per cent risk of internal conflict in the course of any five-year period. And this risk is increased by factors such as economic inequality, social and ethnic tensions, and the country's dependence on its natural resources. Limited economic growth, continued poverty, and lack of progress of political processes in the years following the end of a conflict are unquestionably significant factors increasing the risk of the conflict flaring up again.[11]

In 2007, the OECD adopted ten fundamental principles for how donor countries should behave in providing development assistance to fragile states. Correspondingly, in the Dili Declaration of April 2010, a number of the countries that are normally regarded as fragile (including Afghanistan, Burundi, and Timor-Leste), drew up their own principles for peace and state building (the G7 initiative). While there are differences in tone, there is emphasis on the same elements which also appear in the report on peacebuilding which the UN secretary-general issued in June 2009, after comprehensive consultation with the UN member states.[12]

The common elements which emerge in the great majority of peacebuilding strategies focus on the following five issues: one, stabilization of the security situation and the creation of sufficiently physical security for the civilian population; two, the provision of basic services, such as water, health, and education; three, ensuring employment, at least for young people and ex-combatants; four, stabilizing and strengthening the political processes in the country; and five, building up the administrative capacity necessary for the rebuilding of the most important institutions of a society, including the judicial system, and for the drawing up and implementation of long-term development strategies.

In order to develop a coherent strategy which can address these five issues, it is necessary to clarify three issues which affect them all.

First, are there national circumstances or relationships that can contribute to the creation of greater political cohesion and which can be a vehicle for peacebuilding activities? It is essential to create as many connections and contact points as possible between the former opposing sides, in order to break down the former patterns of hostility and images of "the enemy."

Second, are there any local existing capacities, of any kind, which can be built on in the post-conflict period? This also applies to productive capacity and thus the scope for stimulating economic growth.

Third, has the international community invested sufficient political and economic capital in assisting the country in question? In general, the less the scope for strengthening national cohesion after a conflict, and the smaller the capacities of a country, the greater will be the need for international assistance. This applies both politically in relation to the negotiations of a peace agreement and ensuring that it is complied with, and economically in relation to securing the speedy and efficient provision of critical social services.[13]

CIVILIAN CAPACITY

In its *World Development Report 2011: Conflict, Security, and Development*, the World Bank focused on the almost forty countries in the world that are seriously affected by internal conflicts. The bank produced the WDR following extensive international consultations, including with the major UN organizations, and there is broad agreement about its conclusions: more than anything else, internal conflicts and widespread violence keep a people locked in poverty, and in order to break out of this conflict trap it is essential to give some impetus to a positive development process.

The World Bank points to three areas as decisive for a country being able to create this kind of positive momentum: the creation of the necessary security for its people, the establishment of a properly functioning justice system ensuring fair and equal treatment, and the creation of employment opportunities for the unemployed and underemployed, especially among young people. The key words are *security*, *justice*, and *jobs*.[14]

Depending on the circumstances, the achievement of sufficient progress in these areas requires the existence of effective government institutions which can: ensure security and justice (police, courts, public administration), create the proper legislative frameworks and conditions for productive investment of domestic resources, ensure that remittances from overseas workers are used productively, and attract foreign direct investment and the accompanying transfer of management skills and technology. For the UN system it is essential that the buildup of institutional capacity in these areas should be a core element of the peacebuilding operations from the start, and preferably as soon as the circumstances on the ground permit.

In the spring of 2011, in parallel with the World Bank's *WDR*, an independent UN group of experts in their report on Civilian Capacity in the Aftermath of Conflict emphasized the need to focus on countries' own existing capacities as a basis for peacebuilding early on in conflict situations. This aspect has often been undervalued and the expert group called on the UN system to identify and make better use of such capacities.

To the extent that there is a need for international advice and expertise, the group proposed that the UN system should develop more flexible and pragmatic methods for recruiting such expertise, following the model used for the UN's peacekeeping operations: identification of precise needs for technical assistance, asking the member states to submit offers, and selecting providers. It was suggested that greater use should be made of the expertise of neighbouring countries and of developing greater South-South co-operation in the area of technical assistance.[15]

Peacebuilding in the aftermath of conflict will be one of the most important tasks of the United Nations in the years to come. It is an area in which the UN has a clear comparative advantage and should be able to mix a number of different tools and interventions be they humanitarian, political, military and technical assistance (capacity building), and where the scope for effective coordination of the different interventions is unique.

But the results should not be taken for granted. Peacebuilding requires strong leadership of the overall UN system, as well at country level. It depends on an expressed willingness to listen to, and respect, the political priorities of the country in question. It requires strong coordination skills, and instruments, not only among the UN bodies and programs but across the whole range of assistance programs, including bilateral and other multilateral activities. It must be rooted in clear national ownership and leadership, and at the same

time it also requires that the international community makes sufficient means available, not merely during the first years after peace has
been restored, but for the many years that it will take before a country is able to stand on its own feet.

As a rule of thumb, the recovery and reconstruction of a country
after a conflict takes at least as long as the duration of the conflict
itself. For Liberia, which emerged after fourteen years of civil war in
2003, this means that in 2012 the peacebuilding process had reached
just about halfway. It will take most of the next decade for Liberia just
to reach the economic level it had before the civil war.

This requires patience, but patience is not the most plentiful commodity in a country just emerging from years of civil war, with high
hopes and large generations of young people eager to find their place
in the world.

PART III

Freedom

The meetings of the UN General Assembly usually take place in the impressive General Assembly Hall. Here, over the years, changing generations of politicians and diplomats from all over the world have both spoken and listened intently to the words of others which might indicate a political opening or suggest possibilities for finding common ground. But after sixty years' use, the building is worn out; part of the ceiling recently collapsed and a few days before Christmas there was a gas leak causing a complete evacuation of the building. For this reason the Assembly is meeting in the temporary North Lawn Building on 21 December 2010. The architectural design and the building standards are on a level with the best that IKEA's self-service warehouses can offer – concrete floors, exposed pipe-work, fluorescent lighting, and only the most essential electrical installations. It is quite evident that these meeting rooms are temporary.

On the agenda is the adoption of a resolution, sponsored by the Nordic countries, on extrajudicial, summary or arbitrary executions. During the previous discussion in the Third (Human Rights) Committee, a small majority of member states succeeded in removing a reference to sexual orientation – a term which usually refers to gays and lesbians. Homosexuality is still punishable in many countries, and a great number of countries do not recognize the human rights violations and the persecution that homosexuals suffer. The Committee vote was an eye-opener. The United States, the Nordic countries, and a number of other European countries had their ambassadors around the world make demarches with their host countries – essentially lobbying hard – with the clear message that the reference should be restored. The United Nations should continue to demonstrate that there is a need for special efforts to protect sexual minorities against discrimination and persecution.

These diplomatic efforts are rewarded and the reference is reinstated. However, the losing side does not give up. Many countries are angry about what they consider as undue Western pressure and – as they see it – a desire to dictate how other countries shall legislate with regard to affairs that they consider entirely domestic. They make it clear that they have no intention of changing their prohibitions of homosexuality just because the UN adopts a resolution. Zimbabwe's Ambassador to the UN expresses this resistance most sharply, saying: "We will not have it foisted on us. We cannot accept this, especially if it entails accepting such practices as bestiality, paedophilia and those other practices many societies would find abhorrent in their value systems."

Human rights? Cultural conflict? Religion? Which fundamental values and human rights apply globally and what are the limits to what others can – and ought to – interfere?

7

Human Rights

All human beings are born free and equal in dignity and rights. They are endowed with reason and conscience and should act toward one another in a spirit of brotherhood ... Everyone has the right to life, liberty and security of person.

Universal Declaration of Human Rights, 1948, Articles 1 and 3

THE INTERNATIONAL HUMAN RIGHTS SYSTEM

The key role of human rights in international relations and as one of the three pillars of the United Nations is based on the Universal Declaration of Human Rights of 1948.

The idea of a society based on laws which govern individuals' relations with each other and the relations between the individual (or particular groups of individuals) and the state, has its roots in the distant past of human history. All cultures and civilizations have had to address the question of the rights of individuals in their ethical, moral, and religious thinking and in their political systems. However, it was not until the seventeenth and eighteenth centuries that citizens' rights and political freedoms were expressed in the form that we know today. The English Civil War of the 1640s and 1650s was a battle between Parliament and the King to resist arbitrary monarchical rule and judicial tyranny, and the English Bill of Rights of 1689 provided certain freedoms for citizens as well as the precursor for the principle of "no taxation without representation."

It is not difficult to see a straight line from here and to the two most important political documents of the late eighteenth century: The American Declaration of Independence of 1776 and the French Declaration of the Rights of Man and the Citizen of 1789. Political freedoms were generally defined as being inalienable (derived from nature and part of what it means to be human), equal (the same for all men), and universal (applicable everywhere). The industrial revolution in the nineteenth century created the basis for giving more substantive content to economic, social, and cultural rights, which came to the fore right after the First World War with the establishment of the International Labour Organization (ILO) in 1919. This was a clear reflection of the strong international focus on social reform and labour issues which had emerged during the war.

However, it would take another world war and yet more millions of fatalities before these endeavours were brought together in a normative synthesis of human rights. The Universal Declaration of Human Rights was first and foremost a statement of international agreement on the fundamental observation that human beings have rights by virtue of being human, and that there are universal limits to how bad states can treat their own citizens. Together with the Nuremberg trials of the Nazi war criminals in 1945–46, and the adoption of the Genocide Convention in 1948, the Universal Declaration was a clear statement that governments' conduct vis-à-vis their own citizens was no longer a purely domestic matter in respect of which others were not entitled to intervene.[1]

The eventual agreement on the Universal Declaration was not something that could be taken for granted. The background to the idea of drafting a Universal Declaration – a set of universally agreed norms and standards of human rights – was a fairly broad dissatisfaction that the UN Charter itself had only limited references to human rights. In the draft UN Charter drawn up at Dumbarton Oaks in the autumn of 1944, the three main victors in the Second World War (the Soviet Union, the United Kingdom, and the United States) had only given peripheral attention to the issue of human rights, and even at the San Francisco Conference in 1945 the three major powers did not show any significant interest in the issue.

At the same time, a number of American civil rights organizations and some of the Latin American member states especially were highly dissatisfied that the UN Charter so clearly emphasized the principle of non-intervention in the affairs of other states (Article 2[7]). These forces came to regard a stronger emphasis on human rights as a counterweight to this and therefore actively pursued the drafting of a human rights declaration. Their efforts led to the establishment of the UN Commission on Human Rights (UNCHR) in 1946 as a subsidiary body of the UN Economic and Social Council (ECOSOC). As its first task, the new Committee was entrusted with the preparation and drafting of a general declaration of human rights to be put before the General Assembly.

This was no easy task. In Europe, the Iron Curtain, which Winston Churchill had already referred to in the spring of 1946, had been drawn ever tighter, especially after the Communist coup in Prague in the spring of 1948 which drew Czechoslovakia fully into the Soviet bloc. The United States and the Soviet Union appeared as more and more clearly diametrically opposed powers in the postwar international system.

The fact that the negotiations on a universal human rights declaration nevertheless proved successful was due primarily to the fact that the Human Rights Committee was chaired by Eleanor Roosevelt, the widow of President Franklin D. Roosevelt. It was Mrs. Roosevelt who, with great integrity and authority and with the aura which the Roosevelt name still carried throughout the world, was able to bridge the increasingly tense ideological-political negotiating divide and to eventually get agreement on the necessary political compromises. The UN General Assembly adopted the Universal Declaration on 10 December 1948 – with forty-eight votes in favour, none against, and only eight abstentions.[2]

The main emphasis of the Universal Declaration is on individual rights and fundamental freedoms, and on civil and political rights rather than economic, social and cultural rights. There is effectively a hierarchy of rights in which civil and political rights are defined fairly precisely in Articles 4–21, while economic, social, and cultural rights are formulated in more general terms in Articles 22–26.

One of the main architects of the Universal Declaration, the French lawyer René Cassin, who was later awarded the Nobel Peace Prize for his contribution, summed it up that the economic, social, and cultural rights were *nearly* as important as the civil and political rights. He argued that the civil and political rights were more fundamental and more easily achievable, while economic and social rights could only be achieved gradually, requiring interaction between national efforts and international co-operation.[3]

The idea was that the Universal Declaration should be followed by a binding human rights convention, but it turned out to be impossible, in the midst of the Cold War, to integrate the two sets of rights in one instrument and instead it was agreed to draw up two comprehensive international conventions: the International Covenant on Civil and Political Rights (ICCPR) and the International Covenant on Economic,

Social and Cultural Rights (ICESCR). The 1948 Universal Declaration and these two international conventions, which were both adopted in 1966, constitute the fundamental international norms and standards in the area of human rights (often referred to as International Bill of Human Rights). The Universal Declaration in particular has formed the basis for a number of regional human rights conventions, including the European Convention on Human Rights (ECHR).

In the late 1940s, the member states agreed to start the process of drawing up a number of more specific human rights conventions. The most important of these are: the Convention on the Prevention and Punishment of the Crime of Genocide (1948), the Convention Relating to the Status of Refugees (1951), the International Convention on the Elimination of All Forms of Racial Discrimination (1966), the Convention on the Elimination of All Forms of Discrimination against Women (1979), the Convention against Torture and Other Cruel, Inhuman, or Degrading Treatment or Punishment (1984), and the Convention on the Rights of the Child (1989). The most recent of these conventions, the Convention on the Rights of Persons with Disabilities, was adopted in 2006. Some of the key conventions adopted by the ILO also belong in this context. For example, ILO Convention 87 on Freedom of Association and Protection of the Right to Organise (1948) and ILO Convention 98 on the Right to Organise and Collective Bargaining (1949) are also core international human rights conventions.

The United Nations' human rights activities thus run on two parallel tracks. On the one hand, by virtue of signing the UN Charter and thereby accepting the Universal Declaration, member states undertake to abide by the more general and universal obligations inherent in these founding documents. Politically, these obligations are followed up in the General Assembly and in the Human Rights Council (HRC) which was established in 2006 to replace the Commission on Human Rights.

On the other hand, there are a number of more specific and detailed human rights obligations which individual member states accept by ratifying the various human rights conventions. These obligations follow from the terms of each convention and they only affect those states which ratify them. Thus, if a member state has a skeleton in its closet, it may be tempted to refrain from ratifying a convention. But there is, of course, a political price to pay by not ratifying, as this can easily be interpreted as an admission of guilt or at least as an acknowledgement of the existence of a serious problem within that country.

There are great differences in the number of countries that have ratified each of the most important human rights conventions. At the top of the list is the Convention on the Rights of the Child, which all UN member states have ratified, with the exception of the United States and Somalia. The Genocide Convention (142 member states) and the Torture Convention (151 member states) have been ratified by fewer states. In most cases, there are optional protocols to the conventions, in which member states allow their own citizens to file complaints about that state's compliance with its obligations under the convention. The convention system and the complaint procedures will be illustrated in more detail below on the basis of the Convention against Torture.[4]

The development, over time, of a comprehensive set of international human rights obligations has been the subject of many political clashes in the United Nations. These clashes were particularly strong between the West and the East during the Cold War, but they have also taken place between the North and the South as new member states joined the UN. Sometimes there have been clashes across all four-quarters of the globe.

WHICH KIND OF HUMAN RIGHTS?

Political differences between the member states of the United Nations have to a large extent been centred on the relationship between the clearly defined individual civil and political rights and the more vaguely defined economic, social, and cultural rights. As their starting point, human rights concern the rights of the individual against the power of the state – the zone of inalienability and inviolability which every person has and which no state and no government is entitled to infringe. But human rights are also economic, social, and cultural rights, where the focus is more on what individual citizens can expect of the state, and thus what the state has an obligation to provide for individuals – in other words, what a citizen has a right to get and what the authorities must therefore provide. It is here we find the more vaguely defined rights, such as the right to work, the right to an education, and the right to social security, et cetera.

One of the new elements under the heading of economic, social, and cultural rights is the right to water. Among other things, the ICE-SCR of 1966 sets out the right to work, social security, health services, education, and the right of everyone to "an adequate standard of living for himself and his family, including adequate food, clothing and housing and to a continuing improvement of living conditions" (Article 111).

The use of the word *including* means that the stated rights are not exhaustive, and that "an adequate standard of living" includes more than just "food, clothing and housing." On this basis, since 2002 various UN bodies and organizations have worked to define what a right to water would actually mean. It unquestionably means a right to clean drinking water. It probably also includes access to water for washing clothes, food preparation, and personal hygiene. But it probably does not include water for other than household use, such as a right to water for irrigation of agricultural production, which is what by far the greatest proportion of the world's freshwater resources are used for. And it does not mean the right to water free of charge.

Access to clean drinking water is one of the United Nations Millennium Development Goals and one of the goals that will most probably be reached (see chapter 9). In 1990 nearly 30 per cent of the population of developing countries did not have access to clean drinking water, but this share has already been reduced to less than 15 per cent (in line with the target of halving the number of people without access), and there is no doubt that this progress will continue in the years to come. This development highlights one of the fundamental principles related to economic and social rights, namely the gradual achievement of these rights over time. Economic and social rights, such as the right to work or the right to water, are not absolute or easily defined. They express aspirations, goals, and a political obligation on behalf of the government to mobilize the necessary political will and economic resources to provide these rights for as many as possible, and to continually increase provision of services and resources in the area in question. "An adequate standard of living" is far from the same in Mali as it is in Western Europe; but the same is not the case when it comes to the understanding of freedom of expression.

As a human right, the definition of a right to water is still a work in progress. In 2008, the HRC in Geneva appointed an independent expert to examine how the concept could be further clarified, and how various claims and rights could be defined more precisely. This was seen as the first step in the preparation of a normal UN process in which the member states will discuss the issue on the basis of an expert's report, and then presumably demand new reports, new discussions, and finally negotiate an agreement on new international standards or norms in the area. However, a small group of Latin American countries, led by Bolivia, Cuba, and Venezuela, decided to shortcut the process by submitting a draft resolution to the General Assembly in 2010 to declare that the right to water a human right.

On this occasion, agreement on the wording could not be reached, and forty-one member states abstained from voting in the General Assembly, primarily because they regarded the proposal as a hollow political ploy without substantive content, as the right to water was not defined in the resolution and because the work to reach agreement on a definition was still ongoing. Subsequent negotiations in the HRC in September 2010 brought the process back on track and led to an initial agreement – by consensus – about the general framework for the definition of the right to water as both a human right and a development issue.[5]

In the United Nations, much of the debate has focused on the balance between individual rights and fundamental freedoms on the one hand and economic, social, and cultural rights on the other. A number of member states, both in the old East (during the Cold War) and the new South, have tried to change the human rights agenda by getting the human rights system as a whole to focus more on the economic and social rights – and less on civil and political rights. For most countries this change of focus is an attempt to continue the gradual development and adaptation of the international concept of human rights. They do not see this as an either/or issue, but they do recognize that the postwar international human rights agenda did not sufficiently highlight economic, social, and cultural rights.

For other countries, the purpose of this change of emphasis, such as a renewed focus on the right to water, is less altruistic. Some countries deliberately want to shift the spotlight away from their own problems in complying with civil and political rights, and to focus instead at their problems in ensuring their citizens reasonable social standards because of their economic and development limitations. In other words, the aim of these countries is to divert political attention away from what they would be able to do but have chosen not to do (ensure compliance with civil and political human rights and respect the individual freedoms of their citizens), and to turn attention to what they would like to do but are largely unable to do (secure better living standards for their citizens). This attempt to change the international human rights agenda has considerable political appeal for countries that grossly violate the civil and political rights of their citizens.

There is no doubt that the existing comprehensive international human rights standards, as expressed in the Universal Declaration in 1948, did not strike a proper balance between the various rights. As already stated, the idea then was to draw up a more comprehensive convention which would describe the complex of civil, political, economic, social, and cultural rights, but this process was frustrated by the Cold War. Instead, in 1966 the United States and the other Western countries got "their" convention on civil and political rights, while the Soviet Union and its fellow travellers got "their" convention on economic, social, and cultural rights, as referred to above.

It was only some years later, after the fall of the Berlin Wall, at the World Conference on Human Rights in Vienna in June 1993, that it was possible to gather all aspects of the human rights agenda under the same heading and to ensure the clear affirmation of the universality and indivisibility of all human rights, and of the obligation of all states to ensure compliance with them. The Final Report of the Vienna Conference expressed its unqualified support for the values and the view of human rights on which the United Nations is based, and all member states reaffirmed their commitment to the purposes and principles of the Universal Declaration of Human Rights in the light of the development and further adaptation of human rights since 1948.

New problems have come to the fore: racism and xenophobia, ethnic and religious minorities, indigenous peoples, migrant workers, the rights of the disabled, the right to development, self-determination and an increased focus on the rights of women and children. Politically, the Vienna Declaration and Programme of Action is probably the clearest and most profound intergovernmental statement of the comprehensive modern view of human rights, and the balance between different types of rights and freedoms that has been established over time. The Vienna Declaration clarifies that "[a]ll human rights are universal, indivisible and interdependent and interrelated," and that all member states have a duty to promote and protect all human rights and fundamental freedoms, regardless of their political, economic and cultural systems.[6]

NEW HUMAN RIGHTS CHALLENGES

Human rights are international norms and standards that are continually being developed, at both global and at regional levels. For European countries, the ECHR (1950) is generally more detailed and relevant than the United Nations' human rights system, which is why it is normally used by European citizens when complaining about human rights violations.

For the rest of the world, the United Nations system is still extremely important for the work to ensure respect for human rights. The following two examples illustrate this point.

The first example concerns sexual orientation and gender identity in a human rights context; in other words, how to secure the same rights for gays, lesbians, bisexuals, and transsexuals as for all other people. Many countries, particularly Islamic and African, as well as the Holy See (an observer to the United Nations), have problems recognizing that protection from discrimination also covers protection from discrimination on the grounds of sexual orientation or identity. They see this as an acceptance of homosexuality which they do not want to agree to for one reason or another.

Homosexuality is still prohibited in more than seventy countries around the world, and in some places it is still subject to very harsh punishment. In 2008, a group of predominantly European and Latin American countries issued a declaration condemning the persecution of, discrimination against, and stigmatization of people on the grounds of their sexual identity. This declaration was eventually signed by a little over one-third of the UN member states. A counter-declaration, sponsored by Syria on behalf of a number of Islamic countries, rejected the whole concept of sexual identity and saw the initiative as unacceptable interference in the national laws of other member states. This counter-declaration won the support of approximately one-quarter of the member states. The question thus divides the UN member states into two groups of nearly equal size.

In the autumn of 2010, there was a major debate in the General Assembly about sexual orientation in connection with the annual resolution condemning extrajudicial, summary, or arbitrary executions. Given the persecution to which gays and lesbians are subject in many places, the resolution listed the risk of arbitrary execution on the grounds of sexual orientation as equal to that which other groups, such as ethnic and religious minorities, refugees, and street children, might be exposed. The reference to sexual orientation, however, was put to a separate vote and in the first instance it was defeated by seventy-nine votes to seventy in the Third (Human Rights) Committee of the General Assembly. This led the United States and other Western countries to engage in a major diplomatic offensive by approaching the governments of a great number of member states with a view to getting the reference re-inserted in the resolution when it came up for a final vote in the Assembly some weeks later.

The UN secretary-general, Ban Ki-moon, also took up the issue in a statement to the General Assembly in which he made it clear that a prohibition of homosexuality was unacceptable. He summarized the issue in clear but simple terms: "Where there is tension between cultural attitudes and universal human rights, universal human rights must carry the day. Personal disapproval, even society's disapproval, is no excuse to arrest, detain, imprison, harass or torture anyone – ever." The massive diplomatic pressure succeeded, and in the final vote in the assembly, the reference was re-included with the support of ninety-three votes, with fifty against and twenty-seven abstentions, primarily because a number of African member states changed their position.

The second example concerns the legal rights of terrorism suspects. The fundamental rules of natural justice, included in the Universal Declaration, require there to be a presumption of innocence, i.e., that an accused is presumed innocent until the contrary is proved; that an accused is entitled to know what they are accused of; that they are entitled to be informed of the evidence against them; and that they are given an opportunity to defend themselves against the charges.

However, these fundamental rules of justice do not always fit well with the requirements for combatting modern terrorism. An example of this can be seen in relation to the UN sanctions regime against the Taliban in Afghanistan, and against Osama bin Laden and the al Qaeda terrorist network, which was adopted by the Security Council in Resolution 1267 in 1999 and which is regularly updated. These sanctions were introduced as part of international measures against terrorism, and typically involve freezing foreign assets and prohibiting air travel by people believed to be connected to al Qaeda or the Taliban.

The whole sanctions regime was overseen by a special 1267 Sanctions Committee of the Security Council which acted on the basis of unanimity and had the power to decide which organizations and persons are put on the "terrorist list," which all member states of the UN are thereafter required to enforce on the basis of a resolution of the Security Council. Inclusion on the list is often based on information from various intelligence services, more often than not based on intelligence rather than on the kind of evidence which would be accepted in usual judicial proceedings. Intelligence usually takes the form of "indications" and "reasonable assumptions," not hard evidence or even circumstantial evidence, and it usually needs to be treated with great confidentiality, since its disclosure can put its sources at serious risk.

Few people would presumably have any moral issues with the fact that Osama bin Laden was on the 1267 terrorist list for years before his final demise in May 2011. Together with him were almost 500 others who were assumed to have links to al Qaeda or the Taliban. Problems arise when individuals are included in the list by mistake (for example, by having a confusingly similar name with a suspected terrorist), or if the evidence for listing is simply insufficient according to the principles which would normally be applied by the courts. If a person is not informed of the basis for inclusion on the list and does not have the opportunity to refute it, there is an obvious risk of some people on the list ending up like Kafka's Josef K, in a black hole, not knowing what they are accused of, and without the possibility of defending themselves.

This problem is at the heart of the case which a Saudi businessman, Yassin Abdullah Kadi, has brought before the European Union Court of Justice. Kadi's financial assets in EU member states had been frozen since he was put on the UN's 1267 list because of suspicions that he had been financing al Qaeda. Twice, most recently in September 2010, the EU Court of Justice has rejected the European Commission's argument that the EU member states are bound to comply with the decisions of the UN Security Council and automatically transfer any person on the UN list to the EU's corresponding list. The Commission's argument was based on Article 48 of the UN Charter, according to which all UN member states are bound to implement the decisions of the Security Council.

The EU Court of Justice ruled that the UN sanctions regime did not give Kadi the necessary legal guarantees and that his right to due process had been set aside. According to the Court's decision, it is not enough to comply with decisions of the Security Council; there must also be an independent assessment of the case with the necessary legal guarantees, including the problems of satisfying the burden of proof in a case which is based primarily on intelligence. The decisive point in the judgment was that the final decision about the application of European sanctions to individuals who are suspected of involvement in terrorism must be a matter for the EU Court of Justice, and not the UN's 1267 Sanctions Committee.[7]

This ruling sets the scene for a delicate conflict between the EU Court of Justice and the UN Security Council which, in the first instance, the

EU Commission has dealt with by appealing against the ruling once more, and which the Security Council has tried to deal with by improving legal guarantees in relation to the terrorist list. Among other things, co-operation with the UN member states has been strengthened as has the council's monitoring of the persons on the 1267 list. More recently the council has appointed an ombudsperson to assist with requests from suspects to be delisted from the 1267 list.

The Canadian judge Kimberley Prost was appointed as the first ombudsperson in June 2010 with a mandate to require supplementary information from member states for inclusion in the consideration of any delisting. On the basis of her investigations, she will be able to make an analysis of the arguments and present this to the Sanctions Committee, which will then make its decision. It will presumably take some time before it becomes clear whether in practice this arrangement can provide better judicial guarantees for persons who believe they have been unjustly included on the 1267 list. The ombudsperson can only make recommendations indirectly, and the final decision is still taken by the council behind closed doors. In the Kadi case the ombudsperson eventually recommended delisting Kadi, and the recommendation was accepted by the Security Council in October 2012.[8]

The difficult balancing act between politics and law is underlined by the fact that in June 2011 the Security Council decided to divide the terrorist list under Resolution 1267 in two, one for al Qaeda and one for the Taliban. The reason for this is that the process of political reconciliation in Afghanistan would presumably make it necessary, at some point in time, to remove a number of Taliban leaders from the list in order to make them acceptable political partners in Afghanistan. There was a desire not to entertain similar considerations in relation to al Qaeda.[9]

Legal guarantees and due process for suspected terrorists are surely problems which the United Nations and the international community will have to deal with in the coming years. On the one hand, there are the general legal principles of equality before the law and access to evidence; on the other, there is the fact that the authorities do not necessarily wish to give all suspects access to all relevant information, primarily because this could compromise their sources and indirectly reveal what the authorities know and do not know. The threats from terrorist groups are real, and states must, of course, be able to take the necessary steps to protect themselves against terror attacks. So the basic question remains: How is it possible to ensure the necessary legal guarantees, and ultimately the individual freedoms and security for all citizens that we know and value, without unduly diminishing the effectiveness of the efforts necessary to prevent terror? This is not solely a problem for the United Nations or relevant only in relation to the UN terrorist lists. It is a problem which must be dealt with openly as part of the public discourse, and on the basis that it is, and must continue to be, possible to respect human rights and the general principles of a state governed by law, and that the means used in the fight against terror must reflect this.

COMBATTING THE USE OF TORTURE

The Universal Declaration is very clear on torture. Article 5 simply states, "No one shall be subjected to torture or to cruel, inhuman or degrading treatment or punishment." The prohibition of torture is absolute. There are no exceptions.

The UN Convention against Torture and Other Cruel, Inhuman or Degrading Treatment or Punishment was adopted in 1984 and entered into force in 1987. The Convention defines torture as intentionally inflicting severe pain or suffering, whether physical or mental, on a person for the purpose of inducing them to do something specific. Member states that ratify the Convention commit themselves to provisions such as, prohibiting and combatting any form of torture within their own borders, investigating immediately all complaints about torture, making torture a criminal offence, prohibiting the use of evidence obtained by torture, and not extraditing people if there are reasonable grounds for suspecting that they will be subject to torture.

The absolute prohibition of torture is emphasized in Article 2 of the Convention, where it is made clear that "[n]o exceptional circumstances whatsoever, whether a state of war or a threat of war, internal political in stability or any other public emergency, may be invoked as a justification of torture."

The "ticking bomb" scenario, which is often referred to, where it is supposed that the use of torture could force the disclosure of information which may prevent an atrocity, is thus clearly contrary to the convention. It is in any case very dubious, as the combination of circumstances which would produce such a situation would be vanishingly rare. Moreover, law enforcement officers with wide interrogation experience have argued that other interrogation techniques are more effective and produce more trustworthy information than that which can be obtained by using torture. The underlying aim of torture is not to obtain information but to create fear and take revenge. Even if one believes that, under certain circumstances and in wholly exceptional situations, torture can produce usable information, that value must always be weighed against the serious loss of moral legitimacy caused by the authorization and use of torture.[10]

As stated above, with a treaty-based instrument such as the Torture Convention, states must take a positive step to ratify it and thus explicitly accept the legal obligations that follow from accession to the convention. States that ratify the Convention must submit regular reports (every four years) on what they are doing to implement its provisions. These reports are reviewed by the Committee against Torture (CAT), which comments and issues conclusions on the reports of the State Parties to the Convention. In some cases human rights organizations will draw up their own shadow reports in which they may call in question the official reports. Naturally, these shadow reports are also taken into account by CAT.

Of the 153 member states that had ratified the Torture Convention by early 2013, 66 had also recognized the competence of CAT to examine complaints from their own citizens. The right of individuals to make complaints allows citizens who have exhausted national appeal procedures to bring cases about violations of the Convention. There are similar possibilities for bringing complaints in other human rights conventions. Member states will, of course, be provided with an opportunity to respond to such complaints and submit supplementary material, after which CAT can decide, on the basis of the materials before it, whether there has been a breach of one or more of the provisions of the Convention. If CAT believes that there has been a breach, the member state in question will often be encouraged to investigate the case more thoroughly or, in the case of a clear violation, to take the necessary measures and report back to CAT on the issue. CAT does not have the power to enforce its decisions, but countries that have agreed to the right of individuals to complain are assumed to be sensitive to criticism and to generally comply with Committee's recommendations.[11]

There is also an Optional Protocol to the Torture Convention which entered into force in 2006 and which contains two further measures to strengthen the fight against torture. First, it establishes national preventive mechanisms in the individual member states which are intended to focus on prisons and other places where there is a special risk of torture; and second, it allows for unannounced visits to be made by the UN Subcommittee on the Prevention of Torture to police stations, prisons, detention centres, mental health and social care institutions, and any other places where people are or may be deprived of their liberty. By early 2013, sixty-seven countries had ratified the Optional Protocol.

Since 1985, there has been a UN special rapporteur on torture who can look into particular cases and review particular themes. The special rapporteur on torture is appointed by the HRC, and can also review the situation in countries that have not ratified the Torture Convention, including visiting such countries and inspecting their institutions.

However, in practice the special rapporteur's scope for investigation is limited by the fact that there are many countries to which he is unable to get permission to visit. The present special rapporteur is Juan Mendez, who took office on 1 November 2010. His predecessor, Manfred Nowak, focused on prison conditions and in October 2010 he published a report which was highly critical of the Greek authorities' treatment of migrants and asylum-seekers. Unsurprisingly, it is quite common for some countries in the HRC to try to restrict the special rapporteur's mandate and make it more difficult for him to make criticisms in specific cases. However, so far it has been possible to secure a clear and effective mandate.[12]

The Torture Convention, the Committee against Torture, the Optional Protocol, the Subcommittee on the Prevention of Torture, the special rapporteur, country reports, conclusions, complaints, statements, and reports – the whole sum of this network of international human rights instruments is intended to ensure that the prohibition of torture is effective. In order to connect all the dots and provide a common framework for the entire system, and to mark the steady progress of international collaboration in the fight against torture, the General Assembly adopts a comprehensive resolution each year on torture and other cruel, inhuman, or degrading treatment or punishment.

It has often been difficult to ensure broad support for the continued development of international standards which a number of countries clearly do not live up to in practice, and which they – by implication – would prefer to see weakened. Many countries have something to hide in relation to the use of torture and degrading treatment. Topics such as the United States' detention centre at Guantanamo Bay in Cuba, the use of "extraordinary rendition" (the transfer of prisoners for interrogation in another country), and the use of waterboarding (the use of a technique that makes the victims feel they are drowning) in the interrogation of suspects have therefore also been raised during the negotiations.

However, in recent years there has been some success with regard to the continued strengthening of the resolution, both in relation to improved formulations for the protection of individuals and organizations that contact national or international organizations engaged in the fight against torture, and in relation to the agreement of stricter requirements for states to investigate the alleged use of torture. This progress year by year is important. Even though General Assembly resolutions are not binding, in a number of countries the courts do pay attention to these resolutions when considering the state of the law in this area.

The prohibition of torture is absolute. Even if the global fight against torture can hardly be won immediately, it is important – and essential for the UN's ambitions to promote human rights and fundamental freedoms everywhere and for everyone – that the challenge should be taken up again and again, regardless of which country might come under the spotlight. Proportionality is important, and the harshest criticism must always be reserved for those countries in which the use of torture is most widespread and systematic. But the prohibition is nevertheless absolute, and each country must expect to be criticized if it does not live up to the norms and standards as set out in the convention.

Increasing public awareness of torture and reinforcing government measures to combat the use of torture remain significant challenges, not least in those countries where the use of torture and degrading treatment by police and security services is more widespread. In this situation UN collaboration with non-governmental human rights organizations is key; whether Amnesty International, Human Rights Watch, the Association for the Prevention of Torture, or any of the other organizations which are doing important work in this area. Co-operation with torture rehabilitation centres around the world is also important, and helps increase public knowledge of the long-term physical and mental harm than can be caused by torture.

The international fight against torture will continue, both in the UN General Assembly, in the HRC, and under the auspices of the Torture Convention and the human rights bodies and instruments of the United Nations. In order to increase the impact of these efforts, the

UN will have to engage more actively and directly in a stronger public diplomacy campaign directed at political decision makers, police, and security services as well as the general public. Member states can, and should, engage in these efforts alongside the United Nations.

UNIVERSAL VALUES OR WESTERN VALUES?

The United Nations is generally perceived as a value-based – and value-driven – organization, due to the political and moral values inherent in the Charter and the Universal Declaration of Human Rights. This perception, however, is challenged by political disagreements about what this actually means, and especially by differing views on the specific values which define the concept of human rights. Which human rights, for whom, and which practical effects?

As stated previously, during the Cold War the basic political conflict was between the East and the West, on the primacy of civil and political rights versus economic, social, and cultural rights. With the fall of the Berlin Wall, this picture changed dramatically. For a few years in the first half of the 1990s there was a widespread feeling that the world had reached what the American historian Francis Fukuyama called "the end of history," in the sense that liberal democracy had overcome all opposition and that the world had now found its final ideological-political form. It was during this period that Western liberal ideas reached their high point, and this led to the adoption of a set of global norms and standards for which it would probably be far harder to get universal support today: the Vienna Declaration on Human Rights (1993), the International Conference on Population and Development (1994), and the Platform for Action at the Fourth World Conference on Women in Beijing (1995). The idea of "the end of history" faded toward the end of the 1990s, and it vanished entirely with the terrorist attacks on New York and Washington on 11 September 2001.[13]

Today the arguments concerning key sets of values largely concern whether human rights, and civil and political rights in particular, express universal values or whether they are primarily the products of Western thinking. The idea that human rights as we know them are purely Western ideas is directly contradicted by the fact that many other cultural traditions and religions are to a large extent based on corresponding ideas. However, the Universal Declaration omits at least one right which the victors of the Second World War were unwilling to sign up to in 1948, namely the right of a people to self-determination. However, the Vienna Declaration on Human Rights in 1993 gave prominence to the right of all peoples to self-determination, to freely determine their political status, and to freely pursue their economic, social and cultural development.

In many ways, the process of decolonization, which took place from the late 1940s and for some twenty to twenty-five years thereafter, created a United Nations that was very different from the organization that was established in 1945. Many former British or French colonies received their own copies of the Westminster Parliament or the French National Assembly as a kind of coming-of-age present, and often not much more than an additional "best of luck" from their former colonial masters. Especially in Africa almost all the new states were severely affected by their colonial legacies, whether in the form of entirely arbitrary national borders, complex ethnic and tribal mixes, or very limited institutional capacities. On top of this, many new states easily became pawns in the Cold War rivalries and many succumbed to the traditional focus on leadership by a strongman. It is hardly surprising that in the 1970s and 1980s in most of these countries their initial hopes of freedom and prosperity ran aground with many of them ending up as one-party states, ruled by brutal dictators.

But even in these cases traditional democratic political thinking proved its strength. Paradoxically, the universal attraction of the idea of political freedom and democracy has often been demonstrated by the charades by which many dictators have been at pains to show that they also are democratic at the core and that they respect their citizens' right to choose their leaders. "Free and fair elections" have been presented by the yard to the international community, often accompanied by implausible majorities of votes and "spontaneous" popular demonstrations of joy at the outcome when the expected results were announced.

Against this background real encouragement has been found in recent years in the fact that a number of fairly new states have passed the ultimate test of democracy – political elections whereby a new majority in Parliament emerges and the government resigns and peacefully hands over the reins of power the a new government representing a new political majority. However, overall the global situation has not changed much over the last decade. In 2013, the well-known non-governmental American organization Freedom House assessed that forty-seven countries were not free; the number was exeactly the same in 2000 (forty-seven). Freedom House concluded that ninety countries were free (representing forty-three per cent of the global population) and fifty-eight were partially free in 2013; the corresponding numbers for 2000 were eighty-six and fifty-eight.[14]

In relation to human rights and the ideals of freedom in the UN context, there are four particular challenges to the traditional view of the United Nations as a value-driven organization, based on universal values. The background to the prominence of this issue on the international agenda is the changing global balance of power in recent decades, and the gradual shift of the world's economic centre of gravity toward Asia, and especially toward China, India, Japan, South Korea, and the ASEAN countries in Southeast Asia. At the same time there has been a religious radicalization in some countries, especially among the young and especially in the Islamic world, supporting those Islamist forces that want to confront the West.

A number of Islamic countries clearly use the value-based political issues on the UN agenda to show how Islamic they are and thus to demonstrate their religious credentials at no real cost at home. It should, of course, be emphasized that religious radicalization is not only an Islamic phenomenon. The same phenomenon can be observed, though to a lesser extent, in other major religions, including Christianity and Judaism.

The first challenge is the natural feeling of solidarity between developing countries struggling with the same kinds of problem. The tendency to reject criticism from the outside seems in general to be on the increase, and this unquestionably reflects these countries' historical similarities as well as the feeling that "your problems today can be my problems tomorrow." From this perspective it is relatively easy to identify with one's neighbour's anger at being publicly criticized for violating human rights. The notion of "people in glasshouses shouldn't throw stones," and the attitude of "if I support him today, maybe he'll support me tomorrow if I have a similar problem" is an understandable reaction and reflects an entirely understandable degree of political caution.

This attitude generally leads developing countries to support each other and to reject criticism of an individual country in the General Assembly or in the HRC. This trend has probably also been reinforced by closer formal co-operation in a number of regions and by the strong desire for such regional organizations to deal with their own regional problems, as in ASEAN (Southeast Asia), ECOWAS (West Africa), SADC (Southern Africa), and the emerging integration process in the

AU. But the trend can probably also be seen as an expression of a high-er degree of political self-confidence of many countries, reflecting the changing global balance of power.

As a result, it is much harder than previously to get resolutions adopted that are critical of individual countries. In 1999, the General Assembly adopted resolutions criticizing the human rights situations in Afghanistan, Bosnia-Herzegovina, Myanmar, Cambodia, DR Congo, Haiti, Iran, Iraq, Kosovo, Rwanda, and Sudan – some of these even without it being put to the vote. In 2012, it was only possible to get critical resolutions adopted on four countries: Myanmar, Iran, North Korea, and Syria. Ever more developing countries are against the nam-ing and shaming of countries, whichever the country, as an instru- ment of international human rights co-operation.

The second challenge concerns the right to development, which involves an attempt to internationalize the responsibility for ensuring economic and social rights so as to place it more clearly on the shoul-ders of the Western countries. A Declaration on the Right to Devel-opment was adopted by the General Assembly in December 1986. In the vote, only the United States voted against, and eight other coun-tries abstained. The right to development constituted a new form of rights which, in addition to a right to development for the individual, also defined a collective right for peoples and states.

The right to development is only defined very generally in the Dec-laration, primarily as including the fulfillment of and compliance with all other human rights, civil and political, and economic, social and cultural. Thus, for the individual, the right to development is pri-marily a right to participate in a development process that leads to better conditions for all. Seen in this light, the states have both a right and a duty to formulate national policies and strategies which can ensure such better conditions for all, and remove obstacles to the enjoyment of all rights, including civil and political rights. All this is primarily a declaration of intent.

What was politically controversial was that the Declaration also stated that "States have the primary responsibility for the creation of national and international conditions favourable to the realization of the right to development," and that "States have the duty to take steps, individually and collectively, to formulate international development policies with a view to facilitating the full realization of the right to development." In the eyes of the Declaration's critics, this meant that some developing countries could avoid their responsibilities to their own citizens and instead pass this responsibility on to others, not least the former colonial powers and the "rich countries" in general, with demands for increased aid, improved market access, et cetera, as preconditions for these countries living up to their obligations to protect the human rights of their own citizens. In the light of this interpretation, a right to development could very well end up legitimizing many countries' lack of capacity being used to absolve them from well-founded criticism of their absence of political will. This led many Western countries to be somewhat sceptical about the whole idea of the right to development.[15]

The third challenge is the key question of whether the values are truly universal, or whether they merely reflect Western values developed over the last couple of centuries. The question goes further, asking whether human rights may be culture-related and whether, for example, there may be Asian values, as has been argued by some Asian politicians, such as Malaysia's former prime minister Mahathir Mohamad and Singapore's former prime minister Lee Kuan Yew.

If this is so, these Asian values are in part inspired by broadly shared Asian beliefs, especially by Confucianism, which put the emphasis on society, the family, and the collective, rather than on the individual. In this context, social harmony, a consensus culture, community, and authority are seen as stronger and more important forces than the individual and his or her rights and freedoms. In this thinking, individuals must often subordinate themselves to the wider community and primarily see themselves as part of it. In return, they share in the economic prosperity which the community achieves and which is assumed to give greater growth rates that can be achieved under other conditions.

The clearest example of this is China, where the Communist Party has liberalized the economy since the 1980s, but not its political system, and which still reckons that a continued annual economic growth of about 10 per cent will be enough to avoid serious political challenges and popular calls for increased political freedom and a more democratic form of government.

There are many arguments against the existence of such special Asian values. The Indian economist and Nobel Prize winner Amartya Sen has denied the existence of such a connection between the political form of government and economic achievements. There is no evidence that authoritarian systems create more economic growth. On the contrary, democratic and free societies are much more able to deal with crises than authoritarian ones. The whole discussion of special values which stand above or replace the universal human rights has primarily been generated by authoritarian regimes as an attempt to keep hold of power and to resist demands for freedom and democracy.

It has been argued that, even where the economy seems to be successful on the surface, as in today's China, where in the recent decades several hundred million people have been raised from poverty and into the middle classes, and in countries such as Vietnam and Singapore, it is probably only a question of time before internal tensions will appear more clearly. Economic growth and higher standards of living also lead to increased access to global knowledge sharing and political discussions via the Internet. New generations and a fast-growing middle class will be steadily more global in their outlook and attitudes, and they are unlikely to be willing to remain without direct influence on the most important decision in their society. Conversely, it must be acknowledged that these arguments have been made for many years without the predicted demands for more democratic government becoming apparent.[16]

The fourth challenge is a variation of the discussion about whether human rights are relative, but focusing on religion rather than on culture more broadly. The central issue in this context concerns yet another problem of balance: freedom of expression as opposed to defamation of religion, especially in relation to Islam – an issue which the Organization of Islamic Cooperation (OIC) has for many years taken to the General Assembly. In particular, the publication of the Mohammed cartoons in the Danish newspaper *Jyllands-Posten* in September 2005 led to intensified discussion.

Freedom of expression is not absolute. Most countries have laws on defamation, whereby one can incur liability if one spreads false rumours or make false accusations against another. This is considered necessary in order to provide a natural protection of other peoples' rights and freedoms. Pornographic material is prohibited in many countries and is not covered by the usual provisions on freedom of expression, just as considerations for national security can restrict how freely citizens can express themselves in certain situations.

Racist expressions are also not permitted. In a number of countries it is a criminal offence to threaten, insult, or denigrate others on the grounds of their race, skin colour, national or ethnic origin, religion, or sexual orientation. Many countries also have laws against blasphemy, making it a criminal offence to ridicule or insult religious teachings or the worship of God. Precisely what this means is a matter for the courts to interpret, often based on an assessment of the extent of the insulting behaviour and its threat to public order. However, in most Western countries blasphemy laws, if still on the books, are in reality hardly ever enforced. There is no doubt that the freedom of expression in these countries is broadly defined and that restrictions on it are fairly few.

In the context of the United Nations, however, there are conflicting positions on this issue. The OIC countries want to establish an international norm whereby states can restrict freedom of expression if it results in insults of religion, understood as expressions that criticize, offend, or otherwise affront the religious sentiments of those who believe.

Western countries dismiss such restrictions on freedom of expression as unacceptable and as legitimizing entirely arbitrary limits on one of the most important civil and political rights. The view of most Western countries is that the restrictions on freedom of expression in Article 20(2) of the ICCPR are quite sufficient, stating that "[a]ny advocacy of national, racial or religious hatred that constitutes incitement to discrimination, hostility or violence shall be prohibited by law." Western countries in general believe that there is no need for further restrictions on freedom of expression.

From a Western point of view, the real issue in relation to religion and freedom of expression is a very different one, namely the lack of freedom for religious minorities, including Christian minorities in Muslim countries, to practise their religion, despite clear provisions to the contrary in both the Universal Declaration of Human Rights and the ICCPR. Therefore, when the OIC put forward their draft resolution on combatting defamation of religions, the EU member states put forward their counter-proposal on combatting religious intolerance.[17]

The core of this discussion is not whether freedom of expression can be restricted in relation to expressions encouraging violence or discrimination against people of other faiths – it can. The core question is whether such a restriction can be based on anything other than the general considerations of public welfare or public order, and whether offending religious sentiments or offending religions as such can justify restrictions on freedom of expression? In their more recent arguments the OIC countries have referred to a growing Islamophobic tendency and to multiple examples of insults of Muslims and Islamic symbols in Western countries. Their proposal is thus presented as a defensive measure in the light of Western countries' failure to recognize the extent of the problem and as necessary because of the discrimination and incidents to which Islamophobic tendencies often lead.

Western countries in general reject the idea of giving human rights protection to religions. As expressed by the EU member states in their joint explanation of their votes in the General Assembly in November 2010: "International human rights law protects individuals in the exercise of their freedoms, and does not and should not protect religions or belief systems as such." In the view of the EU member states, the solution does not lie in restricting freedom of expression but in a dialogue about the real problems of discrimination which religious minorities may experience.

For Western countries, the OIC proposal is an unacceptable restriction on freedom of expression. To the extent that criticisms of religion take on the character of encouragement to discriminate, hostility, or violence, these are already covered by the prohibition of hate speech in Article 20 of the ICCPR. To the extent that expressions are not of such a kind, then freedom of expression applies, even though many might feel offended by this. From a Western point of view, it has been positive to see the dwindling support over recent years for the OIC's position among UN member states. The voting numbers have been: 2007 – 108 in favour of the OIC resolution, 51 against (primarily European countries and the United States), and 25 abstentions; 2008 – 86 in favour, 61 against, and 42 abstentions; 2009 – 80 in favour, 61 against, and 42 abstentions; and 2010 – 76 in favour, 64 against, and 42 abstentions. Even though the proposal has been adopted each year, the trend has been that of an ever decreasing majority. This eventually made the OIC seek a compromise and, following intense negotiations between the OIC, the EU, and the United States, the HRC in March 2011 unanimously adopted a consensus resolution omitting references to defamation of religion and Islamophobia. What effectively happened was that the OIC countries recognized that their resolution might at some point run the risk of being voted down, and they chose instead to water down their proposal so that it basically reflected the wording of the ICCPR.

But it should once more be emphasized that the issue of religion versus free speech is not only relevant in relation to Islamic countries. In a report in 2010, Freedom House pointed out that both Greece and Poland had religiously motivated restrictions on freedom of expression which were intended to limit criticisms of the dominant religion, reflecting the influence of the Greek Orthodox and Roman Catholic churches respectively in these two countries.[18]

THE WAY FORWARD

Human rights discussions in the United Nations reflect the ongoing global discussions – sometimes very fundamental and more often than not quite heated – of values and of systems of values. New rights and demands are put forward, often resulting in the scope of the classic individual rights being relatively reduced. A number of the new elements are justified and broadly accepted as reflecting the continuing development of the concept of human rights. In other cases, the new ideas are poorly concealed attempts to reduce the impact of individual rights and fundamental freedoms. This distinction is not without importance.

Democratic systems, and the rights of a country's citizens to choose their own political leaders, are an inherent part of human rights. This does not mean that all countries must implement this right in the same way or that all political systems should be alike. Moreover, democracy is not just a matter of being free to vote; it is also a question of political culture, of a strong civil society and free public debate, free and accessible media, as well as strong and effective social institutions that can implement political change. It takes time to build up such an enabling environment, and one should not expect perfection from the very first day. Western Europe has taken centuries to develop the democratic systems and political cultures it has today. And the journey is not over.

The human rights system and human rights values which the United Nations stand for, and which are inscribed in the UN Charter, the Universal Declaration and the various human rights conventions have their roots in the fundamental freedoms formulated in the seventeenth and eighteenth centuries. Even though these rights have been further elaborated in succeeding generations – with economic, social and cultural rights as well as more collective rights – it is still the individual civil and political rights and fundamental freedoms that are at the core of the UN's values. These rights are inherent, equal, and universal.

The United Nations is currently making progress in many areas related to human rights. There is much more information available in the public domain on the human rights situation in many countries, and much greater awareness of violations of human rights in

individual countries, also in Western countries. International human
rights organizations are becoming stronger and their analyses are better documented than before. And in a number of countries with very
difficult and oppressive human rights conditions, popular movements spring up when the pressure becomes too great. The Arab
Spring of 2011 clearly shows how repression can lead to insurrection,
and how today's youth are able to mobilize political pressure against
authoritarian regimes. Overall, there is no indication that the ideas
and values that underpin the United Nations' efforts to promote and
defend human rights are in retreat.

At the same time, there is a feeling that in future human rights may
come under more pressure, primarily because of the shift in the balance of global power and the increased economic strength of some
authoritarian regimes. If, as is usually the case, economic strength is
reflected in the political weight of these countries, this will to some
degree affect the international human rights discourse.

But it must also be assumed that a general strengthening of regional organizations and increased regional economic integration in the
coming years will have a positive effect in the area of human rights. In
some cases strengthened regional co-operation will probably increase
the interaction with and indirect pressure from other countries in the
region on those countries which may have problems of complying
with established human rights standards.

Similarly, it must be assumed that increased contact between peoples, the continued spread of information technology, and the mobilization of Internet-based campaigns will strengthen co-operation
between networks of national, regional, and international civil society
groups. Such a development, combined with the probable and significantly increased political engagement of younger generations may
very well change the rules of the game. If this is the case, then the Arab
Spring may be followed by a warmer summer in other parts of the
world.

It is difficult to predict the future. And precisely because of this it
is important to focus on the basics – to insist that the human rights
norms and standards that have been developed within the context of
the United Nations over the past decades must not be diluted, and
that the values of the United Nations, as expressed in the Charter and
the Universal Declaration on Human Rights, must be upheld as universal values.[19]

8

Genocide and War Crimes

Each individual State has the responsibility to protect its populations from genocide, war crimes, ethnic cleansing and crimes against humanity ... The international community should, as appropriate, encourage and help States to exercise this responsibility ...

UN World Summit Outcome 2005, paragraph 138

SOVEREIGNTY UNDER PRESSURE

"Nothing contained in the present Charter shall authorize the United Nations to intervene in matters which are essentially within the domestic jurisdiction of any state." These are the words of Article 2(7) of the UN Charter, and they are a clear expression of the fundamental aspect of the Charter, that the United Nations has no right to interfere in matters that take place within the borders of a sovereign state.

This means that the United Nations has no mandate to involve itself in the "domestic affairs" or "internal concerns" of a country. States are sovereign and interact with their citizens without interference from outside. They chart their economic and political course and adopt the necessary measures to implement it. They have full self-determination over their own territories, and it is not for others to question how they exercise their national sovereignty. States can, of course, undertake certain international obligation by acceding to international treaties or conventions which limit the exercise of their sovereignty, but the point of departure is a very broad interpretation of state sovereignty.

This is the classic view of states as the real actors in international relations. In the classic view, reflected in the United Nations Charter, what mattered was what happened *between* states and not what happened *within* individual states. States were chess pieces of varying sizes and values, but playing by an agreed set of rules. What happened within a state did not concern others and was not relevant to international relations. However, this view was challenged long before the drafting of the UN Charter. In the nineteenth century, there were those who argued that "they" (usually the great powers, and not always for idealistic motives) ought to intervene in relation to genocide and ethnic or religious cleansing in other countries. Even then the argument was that situations could arise where the overriding considerations of human rights and justice might trump the sovereignty of states.

One example was in Lebanon and Syria in 1860, when France and the United Kingdom intervened to stop widespread attacks on the civilian population in connection with a bloody conflict between Christian Maronites and the Druze population.

The British Foreign Secretary at the time, Lord Russell, made it clear, in terms that seem quite modern 150 years later, that the British government would only offer naval support and would not deploy land troops in order to prevent the massacres, and that he was also in favour of there being a time limit on the mandate for the operation. Russell was afraid that the presence of foreign troops "could provoke a fiercer fanaticism" among the parties to the conflict. In the twentieth century the Armenian genocide in Turkey in 1915–16 was the focus of huge international attention and epitomized what unrestrained attacks and killings meant in a time of modern warfare. The attacks against the Armenians led to political demands for external intervention to stop the killings, not least in the political debate in the United States. However, the military and political preoccupations of the First World War (1914–18) prevented interventions by other countries.[1]

It was the Nazi regime's killing of six million Jews and its attempt to wipe out the Roma people and other Eastern European minorities that was the direct occasion for the drawing up of the United Nation's first human rights convention, the Convention on the Prevention and Punishment of the Crime of Genocide in 1948. In the Genocide Convention, "genocide" is defined as "acts committed with intent to destroy, in whole or in part, a national, ethnical, racial or religious group." The definition of genocide was the subject of hard negotiations, resulting in a narrow definition which did not cover systematic attacks on and attempts to eliminate political or social groups, nor those with a minority sexual orientation.

In the decades since the Genocide Convention the world has witnessed one major attempt after another to eliminate population groups "in whole or in part." Sometimes the international community has intervened and sometimes not, and in some cases interventions have had negative consequences. The terror regime of the Khmer Rouge and Pol Pot in Cambodia caused more than two million deaths between 1975 and 1979 – several hundred thousand directly murdered and many more who died of avoidable starvation and disease. When Cambodia's neighbour, Vietnam, intervened and overthrew the Pol Pot regime, it was Vietnam that was condemned by the Western countries. It was clear that the Vietnamese intervention was not made only, or even primarily, on humanitarian grounds, but it presumably saved many hundreds of thousands of Cambodians from death from privation.

Another example, from the same period as Vietnam's invasion of Cambodia, was Tanzania's intervention in Uganda and the toppling of its then president Idi Amin. Amin was directly responsible for the deaths of more than 100,000 of the country's own citizens in the course of his eight-year dictatorship, but it was his thinly disguised threats against Uganda's neighbour Tanzania that was the official reason for the military intervention. Tanzania's president Julius Nyerere never justified the intervention by reference to Amin's atrocities against his own people.

In contrast to the case of Vietnam, the Tanzanian military intervention was generally accepted by the international community. This was probably in part due to the international prestige enjoyed by President Nyerere at the time and the fact that, unlike Vietnam, he had not placed Tanzania as an ally alongside the Soviet Union during the Cold War. Great power politics, alliances and the balance of power between East and West remained important up to 1989. Major crimes against humanity and genocide were seen and interpreted through this political prism.[2]

In this context, the 1990s was a turning point. In December 1992, the Security Council decided to initiate an operation to impose peace in Somalia, with a view to establishing sufficient security in the country to enable emergency relief operations and ease the effects of the civil war which was ravaging the country. Thirty-eight thousand soldiers, including 25,000 Americans, made up UNITAF/Operation Restore Hope, which made a good start, but in the course of 1993 found it increasingly difficult to convince the local clan-based militias to co-operate.

Developments on the ground increased already tense relations between the UN force and the local leaders and their militias. In June
1993, twenty-three Pakistani soldiers were killed in a confrontation
with General Mohamed Farrah Aidid's militia, and in October 1993,
eighteen US soldiers were killed in the "Black Hawk Down" incident
in the capital Mogadishu. Black Hawk Down (the name related to
the shooting down of two US attack helicopters) caused considerable
shock in the United States, which had to recognize that the UN troops
were not seen as liberators on a humanitarian mission but as just another part of the problem in a complex political and military struggle
between various Somali clans. This recognition led the Clinton administration to withdraw its troops from Somalia. Other troop contributors
quickly followed suit, and on 4 February 1994, the Security Council
took the formal decision to end the UN operation in Somalia.

The experiences in Somalia and of Black Hawk Down are important to a full understanding of what happened – or rather, did not
happen – in Rwanda in 1994. Two months after the Security Council
pulled the plug on Somalia, Rwanda's president was killed when his
aircraft was shot down on its way back to the capital Kigali from Dar
es Salaam in neighbouring Tanzania.

This triggered one of the bloodiest genocides of recent times. The
UN peacekeeping mission, United Nations Assistance Mission for
Rwanda (UNAMIR), under the leadership of the Canadian general
Roméo Dallaire, numbered about 5,000. They looked on, powerless,
while in the following hundred days, parts of the Hutu population,
with the active support of the Hutu-controlled military and police
forces, killed hundreds of thousands of the Tutsi population. Altogether about 800,000 Tutsis and moderate Hutus were killed, mostly
with machetes and knives, and neither the United States nor the
United Nations did anything effective to stop this extensive and pro-
longed genocide. President Clinton later acknowledged that the lack
of an American reaction, once it became clear what was going on in
Rwanda, was the biggest mistake of his eight-year term of office as
president.

Ten Belgian UN soldiers were killed on the first day of the genocide, and this led Belgium, by far the biggest contributor of UN
troops, to withdraw its troops from Rwanda. The orders from New
York to the UN force in Kigali were clear: "You should make every
effort not to compromise your impartiality or to act beyond your
mandate, but [you] may exercise your discretion to do [so] should this

be essential for the evacuation of foreign nationals. This should not, repeat not, extend to participating in possible combat except in self-defence." The Belgian withdrawal reduced the UN force to 2,100 troops, and with the Belgian troops went the force's signals and communications capacity. Dallaire had one satellite telephone with a connection outside Rwanda.

The United States demanded the full withdrawal of the UN troops. The Security Council decided to reduce the UN force to 270, with a purely observer role. However, some troop contributors maintained forces above this level so that the force remained at about 500 who did what they could, without the use of weapons, to show the UN flag and to limit the killings. It was first toward the end of June, nearly three months after the start of the mass killings, that international forces were deployed in Rwanda in the form of French troops who created a safe area in the southwest of the country. By that time, the mass killings had begun to diminish. The Hutu leaders had achieved what they wanted.

In the following year, in July 1995, there was another decisive event, this time in the Western Balkans. The dissolution of Yugoslavia at the beginning of the 1990s, and the gradual establishment of seven new states to replace it (Bosnia-Herzegovina, Croatia, Macedonia, Montenegro, Serbia, Slovenia, and most recently Kosovo) led to years of civil war and conflict.

The town of Srebrenica, in Bosnia and Herzegovina, was designated a safe area, protected by a few hundred lightly armed Dutch soldiers who were part of the United Nations Protection Force (UNPRO-FOR), to which the Security Council had given a mandate primarily to monitor the ceasefire between Bosnia and Croatia. On 11 July 1995, the Bosnian-Serb General Ratko Mladić entered Srebrenica, and over the following days his troops separated and then killed more than 7,000 Muslim men and boys. This was the biggest mass killing in Europe since the end of the Second World War. The Dutch troops had neither the resources, nor the support, nor the mandate to defend the city against Mladić's forces.[3]

Apart from providing the political background to the changes in the UN's concept of peacekeeping operations set out in the Brahimi Report (discussed in chapter 5), the events in Mogadishu, Kigali and Srebrenica also prompted renewed consideration of whether and to what extent the international community had a duty to react to genocide and other crimes against humanity. In many ways this was a return to the debate from the nineteenth and early twentieth centuries: are a country's domestic affairs solely a matter for that country, in particular if those in power systematically try to eliminate whole groups of the population? Was there nothing which, in some situations and on the basis of a humanitarian imperative, should override the state sovereignty defined in Article 2(7) of the UN Charter?

Those questions were picked up by politicians and academics around the world. In Denmark, for example, the Danish Institute of International Affairs (now the Danish Institute for International Studies [DIIS]) was asked in 1999 to draw up a report on the political and legal aspects of possible humanitarian intervention in situations where there are gross violations of human rights threatening the lives of large numbers of innocent people.

The report identified four different approaches to the question: a status quo strategy in which, pursuant to the UN Charter, any humanitarian intervention requires an explicit mandate from the Security Council; an ad hoc strategy under which humanitarian intervention is seen as an emergency *sui generis* exception to the general principle of international law when action by the Security Council is blocked, usually by a veto of one or more of the permanent members; an exception strategy under which an attempt is made to develop a subsidiary right in international law to undertake a humanitarian interventions regardless of the Security Council if the council is unable to act; and a general strategy, which would be the most extensive strategy and which would seek to develop a general right for humanitarian intervention, regardless of the Security Council, along the lines of the general right of self-defence (which is stated in Article 51 of the UN Charter).

The report did not provide final recommendations. It emphasized that the status quo strategy only makes sense if in practice it is developed by seeking greater consensus in the Security Council (status quo plus), i.e., in order to retain the Security Council's unique position in international law, its members should be more responsive to situations which might spur action being taken outside the council and therefore should be more pro-active in contributing to solutions. The report clearly recognized that there is a growing need for a safety valve to prevent an impasse in the council hindering international efforts to prevent humanitarian tragedies, and that the solution to this problem is to be found by combining the approaches of the first two strategies. The primary strategy thus would be to have a more effectively functioning Security Council, supplemented by an emergency exception in situations where a humanitarian imperative makes intervention necessary, and ensuring that any such intervention should be carried out in a way that does not fundamentally challenge the legitimacy and status of the council.[4]

The Danish report was completed in October 1999, and its conclusions were, of course, greatly influenced by the situation in Kosovo earlier in 1999 where, because of Russian and Chinese opposition, the Security Council had been unable to counter ethnic cleansing by the Serbian president Slobodan Milosevic of the Albanian majority in the province of Kosovo which was then still a part of Serbia.

The Security Council's paralysis concerning Kosovo led to a decision by the United States, together with its allies in NATO, to start bombing targets in Serbia. It is not hard to see NATO's decision in relation to Kosovo both as a reflection of the situation in the region and of the shame felt over what had happened in Rwanda and Srebrenica. Perhaps it also demonstrated that more attention is paid to these kinds of atrocities when they are committed closer to home. Kosovo was a part of Europe and had suffered its share of tragedy during the Second World War. The political situation in which a clear majority of the council favoured intervention and where the humanitarian imperative was obvious – in the form the ethnic cleansing of Albanians and the creation of massive flows of refugees from Kosovo to the rest of Europe – gave the decision to intervene militarily a different legitimacy. In this way, the NATO decision to initiate the bombing of Serbia was quite different from the US intervention in Iraq in 2003, when there was no acute humanitarian situation which could explain or justify the intervention, nor a majority in the council for such a military intervention, as discussed in chapter 4.[5]

RESPONSIBILITY TO PROTECT – R2P

The situation described above was also considered by an International Commission on Intervention and State Sovereignty (ICISS) in Ottawa, appointed to clarify the issue of national sovereignty versus humanitarian protection. The ICISS's report formulated the concept of the responsibility to protect (R2P) in an attempt to emphasize the need first and foremost to protect the victims of widespread crimes against humanity. The rights of the victims and their protection should be the focus of attention, and not the "rights" of other states to intervene. This difference is not mere semantics; it decisively alters the approach to the issue.

The ICISS report started from the definition of state sovereignty. Externally, sovereignty means that all states are equal and that therefore each state is bound to respect the sovereignty of other states, as is made clear in Article 2 of the UN Charter. Domestically, state sovereignty involves an obligation to respect the personal dignity and rights of all the state's citizens. The key to this concept is sovereignty as responsibility. The sovereignty of states should be considered as being freedom with responsibility and is therefore conditional on the state being able to fulfill its responsibilities, both in relation to other states *and* in relation to its own citizens.

The ICISS defined this responsibility at three levels:

- Responsibility to Prevent: The prevention of internal conflicts and major crimes against humanity is the key challenge. Problems must be dealt with early, before they become major issues. It is the responsibility of each state to ensure this, but it is also the responsibility of the international community to help in this regard.
- Responsibility to React: If a state is unable or unwilling to solve problems relating to its responsibility to protect its own citizens, it may be necessary for the international community to react. A variety of means can be used: political pressure, sanctions and, in extreme cases, military intervention.
- Responsibility to Reconstruct: If the reaction, whether political, economic, or military, has its intended effect and the problems are solved, it is important that the international community is actively involved in rebuilding institutions and initiating positive social developments as a whole, so that the problems do not recur.

Politically, the most important element of R2P, as defined by the ICISS, concerns situations where a state has no intention to solve the problems causing gross human rights violations, atrocities, and crimes against humanity, usually because the state itself is directly or indirectly responsible for these crimes, and has an interest in their continuation.

Where a state has the political will but not the capacity to deal with such situations – for instance, if its security forces are too few and not sufficiently trained – in most cases it will accept offers of outside assistance to solve the problems. It is the *unwillingness* of states and political leaders to fulfill "sovereignty as responsibility" that is at the core of the R2P discussion. In other words, the situations where political leaders, sometimes intentionally and sometimes by making the wrong choices, step by step take the wrong course leading them to neglect or outright disown their responsibility for their own citizens and the rights of these citizens – and thus failing in their most important political responsibility.

In these cases the basic approach is to start with mild pressure from the outside, then gradually increase it as required. There are many different kinds of sanctions that states can apply to each other, such as excluding a country from regional organizations or from participating in international collaboration, as with the exclusion of Libya from the UNHRC in March 2011 in reaction to the threats of the Gaddafi regime.

There are also the classic measures of breaking off diplomatic relations, or newer measures such as imposing travel restrictions on named persons so they are unable to travel to Europe or the United States. Other possibilities include landing prohibitions for air traffic; stopping commercial flights to a country; stopping weapons exports and military co-operation; financial sanctions, such as the freezing of assets both of states and of individuals; import or export restrictions or careful control of specific products to stop the sale of particular goods, such as blood diamonds. This list is not exhaustive.

It is important to assess what the effect of these sanctions will be in each case and who will be affected by them. General trade restrictions have a tendency to affect poorer segments of the population the hardest and not necessarily those in power. The international community increasingly relies on the use of targeted sanctions ("smart sanctions") that seek primarily to affect political and military leaders and their families, such as preventing those targeted from enjoying their annual shopping trips to London or New York, or having their sons and daughters accepted by prestigious Western colleges and universities.

Where there are major atrocities and crimes against humanity that genuinely shock the conscience of mankind, and where political pressure and sanctions do not work, military intervention may be necessary. The ICISS report suggests a number of criteria that should be fulfilled before military intervention in another country can be justified. These are to a large extent based on the classic justifications for a "just war": the extent and nature of the violence must be capable of justifying intervention ("just cause"); and the intention must be to prevent the violence, not to alter national borders or conquer territory ("right intention").

Moreover, military intervention should only be considered when other possibilities have been exhausted ("last resort"), the military means must be adapted to the purpose of the intervention, and of course the operation must respect the rules of war and international humanitarian law ("proportional means"). It must also be probable that the action will succeed and that a misjudged intervention will not make the situation worse ("reasonable prospects"), and that the intervention can be justified under international law ("right authority").

This last requirement leads back to the previous discussion of the Danish report, that only the UN Security Council can actually authorize such military intervention. Any attempts to by-pass the Security Council will risk undermining not just the council but also international law and a world order based on right and not only on might. The way forward, therefore, to a large degree depends on the council being better able to deal with these questions. Two issues are highlighted here: how the five permanent members use their veto power and the need to establish a code of conduct for the permanent members; for example, not to impose a veto in connection with military interventions made for humanitarian or human rights reasons which have the support of a majority of the Security Council and where the permanent member in question does not have essential national interests at stake.

If the Security Council is unable to adopt a decision to intervene because of a veto, the ICISS primarily considers the possibility for *regional* organizations to act instead. This can be partly justified under Article 52 of the UN Charter (though still based on a mandate from the council), but of course it also requires a willingness to act at the regional level, especially among the neighbouring countries.

This is not always the case, though since the publication of the ICISS report in West Africa ECOWAS in particular has been much more dynamic and prepared to assume greater regional responsibilities. The ICISS report concluded that it would not be possible to find international agreement on any criteria for military intervention other than under a mandate from the Security Council. It is, thus, all the more important that the council should rise to the occasion and act in situations where the conscience of the world is seriously challenged.[6]

The R2P concept and the essential arguments in the ICISS report were included in the report of the special panel appointed by the UN secretary-general to prepare for the World Summit in 2005. At the same time, the panel made it clear which kinds of crimes ought, in its view, to be relevant to R2P, namely: genocide and other mass killings, ethnic cleansing, and serious crimes against humanity, which a government has shown itself to be powerless or unwilling to prevent. At the same time, R2P was described as an "emerging norm," the implications of which were still being considered. The panel's report was accompanied by the secretary-general's own report to the World Summit: *In Larger Freedom*. The then secretary-general, Kofi Annan, had personal reasons for engaging so closely with the work on R2P. In 1994, as head of the UN Department of Peacekeeping Operations, he had been very late in acknowledging the genocide in Rwanda and thus bore some of the responsibility for the United Nations' failure to react earlier and with greater effect than was the case.[7]

The decisive breakthrough for the concept of R2P came at the United Nations World Summit in September 2005, where agreement was reached on two paragraphs on R2P in the World Summit Outcome (paragraphs 138 and 139) which deserve to be quoted in their entirety:

138. Each individual State has the responsibility to protect its populations from genocide, war crimes, ethnic cleansing and crimes against humanity. This responsibility entails the prevention of such crimes, including their incitement, through appropriate and necessary means. We accept that responsibility and will act in accordance with it. The international community should, as appropriate, encourage and help States to exercise this responsibility and support the United Nations in establishing an early warning capability.

139. The international community, through the United Nations, also has the responsibility to use appropriate diplomatic, humanitarian and other peaceful means, in accordance with Chapters VI and VIII of the Charter, to help to protect populations from genocide, war crimes, ethnic cleansing and crimes against humanity. In this context, we are prepared to take collective action, in a timely and decisive manner, through the Security Council, in accordance with the Charter, including Chapter VII, on a case-by-case basis and in co-operation with relevant regional organizations as appropriate, should peaceful means be inadequate and national authorities are

manifestly failing to protect their populations from genocide, war crimes, ethnic cleansing and crimes against humanity. We stress the need for the General Assembly to continue consideration of the responsibility to protect populations from genocide, war crimes, ethnic cleansing and crimes against humanity and its implications, bearing in mind the principles of the Charter and international law. We also intend to commit ourselves, as necessary and appropriate, to helping States build capacity to protect their populations from genocide, war crimes, ethnic cleansing and crimes against humanity and to assisting those which are under stress before crises and conflicts break out.

Many were surprised that it was possible to get agreement on R2P as part of the World Summit Outcome, and it soon became clear that a number of countries subsequently felt that the political compromise went too far. The interpretation of R2P which the UN's then 191 member states accepted by agreeing to the World Summit Outcome was a clarification of the scope of application of R2P, which was limited to cases of genocide, war crimes, crimes against humanity and ethnic cleansing.

The first three of these crimes are defined in the relevant conventions and in the Statute of the International Criminal Court (ICC). Ethnic cleansing is less precisely defined in an international context, but in practice it is difficult to imagine ethnic cleansing that does not also involve one or more of the other three mass atrocity crimes.

In line with the ICISS report, the World Summit Outcome emphasized the states' own responsibilities for preventing these four crimes which are covered by R2P. If a country is not able to solve a problem itself, the international community has a responsibility to assist it, and to help build up the necessary capacity to prevent or deal with critical situations which could lead to such crimes. And finally, the international community has the possibility of taking collective action "in a timely and decisive manner" if a country is not able or not willing to deal with the situation.

However, this latter provision presupposes that there is a mandate from the Security Council to do so on the basis of the UN Charter, and that the authorities of the country in question are "manifestly failing to protect their populations from genocide, war crimes, ethnic cleansing and crimes against humanity." It is also stated that the further development of the concept of R2P should take place in the UN

General Assembly rather than in the Security Council, so that all countries can participate in this work.

In 2009, Annan's successor, Ban Ki-moon presented a report to the General Assembly on the implementation of R2P. The report followed extensive consultations with member states and its general tone was cautious. The most important thing for Ban Ki-moon was to hold on to the bridgehead won at the World Summit, and to prevent the member states from trying to roll back the concept of R2P.

The secretary-general had no illusions that it would be possible to make rapid progress in further developing the concept. What was important was to hold on to and consolidate the progress already achieved, which was in itself a clear step forward in relation to the traditional strict definition of the sovereignty of states and the principle of non-intervention in their domestic affairs. In order to succeed, it was important to build up trust, particularly among the developing countries which appeared to be most sceptical about the R2P concept.[8]

The debate in the UN General Assembly in July 2009 revealed broad support for further development of the R2P concept. More than ninety countries spoke, and a number of countries which had previously expressed certain reservations about R2P including, Brazil, China, India, and Russia, now appeared to be more positive about it. However, unsurprisingly there are still a number of countries, including Bolivia, Iran, North Korea, Sudan, and Venezuela, which were whole-heartedly opposed to R2P and to the efforts to develop it as an international norm. In his introduction to the report, the secretary-general emphasized, in line with the ICISS report, that sovereignty and responsibility were mutually supportive principles, and that what mattered was how, not when R2P would be implemented.

As expected, many developing countries attached great importance to the obligation of the international community, and not least the Western donor countries, to help poorer countries with assistance aimed at preventing and counteracting R2P situations. In this context the focus was on the capacity of countries to deal with such situations rather than on their willingness to do so, and on prevention as a political and social priority.

Unsurprisingly, the question of military intervention caused the greatest uncertainty in the debate. In addition to the Security Council's ability to act and the issue of the veto, there was particular concern about the selective use of enforcement measures for political purposes other than those officially stated, and the lack of precision about the mechanisms which should be used in a crisis to trigger an R2P decision.

Many countries, especially those sceptical about the concept of R2P, called for reforms of the Security Council as a condition for the council having the necessary political legitimacy to authorize R2P interventions, while other countries expressed their support for the idea that the permanent members of the Security Council should be reluctant to use their veto in R2P situations – something which the secretary-general had emphasized in his introductory statement.

Despite the generally positive acceptance of R2P by the member states, both in 2005 and in 2009, it is clear that, as a concept and as an aspiring norm of international law, R2P risks becoming a victim of its own success.

The term *responsibility to protect* trips easily off the tongue, and it is tempting to use it in contexts where it does not belong. The broad political acceptance of R2P, even among developing countries, is clearly conditional on its scope being limited – "a narrow, but deep concept" as the secretary-general has explained it. Many countries will clearly start feeling uncomfortable if and when the concept is used more loosely and in situations other than those intended – often linked to very direct and vocal demands for military intervention. An example of this was when Cyclone Nargis devastated vast areas of Southeast Asia in May 2008, with Myanmar and the Irrawaddy Delta in particular being badly affected. The ruling military junta at the time was initially fairly reluctant to accept humanitarian aid from outside, and the French foreign minister, Bernard Kouchner, whose humanitarian credentials as one of the founders of Médecins Sans Frontières cannot be denied, used the concept of R2P as the political basis for suggesting that humanitarian aid should be delivered without the permission and co-operation of Myanmar's authorities. France at that time had a warship carrying emergency-aid materials at sea off Myanmar. The French R2P argument, and the thinly disguised threat of military intervention to secure humanitarian access, was definitely not helpful to the United Nations negotiations with the government on gaining access for emergency assistance. Among others, the British ambassador to the United Nations had to state publicly that R2P could not be used for purely emergency situations, and on that basis the UN succeeded in getting the agreement of the Myanmar government for the delivery of humanitarian assistance.[9]

In order to avoid discussions about R2P being only about military intervention, the United Nations has pointed to the situation in Kenya after the election in December 2007 as an example of a more pro-active and political application of the concept. The election had resulted in a dead heat between President Mwai Kibaki and the leader of the opposition Raila Odinga. The political confrontation rapidly deteriorated into ethnic riots, especially in the Rift Valley. Several hundred thousand people fled to other parts of the country, and more than 1,300 people were killed in the clashes.

Former secretary-general Kofi Annan, and a number of other African leaders, sought to mediate, supported by the UN. They were successful; civil war in Kenya was avoided and a fragile government of national unity was established with Kibaki as president and Odinga as prime minister. From the start, Annan used this situation in Kenya as an example of an early external intervention of a more preventive and conflict-resolving nature within the framework of the R2P concept, and as an alternative to military intervention once things have gone too far.[10]

Since 2008 the United Nations has referred to the responsibility to protect on many occasions, primarily in public advocacy speeches by the UN high commissioner for Human Rights or by the secretary-general and by his close colleagues. In addition to Kenya, such references have been made in relation to Bahrain, Côte d'Ivoire, DR Congo, Guinea, Libya, Sudan, Syria, and Yemen.[11]

With regard to the situation in Libya at the end of February 2011, the Security Council adopted a resolution, the preamble to which contained a reference to R2P in one of its recitals: "Recalling the Libyan authorities' responsibility to protect its population." This was the first occasion on which the council explicitly referred to R2P in connection with sanctions. This occurred when, in relation to its demand for the Gaddafi regime's immediate cessation of the use of violence, the council introduced a weapons embargo on Libya, as well as travel restrictions on named individuals and freezing their assets in other countries (this applied in particular to the Gaddafi family and its closest advisers).

On 17 March 2011, the Security Council decided to authorize the use of all necessary means to protect civilians in Libya (see chapter 4). This resolution was adopted with the support of the African members of the council, though they had some concerns that this decision would link R2P to military intervention and "regime change." From the perspective of the African member states and of many other developing countries, it is essential that the use of R2P should be based on all three pillars of the World Summit Outcome of 2005: a basic national responsibility to protect; provision of external support, if needed; and the possibility of sanctions or other coercive measures, authorized by the Security Council, if a government is shown to be "manifestly failing" to protect its population. From the African point of view, there is also a strong focus on R2P as a concept in which regional organizations must be closely involved, not least in the area of conflict prevention.[12]

The discussion of the mandate for intervention in Libya – and of whether it was stretched from protection of civilians to engineering regime change – has, of course, also affected the debate on R2P. The Brazilian government has introduced the concept of responsibility while protecting in order to focus more on preventive action and to exhaust all other possibilities before coercive measures are introduced. In his most recent report the secretary-general outlines five lessons learned about R2P: that each situation is distinct and that methods and tools will therefore differ; that the basic principles should nonetheless by applied consistently, to avoid double standards; that measures under all three pillars may reinforce each other; that an effective and integrated strategy is needed, combining elements of both prevention and response; and, finally, that the role of regional partners must be strengthened.[13]

DEALING WITH IMPUNITY

In connection with its resolutions on Libya in February 2011, the Security Council unanimously decided to refer the situation in Libya to the Prosecutor for the ICC.

The ICC was established in 1998 by the Rome Statute, which is the ICC's legal basis. The court began its operations in July 2002, once the necessary sixty countries had ratified the statute. By 2013, 122 countries had accepted the obligations under the Statute, primarily allowing prosecution before the Court for genocide, war crimes, and crimes against humanity committed (after July 2002) on the acceding country's territory or by citizens of the country. The ICC is complementary, meaning that it only becomes involved in cases which national courts cannot or will not deal with satisfactorily.

The fact that neither China, Russia, nor the United States have ratified the Rome Statute is, of course, a political problem for the ICC.

The Libya decision was the second time the Security Council had referred such situation to the ICC. On the first occasion, in relation to the Sudanese government's responsibility for mass killings in Darfur, China, Russia and the United States, together with Brazil, abstained in the vote in the council in March 2005. On the second occasion the United States – under the Obama administration – voted in favour.[14]

In addition to pursuing cases referred to the ICC by the Security Council, as in the cases of Sudan and Libya, the Office of the Prosecutor can naturally also investigate and, if necessary, prosecute relevant cases concerning countries that have ratified the ICC Statute. So far, on the basis of requests from the countries concerned, the ICC has initiated investigations in the Central African Republic, DR Congo, Kenya (the consequences of the riots in 2007–08, opening up investigations on the roles of Uhuru Kenyatta and William Ruto, who in April 2013 were sworn in as president and vice-president of Kenya respectively), and Uganda. In the case of Sudan, a warrant has been issued for the arrest of President Omar al-Bashir. The fact that so far all cases have involved African countries and that a warrant has been issued against an African head of state still in office has to some extent weakened the previously strong African support for the ICC.[15]

The establishment of the ICC is the response of the international community to the two questions which naturally arise in the wake of the increased focus on mass atrocities and gross violations of human rights. What is done to hold those guilty of such crimes to account? And what steps are taken to ensure that these kinds of atrocities do not happen again?

The answers to these two questions do not always point in the same direction. On the one hand, there is the requirement that those guilty of heinous crimes should be punished, which applies in particular to genocide, war crimes, crimes against humanity, and ethnic cleansing, for which impunity cannot and should not be tolerated. On the other hand, there is the desire to limit the extent of the crimes and to put a stop to them in a way that enables societies to function afterwards and as far as possible to reconcile the opposing parties and establish a situation where there is a reduced risk of renewed hostilities. In some cases this can require coming to an understanding with criminals – which may only come at a price.

The Nuremberg trials in 1945–49 after the end of the Second World War were a relatively simple political problem. The trials constituted the international judicial settlement of the crimes of the leaders of the defeated Nazi regime, most of whom were sentenced to death and executed for their crimes against humanity. The prosecution of these cases and the presentation of comprehensive evidence were intended to ensure that the citizens of the Allied countries (not least the United States) could see that their efforts and sacrifices during the war had been justified, and that the war had indeed been a fight for survival against evil incarnate. Similarly, it was important to show the defeated German population what crimes had been committed in their name, in order to achieve a clear-cut political and moral break with the past and create a firm basis for the reconstruction of a new Germany. However, situations are not always as clear as this.

The complexities are apparent particularly at the conclusion of a civil war. There are winners and there are losers, and on some occasions the situation is more clear-cut than on others. But in all cases the parties have to live together afterwards. It is necessary to balance the parties' differing political and sometimes ethnic interests, and in many cases decisions will also have to take into account the military strength and popular support at the time when an agreement is entered into. For example, in Lebanon the unequal parliamentary representation of Christians and Muslims, for historical reasons, was becoming increasingly demographically unequal and this was one of the causes of the civil war in 1975. More equal representation in future was therefore a key element of the Taif Accord in 1989 which brought the Lebanese civil war to an end.

The United Nations often plays a central role in the political processes bringing conflicts to an end. This of course particularly concerns the Security Council, whose encouragement to end hostilities can be decisive for an agreement or a ceasefire. But it also applies to the secretary-general and his colleagues in connection with the often very long, drawn-out peace negotiations that we have witnesses in recent years in relation to conflicts in Africa. In many such situations what is usually referred to as the "good offices" of the secretary-general play an important role in finding agreement. Good offices normally means the secretary-general's – and his collaborators – possibilities for meeting with all the parties to a conflict, for taking the initiative to bring them together and create a productive negotiating environment, and for putting forward proposals for solutions when the critical time comes.

One example out of many in recent years is the negotiations in Zimbabwe in 2008 on the power-sharing formula which was needed as the basis for the formation of a government of national unity. The two parties, President Mugabe and the opposition leader Morgan Tsvangirai, were assisted in this endeavour both by other countries in the region, not least South Africa and its then president Thabo Mbeki, and by one of the United Nations' best diplomats, Haile Menkerios, who helped draw up the political agreement.

One of the problems Menkerios encountered was Mugabe's demand for a general amnesty to be included as part of the agreement, i.e., that the parties should agree to draw a line in the sand and accept immunity for crimes committed in the past, so as to make a new beginning. Menkerios could not accept this on behalf of the UN, just as the United Nations has refrained from doing since the question first came up in 1999 in Angola, and subsequently in Sierra Leone, Sudan, and Uganda. In the view of the UN, under international law an amnesty cannot be granted for crimes such as genocide, war crimes, crimes against humanity, or other serious violations of human rights (including torture, arbitrary executions, forced disappearances, and sexual violence), or international human rights law.[16]

Thus, the United Nations cannot accept relinquishing the possibility of prosecuting war criminals in order to get them to accept a political agreement. No one should be able to obtain impunity as a precondition to accepting a peace agreement.

Peace and justice naturally go hand in hand, and so must the implementation of peace agreements and judicial accountability for atrocities committed in the past. But there may still be some room for manoeuvre with regard to how and when such accountability is actually dealt with. This need not be the first thing a new government does. As stated above, the International Criminal Court is a complementary court, and to the extent that countries can themselves build up the capacities of their legal systems to hold people accountable in a proper manner, the countries' own courts will deal with these cases rather than the ICC. It is expected that a number of countries that have ratified the Rome Statute and accepted the ICC will, for this reason, want to strengthen their capacities in this area with a view to conducting their own judicial settlements.

However, there is also a political reality. When after eight years of brutal dictatorship, Idi Amin was driven out of Uganda by Tanzanian forces, he sought refuge first in Libya and then in Saudi Arabia, where he lived for many years until his death in 2003. This was the same Saudi Arabia to which Tunisia's dictator Ben Ali fled after the popular uprising in Tunis in February 2011.

In these cases it must be assumed that these escape routes often help ensure a quicker transfer of power than would otherwise be the case and, thus, helps limit the human costs of the forced transfer of power. In some cases asylum for political leaders is a direct part of the diplomatic bargain for a political solution, as seen in the case of Côte d'Ivoire, where asylum for President Gbagbo and his family was a key element in the negotiations conducted by South Africa, the AU, and ECOWAS in the spring of 2011 with a view to getting Gbagbo to step aside in favour of the newly elected President Ouattara. However, in this case this became irrelevant when Gbagbo chose to continue to fight until his forces were overcome and he was finally arrested.

In connection with changes of government following democratic elections it is not unusual for the new government to draw a line under the misdeeds of the past, in the interests of stability. When Mwai Kibaki won the presidential election in Kenya in 2002, the outgoing president Daniel arap Moi packed up his belongings and moved from the presidential palace to his large country estate, taking with him several hundred million dollars' worth of booty from decades of corruption, and leaving it to the new government to expose to the public the police torture cells in the basement of Nyayo House. Any talk of calling Moi to account was politically unrealistic; it would destabilize the country and risk initiating ethnic conflict.[17]

These few random examples merely underline that it is not always easy to enforce the principle of not allowing any de facto form of amnesty or impunity for dictators with a murky past when they withdraw or are pushed out – especially if they still have a power base and political influence in their country. Breaks with the past are not always as clean as one might like. However, it is evident that this situation is changing around the world. It is much less likely today than it was in 1979 that there would be global acceptance of Idi Amin's enjoyment of a peaceful retirement in Saudi Arabia, after having carried out extensive ethnic cleansing and overseen the killing of several hundred thousands of his fellow countrymen.

The broad support for the International Criminal Court, and the focus on genocide, war crimes, and crimes against humanity as being particularly heinous and intolerable and as crimes that must be prosecuted, sends a clear signal that the majority of UN member states want to put an end to impunity for such crimes. So far the International Criminal Tribunal for the former Yugoslavia (ICTY) has brought prosecutions for 161 cases of genocide and war crimes during the

Balkan wars of the 1990s; 136 of these have been decided. The International Criminal Tribunal for Rwanda (ICTR) has brought prosecutions for 75 cases of genocide in Rwanda in 1995, and has decided 58 of these.

The Special Court for Sierra Leone (SCSL) is a hybrid court, established jointly by the UN and Sierra Leone. This Court has brought twelve cases, of which the most prominent was the prosecution of Liberia's former president Charles Taylor, ending with his sentencing in The Hague to fifty years in prison. Finally, in 2006 a special tribunal (the Extraordinary Chambers in the Courts of Cambodia [ECCC]) was set up to deal with the genocide instigated by Pol Pot's Khmer Rouge regime in Cambodia from 1975 to 1979. The Cambodian tribunal is witness to the fact that it is possible to bring prosecutions for crimes against humanity and genocide even many years after the events. Four prosecutions have been brought so far. The cost of bringing such prosecutions is considerable, and for this reason they are mainly brought against those indicted for the worst atrocities.[18]

In addition to ensuring that there is a full measure of justice, and that those responsible are held to account for their actions, transitional justice is often part of a wider picture seeking to combine the judicial settlement of accounts with political and popular reconciliation, and thus contribute to a process of moral and political regeneration following the terrible crimes and suffering faced by the population at large.

Even in situations where *realpolitik* may limit the scope for transitional justice, it will often be possible to reveal what in fact happened in the past and to provide reparation to the victims for some of the pains they have suffered. Truth-and-reconciliation commissions are one way of doing this. They are not new. Even though they are best known from South Africa's process in 1995–98 of coming to terms with the crimes of the apartheid era, these kinds of commissions have been used in one form or another in many countries since the 1970s.

Truth-and-reconciliation commissions have not only operated in developing countries. After reunification in 1990, Germany set up a commission to investigate the repression in East Germany from 1945 to 1989. Truth commissions generally have to perform a difficult balancing act. It can be difficult for some victims to recall traumatic experiences. This applies particularly in cases of sexual violence, where in some cases there may be social stigma attached to making it known publicly that one is a victim. On the other hand, some victims can have a powerful urge to tell their stories and can see this as part of the healing process. The relationship between uncovering the facts by truth-and-reconciliation commissions and any subsequent prosecution on the basis of such facts is also a key question which needs to be clarified in advance.

In some cases the conditions are clear from the start. In South Africa, the Truth and Reconciliation Commission which was led by Archbishop Desmond Tutu heard a total of about 21,000 victims and witnesses, of which 2,000 were heard in public hearings, broadcast by radio. It was decided in advance that perpetrators could avoid prosecution for politically motivated crimes in return for telling the whole truth about their actions. The Commission thus received more than 7,000 applications for amnesty, and the most significant of these were dealt with in public hearings at which the perpetrators were confronted with their victims.

In the Chilean investigations into the Augusto Pinochet era (1973–90) a similar promise of amnesty was given in advance ("truth, but no trials") as part of the political settlement on the basis of which Pinochet stepped down as president in 1990. It was ironic that the commission report was instead used as the basis for a Spanish prosecution, leading to Pinochet being briefly detained in London, before he was released on health grounds. There have been other cases where the reports of truth commissions have been direct precursors to judicial proceedings. This was most clearly the case in Argentina after the end of military rule in 1983.[19]

It is clear from these examples that the United Nations is far from alone in dealing with the most serious violations of human rights: genocide, war crimes, and crimes against humanity. But the UN – the General Assembly as well as the Security Council – is playing a decisive role in the current development of the "responsibility to protect" from an emerging international norm into an important feature of international law.

This applies both to the very basis for the R2P concept – clarifying the definition of sovereignty – and strategically with regard to the planning and timing of the ensuing steps which must be taken to ensure that R2P becomes an integral part of international law. An important aspect of this is recognizing that all three pillars of R2P may reinforce each other and that, more often than not, it will be necessary to combine prevention and response. The Western countries' primary focus on the third pillar, and right of the international community – with the Security Council's blessing – to intervene if a state is not willing to take action itself, would not encourage the acceptance of R2P by developing countries which naturally put the main emphasis on the first two pillars.

Looking to the future, further consolidating the progress which R2P represents will be one of the United Nations' most important challenges in coming years in the area of international law. The clear reference to R2P in the Security Council's decision in the spring of 2011 to authorize the use of force to protect the civilian population of Libya, and the range of views on NATO's air operations in Libya, have put even more focus on R2P and how the concept is to be further defined.

Those countries that have been hesitant about R2P have hardly been reassured by the operations in Libya. The opposing views were expressed in the debate in the General Assembly in July 2011 on the role of regional organizations in the implementation of R2P. On the one hand, Secretary-General Ban Ki-moon emphasized that, on the basis of references in both the Security Council and the HRC, R2P had now become an operational reality. On the other hand, countries such as Cuba and Venezuela, in particular, tried to put their foot on the brake and stressed how limited a basis there is for R2P in international law. In their contributions to the debate, China, Pakistan, and Russia also strongly emphasized state sovereignty and territorial integrity.[20]

At the same time, the United Nations wants to intensify the fight against impunity. One way to do this is for the Security Council to refer more cases to the ICC. Decisions on this ultimately lie with the five permanent council members. Increased support by the United Nations for transitional justice initiatives, where relevant, is something on which the secretary-general can take the lead. This applies not least in connection with the UN's political mediation and activities related to conflict prevention – and in the context of the expected increased involvement of the UN system in fragile and conflict-affected states. In these situations, the UN could put greater emphasis on including justice systems and the development of political and administrative capacities within the framework of R2P, as was the case in Kenya in 2008.

A stronger and more explicit focus on R2P could also mean that several countries would be better able to meet the two-fold challenge that runs throughout this chapter: to ensure that there is accountability

and justice for what has happened in the past; and that both accountability and justice are implemented so as to strengthen national reconciliation processes, helping to build new democratic institutions
that are strong enough to withstand the ghosts of the past. To lead
countries in this direction and to help them implement the specific
measures that can ensure this, will be important tasks for the United
Nations in the future.

PART IV

Development

A meeting in Monrovia with the Liberian minister for justice on 28 January 2010. The minister's office is somewhat knocked about and worn, the curtains are drawn to keep the bright sunshine out, and the noise of the air conditioning is almost deafening. Like all the other Liberian ministers I have spoken to, the minister for justice is very satisfied with the UN system's activities in Liberia. But she is also worried.

She thinks that too much attention is paid to the security sector in Liberia – to reforms of the military and the police – and too little attention to the justice system as a whole, in other words the courts, traditional conflict resolution, and the detention facilities. She points out that the courts have major capacity problems and are a bottleneck in the justice system. She does not try to hide the fact that there is widespread corruption among the judges, and says that the government would like to be able to crack down on such corruption.

At the same time, if the government does come down hard on corruption, this would immediately create a new problem. There are simply not enough well-qualified candidates in Liberia to fill all the vacancies for judges. This is not a capacity problem that can be dealt with quickly – it takes a long time to educate and train judges. The minister also regrets that the Liberian justice system has been modelled on the US legal system. This means there is widespread use of juries, which are both ineffective and provide opportunities for even more corruption. But she believes that the most urgent problem is the detention facilities.

A few days later I have the opportunity to visit the central prison in Monrovia, which contains two-thirds of all the prisoners in the country. The prison was built to house 350 prisoners. On the day I visited it, it has 744 prisoners – more than twice as many as it was built for. Most of the prisoners are on remand, meaning they are waiting – often for months – for their case to come to trial, even for petty crimes. The stench in the jail is almost unbearable. Only the women prisoners have more or less tolerable conditions.

The minister for justice and the United Nations are looking for donors to help finance the construction of a new prison outside the capital. The site is there, but donors will only support a reform of the prison system as part of an overall reform of the justice system. These discussions take time. And meanwhile the remand prisoners sit and wait.

9

Global Development Goals

The real challenge of development is that there is a group of countries at the bottom that are falling behind, and often falling apart.

Paul Collier, *The Bottom Billion*, 2007

THE MILLENNIUM DEVELOPMENT GOALS

The United Nations plays an important normative role in international development co-operation. The negotiation and adoption of international development goals has been part of the UN's approach to development since as far back as 1970 when the international development assistance goal of 0.7 per cent of gross national income (GNI) was first adopted by the General Assembly. The background to this was the Pearson Report, named after its main author, the former Canadian prime minister Lester Pearson who, in 1969, emphasized the critical (and positive) role of development assistance as an economic catalyst in the poorest countries.

The Pearson Report resulted in a proposal that the industrialized countries should each provide development assistance to developing countries amounting 0.7 per cent of the GNI of the donor countries. This would double the then average level of development assistance provided by the OECD countries, which was 0.34 per cent of GNI in 1970.

The General Assembly resolution of 1970 established that the goal of 0.7 per cent should be reached by 1975. This target was not reached, and it has not been reached at any point in the more than forty years that the target has applied, even though it has been confirmed countless times since by various General Assemblies and at international conferences. Since 1970, the average annual level of development assistance from the OECD countries has varied between 0.20 per cent and 0.35 per cent of GNI, and today only Denmark, Luxembourg, the Netherlands, Norway, and Sweden have reached the 0.7 per cent target.[1]

Development aid or assistance (formally called official development assistance, or ODA) is public financing on concessional terms (thus including loans as well as grants if the terms of the loans contain a significant grant element), with the main objective of promoting the economic development and welfare of those countries which the OECD's Development Assistance Committee has defined as developing countries, or through multilateral development institutions such as the United Nations, the World Bank, et cetera. Thus, military aid is not included as part of development assistance.[2]

The experiences of the 0.7 per cent development-assistance goal illustrate the fundamental problem of such quantitative goals. They are first and foremost declarations of intent which countries can commit to, fully aware that there is no sanction associated with their non-fulfillment, other than the political costs in the eyes of their own public and the political exposure vis-à-vis other countries. However, if the majority of donor countries do not in fact fulfil an international target applicable to them and agreed to by them, then the non-fulfilment negates the target.

However, this situation creates a political platform for those who do live up to their commitments. There is little doubt that the high development-aid budgets of the three Scandinavian countries has been an important element in the general and internationally recognized image of these countries' strong international solidarity and their commitment in the fight against global poverty.

The end of the Cold War in 1989 opened up new possibilities in the area of international development co-operation. In the first instance, there was a fall in the aggregate assistance from the OECD countries in the course of the 1990s as aid was no longer needed as an instrument for winning support from the developing countries in the global political competition between East and West.

The change was normative rather than financial. The 1990s became the decade of the major UN conferences. It started with the World Summit for Children in September 1990. UNICEF's then executive director, Jim Grant, got the idea of using the format of global summit meetings, summoning all the world's heads of state and government to promote the UN's Convention on the Rights of the Child, and to focus on the rights of children in general. Many were sceptical, but UNICEF succeeded in getting the attendance of 71 of the world's then 159 heads of state and government and adopting an action plan to promote the survival, protection, and development of children. There was another UN conference in 1990, the World Conference on Education for All. In the following years conference followed conference: the UN Conference on Environment and Development in Rio de Janeiro in 1992, the International Conference on Nutrition in Rome in 1992, the United Nations World Conference on Human Rights in Vienna in 1993, the International Conference on Population and Development in Cairo in 1994, the Fourth World Conference on Women in Beijing in September 1995, the World Summit for Social Development in Copenhagen in 1995, the World Food Summit in Rome in 1996, and a conference on human settlement.

Politically and in terms of setting international goals and targets these were very fruitful years, where world leaders sought to shake off the yoke of the Cold War with all its ideological confrontations and to look to the future. One of the most important aims for the various United Nations conferences was the adoption of new global goals in a range of areas. Most of these goals had a certain idealistic flavour. Thus, at the World Food Summit in 1996 it was agreed to halve the number of chronically undernourished children in the world by 2015. All countries undertook to implement the policies necessary to achieve this goal, but even though the resolution adopted following the conference was long, detailed, and politically ambitious, it is hard to determine what each country has committed itself to do on the basis of the resolution. Not enough thought was given to how the goals could in fact be achieved.[3]

This situation changed in 2000. Secretary-General Kofi Annan decided to reap what had been sown in the many international conferences in the 1990s – to gather the harvest together and put it in a big heap in the UN's political barn. The key to doing this was the UN Millennium Summit in September 2000, to mark the new millennium, and the means were the Millennium Development Goals (MDGS).

In the first instance, the secretary-general included in the draft resolution for the Millennium Summit a number of the key global goals that had been adopted by the various UN conferences in the course of the 1990s. They were, thus, all goals which had already been politically agreed to by the member states, such as halving the proportion of the poor (defined as those living on less than US$1 per day), and similarly halving the number of people starving and of those who did not have access to clean drinking water.

There were also goals on the right of all children to receive a basic education, reducing deaths of mothers in childbirth by three-quarters and the mortality of infants and children under five by two-thirds. All of this was to happen by 2015. There were many other non-quantifiable goals together with these measurable goals in the draft resolution for the Millennium Summit. In fact, it was only *after* the Millennium Summit that Kofi Annan and Mark Malloch-Brown, as administrator of the United Nations Development Programme (UNDP), made the quantifiable goals into a special category of goals under the heading of the MDGs. The term *Millennium Development Goals* is nowhere to be found in the Millennium Declaration which member states adopted at the United Nations Millennium Summit in September 2000.[4]

This collection of goals was first developed *after* the Summit. The right to basic sanitation was adopted as a new target at the Johannesburg World Summit on Sustainable Development in 2002, and a number of targets and indicators were first defined even later. As they stand today, the MDGs have a highly complex structure, with eight global goals divided into twenty-one targets, and measured by sixty indicators. The baseline is 1990 and the goals are typically to be achieved by 2015, though in a few cases before that.[5]

Seven of the eight goals focus on what the developing countries themselves undertake to achieve, primarily in the social sectors, especially in education (goals 2 and 3) and the health sector (goals 4, 5, 6, and in part 7). The eighth and final goal concerns what the developing countries' partners among the industrialized countries commit to do in order to assist developing countries in their efforts to reach the goals. Goal 8 is less explicitly articulated than the other goals.

This system of development goals has had a dynamic effect on international development co-operation – and on the progress made by the poorest countries – during the more than ten years since its adoption. To start with, goal 3 on promoting equality and strengthening the rights of women only had a partial target, to remove gender discrimination in education systems. However, over time the UN system has developed a set of indicators that have effectively made this a more comprehensive goal for women. In addition to promoting the equal rights of boys and girls to education, indicators have also been developed for women's employment conditions (the form and fre-

The Eight MDGS

	Goal	Key Target
1	Eradicate extreme poverty and hunger	Halve, between 1990 and 2015, the proportion of people whose income is less than US$1 per day
2	Achieve universal primary education	Ensure that, by 2015, all children will be able to complete primary schooling
3	Promote gender equality and empower women	Eliminate gender disparity in all levels of education by 2015
4	Reduce child mortality	Reduce by two-thirds, between 1990 and 2015, the under-five mortality rate
5	Improve maternal health	Reduce by three-quarters, between 1990 and 2015, the maternal mortality ratio
6	Combat HIV/AIDS, malaria, and other diseases	Halt and begin to reverse the spread of HIV/AIDS by 2015
7	Ensure environmental sustainability	Halve, by 2015, the proportion of the population without access to safe drinking water and basic sanitation
8	Develop a global partner-ship for development	Ensure market access for developing countries, development assistance and debt relief

quency of employment), and for women's political participation (proportion of seats held by women in parliaments and assemblies).

These extensions of goal 3 have made it possible to use it as a basis for more general measures to strengthen women's participation in the productive economy, both as employees and as self-employed. This reflects a change in the general approach to the issue of gender equality, where women are now regarded as an economic resource and where it is important for society to benefit from using this resource to the fullest extent possible. As the former World Bank president Robert Zoellick has expressed it, economic equality between men and women is not just a question of social justice and fairness, it is also "good economics."

Similarly, goal 5, on the maternal health of women, has been expanded from only covering the reduction of deaths in childbirth to include a new partial goal on the right to reproductive health, supported by indicators about access to controls and support from trained health care workers during pregnancy, the number of teenage pregnancies, and access to contraception and family-planning advice.

This has made goal 5 an important lever for the work to ensure women in the child-bearing years have access to the form of contraception they choose, and to secure contraception for about 222 million women who still do not have access to it. Various reports have shown that access to contraception is most restricted among the poorest women, women without education, and women in rural areas. The reports also show that only limited progress has been made in the last twenty years and that there has been effectively no progress among the poorest women who have no education.[6]

Goal 8 has always been the most disputed goal. The reasoning behind the goal is that the developing countries, and especially the poorest countries, cannot reach the MDGs without the help of more economically developed countries. Shortly after the formulation of the MDGs, the UNDP initiated an analysis of what was needed in the form of development assistance in order for the poorest countries to be able to make the social investments necessary to achieve the goals.

The report of the UN Millennium Project, under the leadership of Professor Jeffrey Sachs, concluded that the MDGs could be achieved if the industrialized countries doubled their development assistance from the level in 2003 of 0.25 per cent of GNI to 0.44 per cent in 2006 and to 0.54 per cent in 2015, and if this increased aid were targeted at supporting strategies in the developing countries that were directly aimed at reaching the MDGs.

The calculations of the Millennium Project formed the basis for the British government's proposal at the Gleneagles Summit in Scotland in July 2005, where the G8 countries (Canada, France, Germany, Italy, Japan, Russia, the United Kingdom, and the United States) agreed to increase development assistance by US$50 billion in 2010, of which US$25 billion was to go to sub-Saharan Africa. Even though development assistance increased by about 30 per cent in the period 2004–09, not least due to increases in the United Kingdom and the United States, the total level of assistance came nowhere near what the G8 countries had jointly promised in Gleneagles.[7]

While the targets for development assistance in goal 8 are without question central to the global partnership, other sub-goals concerns the further liberalization of international trade to allow better access to markets for developing countries, as well as increased debt relief and access to new technology, especially information and communications technology. From time to time these issues have given rise to discussions between developing countries and industrialized countries.

The further liberalization of international trade to a large degree depends on the success of implementing the Doha Development Agenda. The Doha Round is the ninth round of international trade negotiations in the postwar era, and the first since the Uruguay Round which ended in 1994. The purpose of these trade-negotiation rounds has been to achieve greater global liberalization of trade by agreements on balanced reductions of tariffs, quantitative restrictions, and other barriers to trade between countries. Over time, it has become ever more difficult to reach agreement between different groups of countries due to their differing interests, and the Doha Round has stalled since 2001.

Even without the Doha Round, United Nations' statistics show that developing countries, especially the poorest ones, have obtained better market access over the last ten to fifteen years, particularly for agricultural products. Also, since 2000, industrialized countries have supported the most heavily indebted developing nations with various forms of debt relief, primarily through the World Bank and the IMF, which have markedly reduced both their debt burdens and their debt repayments. As for technology, there is a question of whether developing countries should have access to new and patent-protected technology on market terms or on preferential terms. This issue has to a certain degree been pushed aside by the experiences from the remarkable extension of access to mobile telecommunications in Africa over the last ten years, driven by the market opportunities in this area, and underlining the basic experience that transfer of technology follows investment. All in all, there is much to prove that the partnership between North and South is genuine and is supported by shared interests in further deepening the globalization process.[8]

There is no doubt that the MDGs, and especially the goals for education and health, have been the UN's most essential contributions to international development policy in recent years. These goals are easy to understand and to communicate. They focus on the individual man or woman, boy or girl, and that individual's prospect of getting a basic education or to avoid the most serious communicable diseases and the MDGs thus have been a strong communication tool. Even if these goals are not actually expressed as rights, they are considered just and reasonable and as something that all human beings should have the possibility of obtaining.

Taking infant mortality as an example, in 1990 12.4 million children died under the age of five. This is equivalent to 30,000 children dying every day. By 2011, this figure had fallen to 6.9 million children, 15,000 child deaths per day fewer than in 1990. The greatest progress has been made in North Africa, the Middle East, and Latin America, where infant mortality has been more than halved. But good progress has also been made in many poorer countries, such as Bangladesh, Timor-Leste, Ethiopia, Liberia, and Nepal.[9]

Children under the age of five die from what are generally considered illnesses that are easy to treat, such as diarrhea, pneumonia, and malaria. These illnesses can be treated by simple means such as vaccinations, medicines, nutritional supplements, breastfeeding, and clean drinking water. However, even these simple remedies require a functioning health system.

On a global basis infant mortality has been brought down by more than 40 per cent between 1990 and 2011. The target is to achieve a reduction by two-thirds by 2015. In order to achieve this goal a further 3.5 million children's lives must be saved each year in 2015 compared with 2011. Can it be done?

According to UNICEF, this may be achieved. UNICEF's new equity strategy, which was put forward in the autumn of 2010, turns the efforts made so far through 180 degrees, and UNICEF's assessment is that several million children under the age of five can be saved from dying. This requires more focused investment to reach the most vulnerable and marginalized 20 per cent of children rather than, as hitherto, seeking to help the many children who are easiest to reach, here and now.

The new strategy, which so far only applies to health but will also be pursued in the area of education, means there is a renewed focus on targeted investment to reach the very poor and underprivileged, by using tested and cost-effective measures, removing bottlenecks in the supply of social services to the poorest, and working through local communities.

In many ways, the equity strategy makes a break with the most recent years' focus on the next-least poor, whereby it is possible to help many and to give assistance quickly and thus meet the quantitative targets which the international community has prioritized in the MDGs. In this context, it is often too difficult and time-consuming to reach those people who are the most socially, economically, and often geographically marginalized. The new thinking behind the equity strategy is not only a sign that the world has become wiser, it also reflects the fact that over the last ten years new cheaper medicines have become available for treating diarrhea and lung infections, and that access to mosquito nets for preventing malaria has also been much improved.

These facts have greatly improved the practical possibilities of reaching the poorest parts of the population. Everything points toward the possibility of making continued progress by more intensive efforts to reach the weakest and most marginalized parts of the population, where birth and illness rates are higher than in other groups.[10]

The MDGS are global goals. It is already possible to predict that some of the goals will be reached by 2015. Goal 1, to halve the proportion of people living on less than us$1 per day in 2015 compared with 1990, was well on the way to being achieved before the financial crisis struck in 2008, and it is highly probable that the goal will be reached despite the crisis. This is primarily because of the strong economic growth in China, India, and other countries in Southeast Asia, which has lifted hundreds of millions out of poverty. There has been less progress in sub-Saharan Africa, where the proportion of the poor has only fallen from 58 per cent in 1990 to 51 per cent in 2005, and where there is a long way to go before the proportion of the poor is halved.

There has also been good progress on goal 2, on access to a basic education for all. Globally, the proportion of children attending school has risen from 83 per cent in 1990 to nearly 90 per cent in 2008. However, there are still more than 60 million children aged twelve to fifteen who do not go to school, and there is a need for targeted measures to reach them. Experience shows that school attendance can often be increased by quite simple means: abolishing school fees, introducing school meals, cash payments to the poorest families that send their children to school, separate toilets for boys and girls, and better teacher training are some of the most important parameters for success. A country such as Tanzania, where only half the children went to school in 1999, had achieved almost total school attendance by 2008. Here the challenge is to hold on to the children for the whole period of schooling. This requires renewed focus on the quality of teaching and on the possibilities for secondary education, including vocational training.

Access to clean drinking water, a target under goal 7, has also increased markedly; the goal was actually achieved by 2010, five years ahead of the target date of 2015. Two billion more people now have access to clean drinking water than in 1990. This is mainly due to massive investments in new artesian wells and water distribution systems, especially in China and India. Conversely, it is already clear that the corresponding target for sanitation, halving the proportion of people without access to basic toilet facilities, will not be reached.

One of the goals that is furthest from reaching its target globally is goal 5, on the reduction by three-quarters of maternal mortality. Around the world, about 287,000 women die every year in connection with childbirth, and 99 per cent of these deaths occur in developing countries. A woman in Africa has a far higher risk of dying in childbirth at some point in her life than a woman in one of the industrialized countries. The number of maternal deaths is falling, but it is still 500 deaths per 100,000 live births for women aged fifteen to forty-nine in sub-Saharan Africa.[11]

While the MDGs are global, since 2000 many developing countries have adopted them as national goals, and used them as the basis for their own development plans and strategies. There was clear encouragement to do this in the UN Declaration from the 2005 World Summit, and there is no doubt that in many countries the MDGs have helped to focus efforts, giving education, health and access to water a more central position in national priorities.

Some countries have had significantly greater success than others. At the same time, influenced by the MDGs, over the last ten years most Western countries have gradually increased their assistance in the MDG focus areas. The OECD countries' total official development assistance in the social sectors has more than doubled between 2000 and 2008, from US$20 billion to US$40 billion. Today, development assistance from Western donor countries is increasingly targeted at education, health, and water rather than on infrastructure or the productive sectors of the economy. There is little doubt that the MDGs have played an important role in bringing about this redirection of development assistance.[12]

MDG SUMMIT 2010

Following the Millennium Summit in 2000 and the World Summit in 2005, it was only natural that there would be another UN summit in 2010 and that this would focus on the prospects for achieving the MDGs, with the aim of mobilizing the political will to intensify efforts toward 2015. A United Nations MDG Summit in 2010 would also send a clear political signal from world leaders that the global financial crisis of 2008–09 should not be allowed to derail international cooperation on the MDGs.

The decision to hold the Summit was taken in the autumn of 2009, together with a decision on the more specific outline of the meeting. It was decided to open up the meeting to greater participation by civil society organizations, NGOs and the business sector than in previous UN Summits. The preparation for the Summit began in March 2010, with a series of meetings between the member states and representatives for UN organizations, civil-society organizations, academia, and the business sector. The background documentation for the summit, reports from the secretary-general, the UNDP, and other UN organizations, were published in the course of May, and negotiations about the Summit declaration began in early June and continued over the summer.

After intense negotiations over three months, agreement was reached on the Summit Declaration in time for it to be approved by the General Assembly a week before the Summit began. The participating heads of state and government thus knew the outcome of the meeting beforehand, and could focus their statements on what each of their governments would do to ensure achievement of the goals by 2015.[13]

The negotiations on the Summit declaration were characterized by differing attitudes, clearly demonstrating the differences in approach of the developing countries – led by Yemen, negotiating on behalf of the G77 – and the approach of the Western countries, with the EU clearly in the lead. The essential issue was the tone of the declaration. Was the glass half full or half empty? Was the world on the way out of the global financial crisis, or would the crisis endure?

This was hard to say, not least because the current data were few and not all consolidated. But there were clearly ideological issues mixed up in this as well. The Western countries believed that a positive declaration from the Summit would in itself have a positive impact on developments and consolidate the first signs of economic recovery. What they wanted was a narrative from the Summit, which told in broad terms that the MDGs had been decisive for much of the progress in the developing countries made since 2000 and that, prior to the financial crisis, the developing countries had been well on the way to achieving most of the goals by 2015. The crisis had set the clock back, and it was now important to make up for lost time and get back on the track toward achieving the goals. For most Western countries the main political message of the MDG Summit should be the reconfirmation of the MDGs by the member states, and a clear statement that the goals could still be achieved, if countries worked together on this and did so with a sense of purpose and direction.

Against this, some developing countries (including especially the more ideologically motivated countries such as Bolivia, Cuba, Iran, Syria, and Venezuela) wanted the declaration to present the financial crisis as evidence that the Western market economy model for development was clearly not working, and that the future for the world lay in planned economies, based on new major financial and technological transfers from the North to the South.

Between these two positions stood the UNDP and the other UN organizations with a very different and much more specific approach to the Summit. The UNDP's position was that in general over the previous ten years the developing countries had gained a wealth of experience from different approaches for achieving the MDGs and that these experiences could be used in the future.

The UNDP put forward its assessment of what had worked and what had not worked. The organization reviewed development results in fifty countries, based on fundamental questions such as: What methods have been most effective in getting children into school? How have agricultural harvests been increased? What are the most important factors for promoting equality? How has it been ensured that the poorest get access to clean drinking water? And not least – how can one learn from the experiences of others? Were there methods which were transferable to other countries or which could be scaled up from small pilot projects to operations across a broad front? And on this basis, what would it cost to achieve the MDGs?

The main conclusions were that many more countries could reasonably expect to reach the MDGs if greater use were made of the knowledge that already existed. Naturally, not all good experiences were applicable everywhere. Conditions vary from country to country, but some things came up again and again as recommendations from the country-specific analyses. In relation to the developing countries, the UNDP emphasized the importance of the following:

- National ownership of the policies carried out and based on principles of good governance. In brief: well-thought-through policies and effective public institutions;
- Increased mobilization of domestic resources to invest more in reaching the MDGs, in other words, more effective and growth-oriented tax systems that can increase government revenues;

- Increased public investment in education, health, water supply and sanitation, and not least in access to these services for women and girls. The creation of synergy between the different activities and the strengthening of social sector interventions through a better social security safety net was also important;
- Greater emphasis on economic growth in order to finance the increased public investments in the long run, while ensuring that the growth is broadly shared and benefits the poorest. Growth should thus be *inclusive*, focusing on job creation also for women. It will be necessary to create more than 400 million new jobs worldwide over the next decade if employment is to keep pace with the increased number of young people entering the labour market; and
- Major investments in energy which does not add to global warming and further climate change, and in infrastructure which is essential for increased economic growth. Without access to energy, in particular electricity, and to a nationwide transport network, it is difficult to raise production much above subsistence level.

The UNDP also underlined the importance of the industrialized countries living up to their promises of increased development assistance. If the promises made at the Gleneagles Summit in 2005 had been kept, development assistance in 2010 would have been US$18 billion more than it actually was, and these funds could have been used to great effect to achieve the MDGs.[14]

The United Nations has sought to promote the partnership between North and South which was the basic idea behind the framing of the MDGs. Responsibility for growth and development is a clear and unconditional national responsibility which each developing country must accept for itself. Without the political will to take on this task, no progress can be made toward achieving the MDGs. But the goals cannot be achieved by will alone if the means are wanting. Thus the OECD countries have to play their role through the provision of the development assistance they have promised. The global partnership expressed in goal 8 requires both sides to live up to their responsibilities.

The UNDP approach had an impact on the negotiations and it was also reflected in the Summit declaration. At the same time there were three additional problems which none of the negotiating parties was really willing to tackle, and which were generally kicked further down the road and not addressed in the negotiations.

The first problem was the 0.7 per cent of GNI goal for development assistance. The developing countries decided quite early on to focus on the implementation of the existing commitments rather than proposing even higher targets. This made good political sense, especially in relation to the EU member states which provide over half the total of development aid in the world and which in the spring of 2005 had promised to increase their collective level of development assistance to 0.56 per cent of GNI in 2010.

Preliminary estimates showed that the EU was far from achieving this goal (in 2010 the EU member states' aid ended up at 0.46 per cent of GNI). What was important for the developing countries was to have a reaffirmation that the 0.7 per cent goal would be achieved by 2015, and this was confirmed by the EU. The coming years will show whether this time there is the necessary political will in Europe to live up to the promises made.

The second problem was the concept of partnership itself. Much has changed over the last ten years. The role of states in international development co-operation has been supplemented by much more active participation by non-state actors, not just in implementing measures but also in the formulation of policies. This applies both to the private sector in general and organizations such as the World Economic Forum, but also to international NGOs and civil-society initiatives which can call on substantial means and which are major partners in some countries, both in the area of humanitarian and development assistance. And it also applies to private foundations, such as the Bill and Melinda Gates Foundation, which are increasingly engaged in development co-operation. These new actors must necessarily be part of the new partnership and their efforts must be coordinated with the efforts of others.

Western countries would welcome representatives from the business world, NGOs, and private foundations having greater opportunities to participate in the work of the United Nations. Naturally, this would not include actual participation in intergovernmental decisions, but a role as active partners having the opportunity to speak in debates and to be more directly involved in informal discussions. Some developing countries are opposed to such opening up to non-state actors, which they see as undermining the intergovernmental character of the United Nations and as a dilution of the classic North-South perspective in the UN (the rich versus the poor). However, the various processes are nevertheless moving toward greater participation of non-state actors. As stated above, there was greater participation of new development partners at the 2010 MDG Summit than in previous UN Summits in New York.

The issue of partnership is even more controversial with regard to those countries that are loosely referred to as the "emerging economies" or the "new and emerging economies," such as Brazil, China, India, Mexico, et cetera, which are increasingly important as investors and aid donors, particularly in many African countries. If one talks of global partnership, from a Western perspective it is important that these emerging economies should accept some of the responsibility for helping the poorest countries.

This applies both to opening their markets to imports from poorer developing countries and giving them financial support in such a way as not to undermine the existing development co-operation. This latter issue particularly concerns the conditionality that is often attached to development assistance in order to ensure that that the assistance is used as effectively as possible. The same conditions are not applied to aid provided by, for example, China or Brazil which have not signed up to the "rules of play" for official development assistance adopted by the OECD. This can cause problems, especially if the developing countries begin to play the traditional donors and new donors off against each other. China is already a significant player in sub-Saharan Africa, through its investments in extractive industries and long-term agreements to secure China's continued access to commodities.

The third problem concerns conflict-affected countries. As stated previously, this term is not politically defined in the UN context. However, the statistics are quite clear. The approximately forty countries that are fragile and which are affected by armed conflicts contain one-third of the world's poorest people. It is also in these countries that one finds more than half of the world's cases of infant mortality and one-third of the cases of maternal death.

It is these countries that, broadly speaking, are furthest from achieving the MDGs and where there is the most obvious need for special efforts to improve the situation. Such efforts may involve help for political processes to end conflicts, and assistance for the rebuilding of security institutions, justice systems, and public administration as well as access to social services – all of which are areas where the UN system has something to contribute.[15]

However, the obvious need to focus on states with weak institutions or limited government capacities, or both, ran up against strong resistance from the G77. A number of middle-income countries opposed making any distinction between different categories of developing countries, which they felt would detract from the challenges and needs of middle-income countries. The result was that the Summit declaration referred to a list of different categories of countries including the least developed countries; landlocked developing countries; small, developing island states; middle-income countries; African nations; and people living in areas affected by complex humanitarian emergencies and in areas affected by terrorism. The focus of the declaration was so dispersed that in reality it had little significance. This is not a new phenomenon; prioritizing is not the strongest point of any Summit declaration. Too many differing interests are represented at the negotiating table.[16]

In parallel with the negotiations on the Summit Declaration, a new international partnership was developed with a view to reinforcing the measures to combat infant and maternal mortality (goals 4 and 5). This involved close co-operation between the UN secretary-general, the UN organizations in the health sector (WHO, UNICEF, UNFPA, and UNAIDS), and other international organizations, private companies (especially from the pharmaceutical industry), major private foundations (especially the Bill and Melinda Gates Foundation), major international development NGOs, professional organizations, and the most involved member states (especially Norway and the United Kingdom).

The participants in this partnership each committed themselves to a range of new specific measures, and it was assessed that these commitments would add up to least US$40 billion from 2010 to 2015. The additional commitments were expected to make it possible for the partnership – Every Woman Every Child – to achieve that the lives of at least 16 million more women and children would be saved, that at least 33 million unwanted pregnancies would be avoided, and that globally 88 million children would avoid being stunted (stunting occurs when a child's natural physical and cognitive development is seriously and permanently impaired due to poor nutrition during pregnancy and in the early years of life). The initiative also provides for a monitoring mechanism, developed in co-operation with WHO, to follow whether the participants deliver what they promised, and to ascertain whether the results would live up to expectations.[17]

Every Woman Every Child is a new form of international co-operation, where the starting point is globally established norms, in this case the MDGs, but where the measures taken to achieve these goals are both limited and expanded in relation to previous purely intergovernmental co-operation. In certain respects, the co-operation is more limited, because not all member states need to be involved. Voluntary participation in government-to-government co-operation mean that countries that do *not* wish to co-operate can simply be left out and that they cannot hold back the process in the same way that they can in the case of usual intergovernmental co-operation. Countries join in with what they have to offer. In the Every Woman Every Child initiative there are more than seventy participating countries taking on commitments, of which only a dozen are traditional Western donor countries.[18]

At the same time, the co-operation is much broader and much deeper because governments are supplemented and complemented by relevant non-state actors, ensuring that all relevant views are represented at the negotiating table when the strategies are developed and also that non-state actors make commitments to undertake specific measures in order to reach the stated goals and objectives. It is the clear expectation that this working method, where the focus is on specific challenges, and on ensuring that all relevant actors are actively involved in such a multi-stakeholder forum, can be a model for similar efforts in other areas in future.

From the UN perspective it will be important to ensure that such initiatives are clearly based on globally established goals and standards, that the normative starting point is universal and that the various initiatives are focused only on implementing what has been agreed upon, merely making the implementation more effective. If this can be ensured, the United Nations will be able to participate as a key partner in such initiatives even though the participation of member states will be less than universal.

There are only a few years left before 2015. At this stage it is clear that some of the MDGs will be reached while others will not. It is equally clear that some countries will achieve or come fairly close to achieving the goals, while other countries will still be lagging far behind. This applies in particular to countries whose progress has been set back by periods of armed conflict or which have never had the capacity or resources to plan and implement the necessary policies and measures.

The United Nations MDG Summit in 2010 showed that there is considerable political support for achieving the MDGs, both from the leaders of the developing countries, who are responsible for making it happen, and from the leaders of the Western countries which, in 2000, undertook to support these efforts through their participation in the global partnership. The progress toward attaining the goals will be closely followed in the coming years, and the UN system will publish annual reports on the outcomes. Thus, it will be possible to see whether the political commitments made in 2010 will be implemented.

NEW INTERNATIONAL DEVELOPMENT GOALS IN 2015?

The Declaration of MDG Summit in 2010 ended by encouraging the secretary-general to start considering what, in 2015, should replace the MDGS as the new international development framework.

The success of the MDGs has made it virtually impossible for the UN *not* to continue global goal setting after 2015. There has been a general reluctance to initiate the post-2015 discussion too soon, primarily so as to avoid detracting from the political focus on actually achieving the goals by 2015, but at the same time, it is realized that if new goals are to be set at a UN summit in 2015, this cannot wait until the last moment.

That was the reason for two major initiatives taken in the summer of 2012. The first of these initiatives was the UN secretary-general appointing a High-Level Panel on the Post-2015 Development Agenda, under the co-chairmanship of Prime Minister David Cameron of the United Kingdom, President Ellen Johnson Sirleaf of Liberia and President Susilo Bambang Yudhoyono of Indonesia. The Panel was mandated to provide a report on the global development agenda beyond 2015, to be submitted in the summer of 2013.

The second initiative was a decision at the World Summit on Sustainable Development in Rio de Janeiro in June 2012 ("Rio+20") to initiate an open negotiating process leading to a proposal to the 68th Session of the General Assembly (September 2013–September 2014) "for sustainable development goals for consideration and appropriate action" (for sustainable development goals [SDGs], see chapter 11). The two initiatives will have to be joined together at some point, leading to the establishment of a United Nations development agenda beyond 2015.[19]

It will be much harder to establish the new international development agenda this time than it was to agree on the MDGs. In 2000, a number of global goals had already been agreed upon which could be used as a basis. One could argue about the composition and weighting of the overall MDG package in 2000, but individually each of the seven substantial MDGs had already been adopted as a global goal during various major UN conferences throughout the 1990s. The situation in 2015 will be quite different, and politically much more difficult to deal with.

Whether the target date for the new United Nations development agenda is set for 2030 or for some other year, it will be natural to carry forward the setting of goals in the social sectors: new goals for health (which may cover more than communicable diseases), for education (extending beyond primary education and also looking at the quality of education), for water, for sanitation, and for nutrition (not only in the fight against hunger, but also better and more sustainable nutrition in general). How gender equality is dealt with will be equally important, whether as a separate goal or a sub-goal under each of the other goals.

For these and for other development goals the system that will replace the MDGs should presumably be formed with a view to the double function of the MDGs. In other words, the goals will be formulated and adopted as global goals, but at the same time their form and character will provide a strong inspiration for the development of national goals and development strategies to reach these goals. This has clearly been one of the main advantages of the MDGs.

It will also be important to add new goals that ensure that the productive sectors and infrastructure investments receive the political attention they need. This applies in particular to energy, where there already is a proposal by the secretary-general for a goal of sustainable energy for all by 2030. This initiative focuses on providing access for all to modern forms of energy (today 1.3 billion people, almost a fifth of the global population, do not have access to electricity), doubling the rate of global energy efficiency, as well as doubling the share of renewables in the global energy mix.[20]

As a supplement to this it will be important for the future international development paradigm to take account of other aspects of global warming and climate change and the additional costs which the poorest countries will have to incur in order to adjust to expected changes in climate and in patterns of precipitation. The number and extent of natural disasters, many of them related to climate change, are increasing and everything indicates that this development will continue in the coming decades, even if the international community begins to tackle the climate challenges more seriously than has been the case so far.

Increasing urbanization is also an issue which should be at the centre of development policy and planning. Today, about half the world's population live in cities. By 2050, this figure will be close to three-quarters. This alone will create enormous infrastructural and social challenges which all countries will have to address.

The fight against poverty will undoubtedly continue to be a central issue, but the face of poverty has changed over the last twenty years, and not least in the last ten, since the MDGs placed it at the very centre of the global development agenda. Global poverty is somewhat different in 2012 than it was in 1990.

In 1990, the great majority (93 per cent) of the then 1.8 billion poor people lived in poor countries (low-income countries with an average annual per capita GNI of less than US$995). Today, the majority (72 per cent) of the world's now about 1.4 billion poor live in middle-income countries (countries with an average annual per capita GNI of between US$995 and nearly US$4,000). This change is largely due to the fact that some countries with large poor populations have experienced strong economic growth.

To a large extent this is due to the economic growth in China and India which, together, contain about 40 per cent of the world's population; but it is also due to changes in countries such as Egypt, Indonesia, Nigeria, Pakistan, and Vietnam. Economic growth in these countries has meant that there are relatively fewer poor people today, which in itself helps explain why the world is well on the way to achieving goal 1 of the MDGs: to halve the proportion of poor people by 2015 as compared to 1990.[21]

Meanwhile the problems of poverty have become more urgent in countries that are affected by armed conflict, where social and economic developments have not been so positive. Here it can be argued that in the future it will be these weak and fragile states and those affected by armed conflicts, particularly in Africa, that will be in need of assistance, both financial transfers and technical advice. The middle-income countries will have much better possibilities for finding their own resources to deal with their problems of poverty. This will especially be the case if these countries are able to establish effective tax systems which can help with income distribution, an essential precondition for reducing and ultimately ending the problems of poverty.

There are three further general problems which will have to be settled in connection with the formulation of a new global development agenda and a new international approach to development.

The first problem is whether it will be possible to formulate goals for the political institutions that are essential for establishing and extending national ownership of the goals in order to ensure growth and development. This refers to goals for democratic and inclusive political processes, effective public institutions, the fight against corruption, et cetera, which often touch on politically sensitive questions in many countries.

The second problem is whether it will be possible to discuss development financing in the broader sense and not only in the context of ODA. Aid naturally plays an important role, particularly in the poorest countries, and it can be a catalyst for essential social change. The OECD countries' promises to provide 0.7 per cent of GNI in ODA must therefore be fulfilled, and countries that may wish to give even more must, of course, receive appropriate recognition for such a commitment.

However, other forms of financing are also important. More money is transferred to developing countries in the form of remittances from migrant workers than in the form of development assistance, and more could be done to ensure that these means are better used for development purposes. Private investments in developing countries vary widely, and are typically concentrated in a limited number of countries. Many developing countries could do more to attract such investment and the transfer of know-how and technology which is often part of it.

Export earnings are naturally very important to the economies of developing countries. Better market access and a more flexible interpretation of the rules of origin will increase many countries' export potential and could be supported by national policies promoting diversification of the economy and increased foreign direct investments.

Furthermore, there are new and innovative means of financing, so far primarily at the planning stage. There are potential financial instruments related to international co-operation on climate change, to the pricing of CO_2 emissions and new transfers to developing countries with a view to achieving economic growth based on new climate-friendly technologies and means of production. There can be other forms of financing, such as a tax on financial transactions (the Tobin Tax) or a tax on plane tickets which have already been implemented nationally in some countries (see chapter 11).

The third problem concerns which actors should be included in global co-operation, and what roles they should play. The United Nations is and will probably remain a forum for international co-operation where the 193 member states play the central role. However, this does not mean that the member states are the *only* actors. As stated previously, we have recently seen much closer co-operation between the United Nations and a number of non-state actors, mainly in the business sector, major international NGOs, and private foundations, all of which play important roles in the globalization process. It is only reasonable to give these new actors a stronger voice in relation to intergovernmental co-operation.

What will be most important in this context, however, will be the future of the classic division between industrialized countries and developing countries, in other words between the OECD countries which have increased in number since the admission of Chile, Mexico, and South Korea, and the G77, which covers about 130 countries ranging from Mali to Singapore. The old "us and them" division of the world does not really apply any more when the OECD countries' share of the global economy is falling, while some of the new and emerging economies, such as Brazil, China, and India, continue to grow strongly year by year, becoming ever more important actors in the global economy.

These emerging economies are countries which, each in their own way, are increasingly engaged in aid and investment, especially in Africa, and it therefore makes less and less sense to talk of development in terms of a North-South issue. What we see is increasingly a development triangle, with the OECD countries in one corner, the emerging economies in the second corner, and the poorest developing countries in the third. The question is whether this should lead to the emerging economies taking on obligations toward the poorest countries in the same way as the OECD countries have done. This is an argument that has not yet been properly addressed in the United Nations context, but if the horizon is shifted from 2015 to 2030 it becomes much more relevant.

All this indicates that in all probability the adoption of a new international development agenda to replace the MDGs by 2015 will be politically complicated. One thing is certain: it will have to take account of the shifts in global power and changing economic strengths, if it is to achieve the same degree of success as the MDGs.

Operational Activities for Development

We want institutions!
Graffiti in Benghazi, Libya, 2011

THE HUMANITARIAN AND DEVELOPMENT SYSTEM

The United Nations is not just a normative organization formulating international development goals at global conferences and summits. The United Nations and the network of organizations, agencies, funds, and programs which the UN system consists of, is also an important operational actor in international development co-operation and it is by this means that the UN gives practical support to its normative functions. The combination of its normative and operational activities is one of the major strengths of the UN system.

From the start international economic and social co-operation has been seen as one of the UN's core areas. Article 55 of the UN Charter makes it clear that the United Nations shall promote higher standards of living, full employment, and conditions of economic and social progress and development. The last years of the Second World War and the first few years immediately after it were very fruitful in this context. New global organizations sprung up like mushrooms. The FAO, WHO, UNESCO, and UNICEF, and others, were all established in the years around 1945.

It was not least the United States under the Truman administration (1945–53) which was instrumental in this initial development of the mandate of the UN. Not only did the Americans launch the Marshall Plan for the recovery of Western Europe in 1947, but they also quickly saw the need to initiate a major aid effort to help what were then called the "under-developed countries." Truman announced this initiative in his inauguration speech in January 1949, where he emphasized the need to help the poorest countries participate in scientific and technological developments by their own efforts.

In the course of 1949, the first UN assistance program was established in the form of the Expanded Programme of Technical Assistance (EPTA), which was the forerunner of the UNDP and was to be financed by voluntary contributions. As its name indicates, from the very beginning its main emphasis was on technical assistance, i.e., advice given by experts in the field, by technical training and through education and scholarship programs. Later, feasibility studies for investment projects were included among the tasks of the UN organizations. In the first years of the Cold War, during which almost all the decisions of the Security Council were obstructed, the UN's operational development activities were largely kept away from ideological confrontations between East and West. EPTA grew throughout the 1950s and other programs were added to it, but in economic terms the measures remained quite modest until the 1960s. It was only after 1970 that there was a major expansion of the development activities of the UN system.[1]

The UN development system has grown organically. New global problems have led to the establishment of new organizations, especially in the area of the environment. All the many UN organizations form a complex network which can be seen in the organizational chart at the end of the book. The most important of these organizations are described in the table opposite.

While the UN system includes more than thirty different organizations, funds, and programs, its development activities are to a large extent concentrated in the five major funds and programs and four major specialized agencies named in the table. These nine organizations are responsible for about 85 per cent of the UN system's total turnover in the areas of humanitarian and development assistance (operational activities). In 2010, all the UN development activities amounted to us$22.9 billion. Thus a little under one-fifth of total international development assistance is channelled through the UN system.

In addition to the development expenditure of us$22.9 billion, in 2010 peacekeeping expenditures amounted to us$7.8 billion, and the UN system's total normative, analytical, and informative tasks came to us$5.3 billion. Thus, in 2010 the total expenditure on UN activities amounted to us$36.1 billion.[2]

The Most Important Humanitarian and Development Organizations of the UN

UN development programs (funds and programs), which include the humanitarian and development organizations of the UN system, which are wholly financed by voluntary contributions, and whose leaders (executive directors) are appointed by the UN secretary-general.

UNDP (UN Development Programme) with a total annual budget of about US$5 billion, which, in addition to having a coordinating role in the UN system, has a relatively broad mandate, including governance, crisis prevention and reconstruction.

WFP (World Food Programme) with an annual budget of about US$4 billion, and particularly focus on provision of food in emergencies.

UNICEF (UN Children's Fund) with an annual budget of about US$3 billion, of which about $1 billion comes from private fundraising, and a focus on children and young people, both in emergencies and in development contexts.

UNHCR (UN High Commissioner for Refugees) with an annual budget of about US$1.6 billion and a mandate that covers the protection of refugees and humanitarian tasks associated with this.

UNFPA (UN Population Fund) with an annual budget of about US$0.8 billion, working in particular with population questions and reproductive health, including family planning and contraception.

UN specialized agencies, which are autonomous organizations with their own budgets and which select their own leaders (directors-general). The specialized agencies often have important normative roles (adoption of international norms and standards) and thus have broader mandates than funds and programs. Their development activities are primarily financed by voluntary contributions.

WHO (World Health Organization), which plays an essential role in the global fight against infectious diseases, including laying down international standards, e.g., for dealing with outbreaks of avian flu, HINI, et cetera.

ILO (International Labour Organization), which dates back to 1919 and formulates international standards for the labour market, including the rights of trade unions and collective bargaining.

FAO (Food and Agriculture Organization), which closely monitors global food production and together with the WHO has developed standards for food safety.

UNESCO (UN Educational, Scientific and Cultural Organization), primarily acts as a meeting place for various professional networks and constituencies.

The UN system is financed in various ways. The basic form of financing of international organizations is by means of assessed contributions, understood as mandatory contributions which countries must pay as a subscription for their membership in the international organization.

Assessed contributions are normally set according to objective criteria (i.e., the ability to pay, thus reflecting the size of countries' GNI, although with some delay), and organizations that are financed in this way have a high level of certainty that the contributions will be paid. This gives these organizations a reasonable planning horizon and means that they are not obliged to invest resources in continuous efforts to raise new funds.[3]

However, most humanitarian and development organizations are financed by voluntary contributions. This applies fully to the UNDP and UNICEF, as well as to a large part of WHO's development activities. The voluntary contributions from member states are provided either as core contributions (often referred to as "regular resources") which contribute to the organization's overall activities, or as contributions that are earmarked for specific activities (called non-core, earmarks or other resources). If one deducts humanitarian contributions, which are by their very nature largely earmarked, in 2010 only about 42 per cent of the total contributions to the United Nations from the OECD countries were given as core contributions. There has been a tendency for the share of core contributions to fall over the last fifteen years, from 72 per cent core in 1994. This means that the general flexibility of the resource allocation of the organizations has been significantly reduced over the last fifteen to twenty years.

The two largest UN development funds and programs – the UNDP and UNICEF – now receive only 20 and 25 per cent respectively of their total income in the form of core contributions. This naturally affects how effective they can be. If uncertainty about financing means that they have to start up a humanitarian operation too cautiously, or if they have to dismiss staff from time to time because of lack of funds, and then rehire them a few months later when funds are received, this naturally affects their operational effectiveness and efficiency.

There is little doubt that the increased tendency to earmark contributions also distorts the UN organizations' operations in individual countries. Instead of there being a more organic program, reflecting the organizations' different areas of expertise and the needs of the partner countries, the UN country programs to a large degree reflect the political priorities and development fads of donor countries.

By far the greater part of the voluntary contributions for the UN's development activities comes from the Western countries, and in particular from European countries. The fact that the contributions are voluntary also means that the donor countries can reduce their contributions from one year to the next if they think that the activities are not going in the right direction or if the organizations are not sufficiently effective in achieving their goals.

This gives considerable influence to the donor countries – as money talks. The UN funds and programs would like to have voluntary contributions committed over a number of years (multi-year commitments), and thus achieve greater predictability of their income, which is difficult for most donor countries. The UN organizations also prefer to have as high a proportion of their income as possible in the form of core contributions rather than earmarked contributions which are less flexible in relation to the development needs of partner countries.

The executive boards of the UN funds and programs are the main intergovernmental bodies for providing the overall political guidelines for the organizations and deciding on the specific allocations of funds to different activities and sub-programs. The donor countries have more seats on the executive boards of the UN funds and programs than their numbers would entitle them to. Thus, OECD countries have one-third of the seats on the Executive Boards of the UNDP, the UNFPA, and UNICEF, and they clearly set the tone for the work of the boards where decisions are almost always taken unanimously. The formal meetings of the boards are supplemented by an ongoing informal dialogue between the senior management of the organizations and their major Western donor countries, which of course further strengthen these countries' influence in UN funds and programs.

UNITED NATIONS ACTIVITIES IN THE FIELD

Most people know the United Nations from its development work in the field, especially from its humanitarian operations. The UN coordinates the major emergency operations, and the WFP, UNICEF, and the UNHCR are among the most important agencies in getting the emergency assistance delivered and distributed. When the world is hit by a humanitarian disaster, as was the case in the summer of 2011 when more than 12 million people were starving in Djibouti, Eritrea, Ethiopia, Kenya, and Somalia – the worst humanitarian crisis in Africa in the last twenty years – the United Nations is always at the centre of the relief efforts.

And the United Nations will always be there. The UN is present in about 130 countries where it has a representative in charge of the local UN office. The UN representative, the resident coordinator (RC), is appointed by the secretary-general and is nominally in charge of all the UN's activities in the country in question. Some of the UN funds and programs are present in yet further countries, so there really is a global system of representation which covers the full spectrum of developing countries to an extent that very few, if any, of the UN member states are able to do.

It is in the field, through its assistance to partner countries, that the UN's humanitarian and operational development activities are tested. It is in these countries that by far the greatest proportion of the almost US$23 billion of development assistance administered by the UN is put to use, and it is here that the results must be seen and measured. It is by its operational activities in partner countries that member states will eventually judge whether the UN system is succeeding in delivering assistance in the manner and in the areas that the countries prioritize and where they see a need for UN support. It is in this respect that one can – and should – ask whether the UN system is providing the right kind of support for countries; whether the partner countries regard the UN system and its various organizations, funds, and programs as effective and as well coordinated; and whether the UN's operational activities have a natural place among other providers of development assistance that one normally finds in the poorest developing countries.

A direct measurement of the demand for the services of the UN system is the extent to which the developing countries that are not among the poorest – i.e., the middle-income countries – will pay for the United Nations' support. This is necessary because the executive boards of the UN organizations have generally decided that their funds should primarily be used in the poorest countries. This means that the major UN organizations use at least half their resources in sub-Saharan Africa, and that very few resources are set aside for middle-income countries, such as most of the countries in Latin America.

Nevertheless, an organization such as the UNDP has programs in Latin America amounting to US$770 million in 2010, of which $734 million was financed by the countries which received the assistance. For the UN system as a whole, in 2010 the government of Panama financed UN activities in the country to the extent of US$82 million, by far the major share of funding of UN activities in Panama. Similarly, Argentina financed UN activities to the extent of US$196 million, Brazil US$111 million, and Colombia US$76 million. Elsewhere, Egypt financed UN activities in the country to the extent of US$72 million. Countries such as China and Mexico also finance a significant proportion of the UN operations in these countries. One must assume that the middle-income countries are satisfied with the professional standard of the services they receive from the UN, and that they would use alternatives if they believed other partners could do a better and more cost-effective job.[4]

What are the main competences of the United Nations in the area of development? The UN is not a player in the area of infrastructure investments in the same way as the World Bank or the regional development banks; the UN does not construct roads or power stations. The UN organizations' strength is in the social sectors, where a number of UN organizations work to ensure the delivery of social services to all, and not least to the very poor. This applies in particular in the areas of health (WHO, UNFPA, and UNICEF), education (UNICEF and UNESCO), and food and nutrition (FAO, UNICEF, and WFP).

However, first and foremost, the UN organizations are involved across a range of development sectors, and their activities are generally characterized by the three core concepts of governance, capacity building, and a rights-based approach. Roughly speaking, governance characterizes a significant part of the UN's operational activities, especially for the UNDP, capacity building is the method used, and the rights-based approach is the key to success in capacity building.

The UN system's role with regard to governance is defined by the organization's basic values. The UN is essentially a political organization, but it is owned by the member states in a highly democratic way. Thus, member states trust the organization, and the United Nations is often in a privileged position as adviser and collaborator for governments.

This means that co-operation with the UN organizations at country level, spearheaded by the RC, is generally regarded as more trustworthy than co-operation with most bilateral aid donors or the EU. This should not be understood as meaning that the UN is better, merely that the relationship between partner countries and the UN is different. In relation to the EU Commission or bilateral donors, partner countries know that there are boundaries that must not be crossed. For example, if a country suddenly starts implementing a wholly irresponsible economic policy, begins systematically violating the human rights of its citizens, or subjects minority groups to persecution, then the government of that country will know that this can have consequences for its development co-operation and can very well lead to a reduction of assistance or, ultimately, to its cessation.

This does not apply to UN organizations unless the programs are suspended by the executive board of the organization in question, and this only rarely happens. Earmarked contributions would obviously be reduced, if the situation in a country deteriorates for some of the reasons mentioned above, but the activities financed by the regular resources will continue. And in contrast to bilateral ambassadors, the UN's representatives will be very careful about criticizing their host country. The political costs for a country of expelling a UN senior staff member (to declare them *persona non grata*) are much less than would normally be the case of expelling another country's ambassador, where one must at least expect a tit-for-tat expulsion and a diplomatic crisis.

The UN's place in the overall architecture of development assistance actors is thus one it occupies for better and for worse. UN staff working in countries that are politically at odds with the rest of the world must be able to perform a difficult balancing act. It will be very difficult and risky for them to maintain close contact with opposition groups, and UN staff will often be witnesses to highly reprehensible circumstances without being able to do that much about them. They may know things which they must be very cautious about sharing with others, but which may also become very useful if and when there is political change in the country and bilateral donors are willing to offer significant increases in their assistance, channelled through the United Nations.

In this situation, without stretching the analogy too far, the UN and the bilateral donors may in effect play a good cop/bad cop routine. The fact that the UN system keeps its lines of communication open, even with countries with which no one else will have any dealings – North Korea is a case in point, or Myanmar before the latest political changes in 2012 – is of course important and it will almost always be useful at some point.

Even though all UN organizations work with governance issues within their areas of expertise, it is the UNDP in particular that has a broader focus on this. In fragile countries, more than half the UNDP's work is on governance issues. This covers everything from support for the establishment of parliaments, municipal authorities and local administration, support for a free press, aid for arranging and holding free elections, drawing up constitutions, planning and supporting reforms of justice systems, including the establishment of courts, building up civil society organizations, combatting corruption, implementing administrative reforms, training civil servants, et cetera. It involves nearly everything to do with developing democratic political systems; a healthy democratic culture in which the government accepts that it is monitored by the press and accountable to the people; a reasonably effective public administration that is capable of functioning centrally (in government ministries) and locally without corruption and the abuse of power; a security apparatus (police) which citizens trust; and a judicial system that settles disputes in a way which has the confidence of the people, making redundant the saying, "Why pay for a lawyer when you can buy a judge?"

Many of these governance issues have a direct impact on those holding political power. Doing away with corruption will significantly reduce the income of some. Free and fair elections mean that those in power risk losing it overnight. A free press means that people in power will be criticized, sometimes unfairly. This too requires a balancing act and close co-operation with bilateral donors that will often be involved in these areas of co-operation and which, by definition, will be better at playing bad cop.

Working on governance issues, both in general and in specific sectors, will largely occur through capacity building (also called capacity development). The UN system is not alone in focusing on the importance of building institutional capacity in developing countries. Other donors and international organizations also work with this as an integral part of their development co-operation programs. However, for the UN system, capacity building is the raison d'être of development co-operation.

Capacity building can be described as the processes whereby people, institutions, and societies as a whole unlock, create, and strengthen capacities over time. It is therefore something that institutions and governments must take ownership of, and it cannot be imposed by external actors. External actors can only provide financial support, guidance, technical advice, training, and help with the development of a supporting culture around the process. The UN organizations' approach to capacity building is based on the idea that even in the poorest countries there is a political will and an ability to create effective institutions, and one must therefore build on local resources in the form of people, skills, and available knowledge and technologies.

This involves creating links between reforms in society in general, targeted institutional reforms, and education and training of individuals. The UNDP has identified four areas that are decisive for whether capacity building will succeed: the institutional basis (legislation, administrative rules, the value basis of organizations), leadership (the ability to inspire and motivate others, and to adapt to new conditions), knowledge (personal and institutional, including knowledge sharing), and responsibility (openness and willingness of institutions and individuals to accept responsibility). Tools have been developed in all these areas to help the UN organizations support local processes.[5]

A significant part of the support for capacity building is technical assistance through advice, training, institutional change, and sharing experiences. Here it is a positive factor that in many ways the United Nation *is* the organization's staff and the sum of their knowledge and experience.

In the example of the situation in Liberia described in chapter 6, the UNDP is referred to as having a presence in that country with a staff of about 280, of whom the great majority were local staff. UNICEF had a team of about 74 and the UNFPA a team of about 25. In recent years the UN system has generally put considerable efforts into strengthening the exchange of knowledge between developing countries, with a greater emphasis on South-South co-operation. The background to this is that in many cases the experiences of other developing countries are often perceived as a more relevant starting point for knowledge sharing than the traditional experiences of Western donor countries.[6]

The rights-based approach to development is also a general approach to development widely shared within the UN system, where the aim is to arrange for practical development activities, including assistance for capacity building in a manner which also increases respect for international human rights standards.

The aim is both to reinforce people's will and capacity to exercise their human rights (as rights holders) and to develop the necessary political understanding and administrative capacities of those who are to respect these rights (the duty bearers). The rights-based approach also involves paying increased attention to combatting discrimination against particular groups of the population. It is based on the active involvement of all groups in the processes leading to the formulation and implementation of government policy and stresses that governments must be accountable to all its citizens for how they deal with the challenges they face.

A specific example of a rights-based approach in practice is the UNFPA's work on sexual and reproductive rights.[7] These rights emanate from the basic human rights conventions and the outcome of the UN International Conference on Population and Development (ICPD) in Cairo in 1994, which defined women's reproductive rights – the right of individual women to decide on their own sexuality and reproduction – and the right of women to be able to access reproductive health services, including sexuality education. Achieving this will require significant changes to the structure of public health systems and education systems (not least in relation to what children and young people, and especially girls, are taught about their rights and opportunities). It will also require intensive dialogues with civil-society organizations, including religious organizations and religious leaders, and active advocacy on behalf of the various organizations and groups involved. The issue of violence against women is also closely linked to this agenda.

At the heart of this issue is the question of women's access to contraception and thus their ability to control the number of their children and the spacing of their pregnancies. In short, this concerns women's possibilities for making free and informed choices with regard to their reproduction and sexuality. There are still more than 220 million women in the world who would like to avoid pregnancies, but who do not have access to family-planning advice and contraception.[8]

To a great extent, this is a question of how individual countries design their health services and how they prioritize between different aspects of health care. What is essential for a rights-based approach is that there should be access for women to the relevant forms of contraception, that acquiring these services should be financially affordable for women, and that there should not be discrimination between different groups of women. Here it is, of course, relevant for those taking part in discussions and decisions at country level to be able to argue on the basis of international norms and standards, even if this does not in itself generate more funds in this area.

The activities of the UN system, particularly those of the UNFPA, on reproductive rights are often controversial. The Holy See and countries such as Malta and a number of conservative Islamic countries are constantly seeking to roll back the global political standard created by the ICPD. For some, and especially the Catholic Church, the whole question of family planning and access to contraception is problematic. For others, it is the issue of abortion that is the main concern. The ICPD is clear on this point. Abortion is not a method for family planning, and everything possible should be done to reduce the number of abortions. But where abortion is not against the law, it must be ensured that it is done safely and does not expose women to unnecessary health risks.

The ICPD does not encourage women to have abortions – quite the contrary. The main emphasis of the ICPD is clearly on what could and should be done for women to avoid unwanted pregnancies, and the more successful this approach is the less relevant the question of abortion becomes.

But the ICPD also reflects the real world. Unwanted pregnancies can never be entirely avoided, and in this case women must have the possibility of having an abortion safely. The figures are alarming; it is estimated that there are about 54 million unintended pregnancies in the world every year, leading to 21 million unplanned births, 26 million abortions (of which 16 million are unsafe), and 7 million miscarriages. Unsafe abortions carried out by quack doctors and untrained "helpers" often lead to serious complications, and, in the worst cases, to sterility and even death. There is a real need for increased efforts to change this situation and access to family planning and contraception is the key to this.[9]

ONE UN AT COUNTRY LEVEL

The UN system is complex. The main coordinating body is the Chief Executives Board (CEB), headed by the secretary-general, where the heads of the seventeen specialized agencies (including the World Bank, IMF, and WTO, which have a looser association with the UN but which participate in the CEB) meet twice a year with the heads of the eleven UN funds and development programs. The more programmatic coordination is undertaken by the UN Development Group (UNDG), under the leadership of the UNDP's administrator. The UNDG has thirty-two members, representing the funds and programs, specialized agencies and relevant entities in the UN Secretariat; the World Bank participates as an observer. It is the UNDG that is responsible for overall coordination and for the adoption of common rules and joint administrative systems related to development activities.[10]

In order to improve coordination at country level, the United Nations has adopted a Delivering-as-One (DaO) approach. The DaO concept was first proposed in the report of the secretary-general's High-level Panel on United Nations System-wide Coherence in 2006, and in 2007 eight countries were selected for a pilot project to test the concept. These were: Albania, Cape Verde, Mozambique, Pakistan, Rwanda, Tanzania, Uruguay, and Vietnam.

The idea of Delivering-as-One is simple: the UN system should function as a single, coherent and easily accessible system at country level in order to achieve an improved division of labour, greater effectiveness and reduced transaction costs, both internally and vis-à-vis the host country. A more explicit agreement on who does what also reduces the constant knocking on the doors of the government departments of the host country, which was a complaint often voiced by partner countries. There should be four reforms at country level – "the 4 Ones":

- One Leader: further strengthening the RC's role in relation to all UN organizations present in the country. This will also require a clear separation of the functions of the local RC and the function as head of the UNDP office (a firewall).
- One Budget: The establishment of an overall budget for the UN activities in each country, and the expected results. The budget is to be based on inputs from each of the organizations and their expected incomes, whether from core contributions or earmarked contributions. Any DaO fund in the country should be included.
- One Program: A joint program to ensure that the UN activities are all linked to national priorities and the activities are coordinated between the various UN organizations.
- One Office: If possible, all the UN organizations should be located in the same building or in the same area to help staff interact and reduce administrative costs.

The immediate assessment from the eight pilot countries that have evaluated their experiences with DaO has generally been positive, regardless of whether DaO has led to the provision of further resources. The

UN's position has been strengthened at country level and the UN system has emerged as a more relevant development partner for the governments. As expected, the transaction costs have been significantly reduced and the overall effectiveness has been improved. Even more could have been achieved if the administrative procedures for internal co-operation within the UN had been further simplified, but that takes time.

The preliminary reports also indicate that DaO's financing and the establishment of its special funds in the individual pilot countries sponsored by the donor countries has clearly been a factor that has helped the project succeed.

As stated, the overall UN budget at country level consists of what each individual UN organization beings to the table. These are the funds – whether from regular resources or other resources – which each organization has generated and has at its disposal at country level and in respect of which the organizations do not necessary feel a special obligation to involve the RC. In order to make DaO even more attractive, the UN and donor countries have established special DaO funds in a number of the pilot countries with new money under the control of the RC. This was particularly the case in Vietnam, where the DaO fund early on amounted to more than 25 per cent of the total annual UN budget of us$65 million; in Tanzania (a fund of us$19 million out of a total UN budget of us$93 million); Rwanda (us$12 million out of us$64 million); and Mozambique (us$13 million out of us$113 million).[11]

In all four of these countries these new funds have had a significant effect, not least by strengthening the RC's position in relation to the individual UN organizations – once again money talks. RCs will have a stronger say in coordination when they have additional means to allocate to UN funds, programs and agencies, and this applies even where the amount is not huge. However, it is also clear that the various UN organizations at country level have some concerns that DaO might mean that they lose the possibility of branding themselves as individual organizations and thus lose their ability to raise further funds themselves in the long term.

It is clear that the DaO funds in the pilot countries will not continue indefinitely and that any such funds will be limited when, as expected, the DaO concept is rolled out to all countries after 2012. In addition to the eight countries in the pilot scheme, more than twenty countries have already introduced parts of the DaO concept locally on their own initiative and in co-operation with the UN organizations. It is difficult to see the DaO concept gaining traction unless the RC is truly empowered and controls part of the total UN budget at country level. How this can be done without new money is a matter for discussion by the UNDG and CEB. It will not be an easy challenge to overcome.

It should be remembered that at country level the UN organizations are subject to a number of harsh realities. The organizations are only financed to a limited extent by regular resources (core contributions). The proportion naturally varies from organization to organization, but it is not unusual for a local head of a UN organization to have perhaps only 20 to 25 per cent of their annual budget financed from their headquarters. The expectation from headquarters is that the rest of the funds needed to implement the country program will be raised locally by the country office, i.e., from bilateral donors, global funds or, in some cases, from the host country.

This makes it important for the country representative and the country office to gain some visibility and to create a positive brand image, and it also takes time and energy to raise the necessary funds. Most country representatives would undoubtedly prefer to receive their funds in the form of increased core contributions or from a local UN funds, rather than vigorously pursuing ad hoc funding opportunities. However, they would not like to have less funding available as a result of possible restrictions on local fundraising.

If this very generalized description of the challenges facing country representatives were to change it would require a cultural transformation of the UN system, where using the ability to raise funds locally as a key indicator of success is given less importance and more importance is attached to the ability of each leader and each organization to act holistically in conjunction with the rest of the UN system. Specifically, in the UN as in other organizations what matters is what signals are sent out by senior management in relation to appointments and promotions. There is no doubt that at present country representatives of UN funds, programs, and agencies are largely assessed on their ability to raise new funds locally.

Despite these challenges, it is obvious that the DaO concept and its further development will be an important factor in increasing the effectiveness of the UN's operational activities at country level. This is clearly recognized by all the organizations at headquarters level, though there are difficulties in keeping up with developments in the form of making the structural measures necessary to support this process, not least in the areas of human resources, budgeting and ICT.

However, politically not all the developing countries are equally pleased with DaO. Some of the less reform-minded countries see the new concept and the empowered role of the RC as undesirable because a strengthened RC, supported by the UN's political mandate, could play a more political role in the host country, perhaps in relation to violations of human rights and the treatment of minorities. In these countries, a more fragmented and technically oriented UN system is often regarded as less of a political risk.

THE UNITED NATIONS, THE WORLD BANK, AND THE G20

While the United Nations' central role in relation to international peace and security is unchallenged, and while the UN's institutional mandate in the area of human rights is broadly accepted, the situation is different with regard to the role of the UN system in relation to global economic co-operation and the international financial and economic systems.[12]

In this area there are a number of other international organizations that have global or regional mandates and which play important roles in international co-operation. This applies in particular to the World Bank and the IMF, the two Bretton Woods institutions named after the New Hampshire town in the United States, where the organizations were established in July 1944. Like the United Nations, the World Bank is an organization with global membership – 187 members compared with the UN's 193 members.

The main difference concerns the voting rights of the member states. While voting in the UN General Assembly uses the well-known principle of one country–one vote, in the World Bank, as in a company with shareholders, the votes of the member countries are determined by their shareholdings. For example, Afghanistan has 0.04 per cent of the votes, Denmark 0.98 per cent and the United States (the biggest shareholder) 14.99 per cent. This naturally gives an entirely different balance of power in the organization. With the reform of the voting power which was adopted in April 2010, the developing countries as a whole have increased their share of the votes, in the first instance to 47 per cent. The industrialized countries thus still have a majority of the votes.[13]

In financial terms, the World Bank is a bigger development actor than the UN system, but only just, and with a more narrowly defined role in relation to the political agenda for development. The Bank is strongly involved in major infrastructure projects and in other important programs, and it has markedly expanded its involvement in developing countries in recent years in order to counter the effects of the financial and economic crises. Even though traditional lending is still an important part of its work, an increasing proportion of the Bank's funds are now provided as grants not linked to specific projects, especially to the poorest countries, and financed by the same donor countries that support the UN system with voluntary contributions. The gradual shift of the Bank's scope of work has created a greater overlap between the activities of the World Bank and those of the UN system, especially the UNDP. This is of course a challenge for both systems.

There has traditionally been a certain difference of approach between the World Bank's (and the IMF's) thinking on development and the thinking within the UN system. To some extent, this reflects the different political bases of the two organizational systems. The Bretton Woods institutions' structural adjustment policy of the 1980s and their demands for developing countries to liberalize their economies (known as the "Washington consensus") was looked at with some scepticism by the United Nations, and it was one of the reasons why the UN system began to think more along the lines of human development as the cornerstone of economic policies in developing countries.

In this context, the UN system, and especially UNICEF, the UNDP and the ILO, developed a more broadly defined alternative to the World Bank's development paradigm; this attracted increasing support, and by the end of the 1990s it was also accepted by the Bank. This development paradigm, with its emphasis on improving health, nutrition, and education, was established as the new international model with the adoption of the MDGS in 2000. Since then the ideological and political differences between the Bretton Woods system and the UN system have diminished and the thinking has to a large degree converged.[14]

The financial and economic crises of 2008–09 brought another important global actor onto the stage in the form of the G20. The G20 co-operation was established during the Asian financial crisis of 1997–98, as a collaboration mechanism between the finance ministers and central bank governors of the world's then twenty biggest economies. The global financial crisis created even greater demands for coordination of the economic policies of the largest economies to deal with the crisis, and on the initiative of the United Kingdom in September 2008 the G20 co-operation was raised to the level of heads of state and government, first in Washington in November 2008 and then in London in April 2009. There was a clear ambition that the new G20 should be the most important international forum for dealing with international economic issues.[15]

The G20 co-operation is to a large extent an expansion of the G7/G8 co-operation which the major Western economies have had since 1975 (expanded to include Russia in 1997). The further expansion to include the major emerging economies is a clear recognition that the global economic balance of power has shifted over the last twenty years and that it is no longer possible to deal with economic crises by coordinating the policies of the industrialized countries alone. It is now necessary to get Brazil, China, India, Mexico, and South Korea on board as well if policy coordination is to be global. Together the G20 economies represent about 90 per cent of the world's economy (if all of the European Union is included), and about two-thirds of the world's population.

There is little doubt that the G20 co-operation in 2008–09 to a large degree succeeded in preventing the crisis becoming even worse and in avoiding the major economies trying to solve their problems by a strategy of "beggar-my-neighbour" as they had done in the Depression in the 1930s, leading to a global downward economic spiral. Since the focus was on the financial sector and on the coordination of national economic policies, it was not a given that the UN should take part in the co-operation, in line with the World Bank and the IMF. However, the UN secretary-general succeeded in getting a place at the table, and when the G20 co-operation was expanded in 2010 to include questions related to development, the UN became a permanent participant.

From the start, the G20 co-operation was viewed with some scepticism by most of the countries that were not invited to take part. This scepticism has since noticeably diminished, partly because the rotating G20 presidencies have been open to the idea of participation of other actors (so that both the AU and ASEAN took part in the G20 Summit in Seoul in November 2010), and partly because the co-operation has not expanded into other policy areas, as many had feared.

Some countries tried to create a division between the G20 as a self-appointed group without legitimacy on the one hand, and the United Nations and its universal membership ("G193") on the other hand.

However, legitimacy can be something one has virtually by definition (as is the case with the UN) or it is something that can be won by hard work and visible results. From this point of view the G20 obtained considerable legitimacy by is handling of the global economic crisis in 2008–09. And it has not escaped notice that the expansion of the G8 to the G20 is a clear signal that the world's economic balance of power is rapidly changing.

It is important to emphasize that the UN has only a limited mandate with regard to international financial and economic issues. The organization's role in relation to global economic governance has primarily focused on development policy and the aspects that are significant for the participation of developing countries, and especially the poorest developing countries, in the global economy. The economic policies of the industrialized countries have only been a subject for UN deliberations to the extent that these policies affect developing countries – which is naturally often the case. Trade policy, protectionism, market access, terms of trade, foreign direct investments, remittances, capital flows, macroeconomic and financial stability, and interest rates – in the UN context all these issues have primarily been seen through the prism of their effects on developing countries.

To the extent that these issues and the interrelationship between them are the subject of G20 discussions, the UN Secretariat will naturally take part in this discussion. From the secretary-general's perspective the G20 is not a threat to the United Nations but an opportunity for a more informal dialogue between and with some of the major actors which can open up the possibilities for decisions in the UN context. The United Nations is quite used to smaller groups of countries discussing issues of common interest and seeking to work out common positions which they then take to the wider membership.

If the G20 countries agree, the group can be a driving force for broader co-operation on development activities in the UN. However, the question is whether it is likely that the G20 countries can agree on much in the area of development. Among other things this will require the new emerging economies in the G20 to state clearly where they actually stand and not, as has been the case so far, to hide behind the G77. More fundamentally, it could also lead to the poorest developing countries beginning to see the concept of rich countries in a different light, not merely encompassing the OECD countries but also the emerging economies. The poorest and least developed countries may then also begin to make demands on the emerging economies, for improved market access, increased debt relief, and development assistance.

What may become the most important feature of G20 co-operation on development issues may therefore very well be its significance for future relations between the traditional developed economies, the emerging economies (especially Brazil, China, India, Indonesia, Mexico, and South Africa), and the large number of poorer developing countries. Eventually this development triangle may question the cohesion of the G77 and the prospects of keeping this very diversified group together in the long run.

COMPETING DEVELOPMENT PARADIGMS

The UN system's operational development activities have always been a battleground for contending development philosophies and ideas. To some extent this naturally reflects the different centres of political power within the system. The developing countries have considerable influence through their overwhelming majority in the General Assembly, and the OECD countries have significant influence through their voluntary contributions and their role in the executive boards of the funds and programs.

Since the 1960s, the General Assembly has often been the scene for clashes between different approaches to development. Developing countries saw the General Assembly as a better platform for presenting their visions and ideas than the World Bank or the IMF, where the industrialized countries were solidly in the driving seat and did not, in the minds of developing countries, seem very willing to take their views into account. However, this changed when Jim Wolfensohn took over as president of the World Bank in 1995.[16]

The clashes between the member states of the United Nations have primarily concerned the overall development policy – and especially the obligations which the former colonial powers had, or ought to have had, to help the new independent countries in Africa, Asia, and Latin America speed up their economic and social development so they could quickly be on a level with the industrialized countries.

Over the years the developing countries have often called for greater financial support, debt relief, increased customs-free and quota-free market access, minimum prices for commodities, access to new technology on non-commercial terms, and for more influence in multilateral organizations, especially the international financial institutions. There have also been demands to have all this without submitting to the various accountability requirements and "conditionalities" which the industrialized countries find necessary to ensure that the means directly or indirectly transferred from the North to the South are used properly and responsibly. The source of ODA remains the taxpayers in donor countries, which is naturally the basis for the requests of donor countries for transparency and sound fiduciary management of ODA.

Throughout the 1970s and 1980s the more ideological North-South confrontation set its mark on the General Assembly, ECOSOC, and on major international conferences. The emergence of OPEC as a new important player in the global economy and the two global oil crises, in 1973–74 and 1981–82, gave fresh impetus to discussions about a new international economic order (NIEO). However, it was not possible to reach agreement on a new global negotiating round with the North-South relationship as the subject of serious discussion.

The end of the Cold War and the ideological victory of the market-based economies of the Western world in the 1990s went almost unnoticed by some delegates in the negotiating chambers of the UN. For a number of years, many of the UN representatives of the developing countries continued to fight the battles of the 1970s and 1980s, and some are still doing so. The explanation for this is discussed in chapter 1, but it also reflects the fact that many of the discussions on international economic and development issues in the General Assembly have become less relevant as operational decisions are taken elsewhere, including by the executive boards of the various UN organizations and in informal discussions between the relevant organizations and donor countries.

As the discussions and decisions of the General Assembly do not have much effect in practice, it does not matter that much if they are sometimes distorted. At the same time, the basic principle of solidarity within the G77 means that those that shout loudest often have the most influence, especially on issues which the great majority of more pragmatic countries have long since written off. This means that the more radical ideologues among the developing countries, such as the ALBA countries in Latin America (especially Bolivia, Cuba, Nicaragua, and Venezuela) often have a fairly free run at repeating their revolutionary speeches from the 1970s and 1980s, while the rest of the world looks on, mildly bemused and shrugging their shoulders.

A recent example of this was the United Nations Conference on the World Financial and Economic Crisis in June 2009. The topic was clearly relevant. The global crisis had gained momentum over the summer of 2008, and a number of world leaders met informally at the Waldorf Astoria Hotel in New York in connection with the opening of the General Assembly in September 2008. These leaders agreed to revive the G20 co-operation at the level of heads of state and government. The United States invited delegates to the first G20 meeting in Washington in November 2008 and the United Kingdom to the next meeting in London in April 2009. In London, the G20 generally succeeded in stabilizing global financial markets and preventing the crisis becoming even worse.

As discussed, the role of the United Nations in these extremely important developments was marginal at best. It was the IMF and to a certain extent the World Bank that were the important institutional players in re-establishing global financial stability following the collapse of Lehmann Brothers.

However, this apparent disregard for the UN was unacceptable for a small group of developing countries, led by Nicaragua whose former foreign minister was president of the General Assembly in 2008–09. These countries succeeded in having a decision adopted to organize a major UN conference on the issue and to involve the American economist and Nobel Prize winner Joseph Stiglitz and a number of other experts in the extensive preparations for this conference. The initiative led to a long and complex negotiation process, based on an unhelpful Nicaraguan attempt to create a new economic world order under the auspices of the UN. Ultimately, the conference was a total failure with a meaningless outcome which few people outside the narrow confines of the UN in New York have ever heard of, let alone read.

Most of the member states, including the majority of developing countries, merely shook their heads in wonder, but accepted the process as long as it did not cause harm elsewhere. Thus, it was not possible to persuade the majority of developing countries that everyone would be better served if the UN focused instead on questions on which the UN system could have made a constructive contribution, for example on the effect of the global crisis on the poorest countries. These were countries which, because they were only integrated in the global financial sector to a limited extent, were not affected so much by the financial crisis. However, they soon felt the effects of the wider economic crisis as the economic slowdown in their most important markets led to decreased global demand and had significant effects on private investors. The poorest countries, including the forty-nine least developed countries (LDCs), were not represented at the G20 and it would therefore have been natural for the United Nations to look after their interests more systematically, rather than to seek to challenge the global economic order per se, as the initiators of the conference suggested.

The UN Conference on the World Financial and Economic Crisis in June 2009 created the impression that the UN did not have anything important to contribute to global crisis management. This not only damaged the UN's reputation, it was also a missed opportunity to pursue a corrective agenda which would have made much more sense.[17]

It is part of the same picture that in an entirely different area but at almost exactly the same time, the UN showcased its relevance in dealing with the food crisis in 2008. The secretary-general acted very swiftly on the first signs of rising global food prices and established a multi-agency task force involving the whole UN system under the leadership of the UN emergency relief coordinator, John Holmes.

The UN organizations proposed a common framework for action to mitigate the food crisis and reduce the increasing food prices which were at that time having a serious negative effect on many food-importing countries. Even though in principle the *Comprehensive Framework for Action* was only a "management view" in the sense that the analysis and the recommendations emanated from the various secretariats within the UN system – and not from intergovernmental negotiations – its political approach was well received by the member states and other international organizations, and it thus became the general political framework for the global management of the food crisis in 2008–09.

The UN approach emphasized the need for increased food aid to protect the poorest from the effects of the crisis, and it also encouraged countries to develop social safety nets to make the poorest segments of the population less vulnerable to fluctuations in food prices in the future. The recommendations further stressed the need to maintain or increase food production from small holdings by providing subsidies for seeds and fertilizer. The recommendations should, of course, be adapted to national circumstances.

At the same time the UN secretary-general was engaged in intensive telephone diplomacy to encourage a number of large food-producing countries not to stop their exports out of concern for domestic food shortages. Stopping food exports to a greater extent than was eventually seen in 2008 would have exerted further upward pressure on food prices and could have led to a much more chaotic situation in a number of countries. Ban Ki-moon's efforts helped prevent this.[18]

CONFLICT-AFFECTED COUNTRIES

The UN's operational development activities are firmly rooted in the mandates of the individual UN organizations and in their obligations to help countries develop the necessary capacities for fulfilling the mandates. This applies to UNICEF's work to promote children's rights on the basis of the Convention on the Rights of the Child, to the support of the UN High Commissioner for Human Rights for countries to implement the human rights conventions they have signed, to WHO's global establishment of common standards for dealing with communicable diseases, and the ILO's efforts to ensure that countries respect workers' rights to organize. The UN system covers a very wide spectrum of activities. There are many, often highly specialized organizations, mandates and interest groups to deal with, and a significant part of the activities focus on fairly technical issues.

However, the essential strength of the UN system, and its most significant potential for further evolution in the coming years, lies in its operational activities in fragile countries and countries affected by armed conflicts. It is in this context that the UN system's global presence, its organizational diversity, its arsenal of different tools (preventive, political, humanitarian, peacekeeping, peacebuilding, and development activities), its focus on governance, capacity building, rights-based approaches, and, last but not least, the system's human resource capacities have the possibility to come together to create a whole which is much greater than the sum of the parts.[19]

It is especially in the area of peacebuilding that the United Nations has a comparative advantage and can really make use of its political mandate, its institutional legitimacy and the general acceptance by the developing countries of the UN as a development partner, which they can trust to assist them, whatever their current conditions.

A recent report published in connection with executive board meetings on the UNDP, UNICEF, and the UNFPA in January 2011, based on analyses of these organizations' operational activities in Liberia, Somalia, Sudan, and Zimbabwe, shows that the UN is considered to be a very important development partner in fragile and conflict-affected countries and as an organization whose obvious capacities for building bridges between different kinds of support measures is firmly backed up by a substantive staff presence in the field. However, the report also points out that the multiplicity of UN organizations working in related areas has created a number of problems which need to be resolved.

This applies in particular to the co-operation between the various UN organizations, and it underlines the need for strong political leadership of UN operations in fragile and conflict-affected countries where the government partners often have fairly limited institutional and administrative capacities. In particular, in relation to the UNDP the report points to the need for a clearer focus to the organization's operations when working with fragile countries and countries affected by armed conflicts, and the need to recruit more staff with the special skills which operations in such countries require.[20]

In essence, the main lessons to draw from this are that all the political challenges which the UN system are mandated to take on, and the reform agenda which the UN system generally supports in the area of development co-operation – involving governance, capacity building, human rights–based activities, better coordination between the different areas of activities, more effective and coherent implementation, and stronger leadership (Delivering-as-One) – are all the more important when dealing with countries that can be described as fragile, with weak institutions and lacking in political resilience. It is in these countries that the UN system seems to have its strongest comparative advantages compared to other development actors.

The question is whether all 193 member states will agree to the UN system focusing more on further expanding and strengthening its operational activities in fragile and conflict-affected countries.

It will never be a question of either/or. The United Nations is and will remain a global organization, and it is essential for the credibility and legitimacy of the organization that it is in principle omnipresent, and thereby able to support the implementation of global norms and standards around the world. However, the recognition of the UN system's global character is not the same as saying that the United Nations must have the same level of presence or of operational activities everywhere. If clear comparative advantages mean that the UN's operational activities ought to be predominantly concentrated in certain countries, one can argue that there is every reason for doing so.

This is, of course, easier said than done. All member states see the UN as *their* organization, and all of them would like a better return for their membership. Many donor countries campaign to have UN offices located in their capitals or to have their nationals appointed to senior positions in the organizations. The middle-income countries think they receive too limited a share of the donor funds which the UN organizations have at their disposal and which the donor countries want to direct primarily at the poorest countries. Some of the poorest countries look at the criteria for the allocation of funds and often demand that adjustments be made to the fixed criteria so as to benefit themselves. Over the years a balance has been found for the allocation of regular resources (core resources) in funds and programs, and it would be very difficult to significantly change this suddenly.

For donor countries, an increase in core contributions, which is clearly what the organizations most need in order to function as effectively as possible, would not in itself provide the clear shift toward increased focus on fragile states which the UN's comparative advantage suggests would be desirable. If the donor countries are to give the organizations and other member states a clear indication that the UN system ought to further expand its activities in the weakest and most conflict-affected countries such as Afghanistan, DR Congo, Liberia, Somalia, Sudan, and Zimbabwe, donors would have to combine increased core contributions (which would improve the overall effectiveness of the UN system, as mentioned) with earmarked contributions for these particular countries. However, in order not to undermine the effectiveness of the organizations, it would be important for such earmarked contributions to be made as flexible as possible, and primarily given to the common funds in the countries in question. This would also strengthen the hands of RCs in applying these funds.

If the United Nations system, and its various agencies, funds, and programs, is to maintain and further develop its comparative advantage as an operational partner at country level it will have to focus more – and provide more funding, more technical assistance, and more leadership competences – on its operational activities, and especially on institutional development, in fragile and conflict-affected countries.

11

Sustainable Development

The Earth is one but the world is not ... Sustainable development is development that meets the needs of the present without compromising the ability of future generations to meet their own needs.

The Brundtland Report, 1987

ENVIRONMENT AND SUSTAINABLE DEVELOPMENT

Issues related to the environment were first put on the international agenda at the UN Conference on the Human Environment in Stockholm in June 1972. Until then concern about pollution and the degradation of the environment had been sporadic. Even though environmental movements had emerged in a number of countries in the 1960s, environmental issues were still not that much of a concern to most people. The overall approach at the Stockholm Conference also reflected that the environment and the related discussion of natural resources were seen from the perspective of decolonization and national sovereignty, with the emphasis of each country's national ownership of its own natural resources, but at the same time emphasizing that each country should administer these resources in a way that did not harm other countries.

Representatives of many developing countries went to Stockholm with a fairly sceptical mind-set, seeing the 1972 Conference as a thinly disguised attempt by the industrialized countries to impose on them co-responsibility for the necessary environmental global clean-up after many years of unimpeded pollution primarily by the industrialized countries. The developing countries were also concerned that the various environmental requirements would put a brake on *their* economic growth and industrialization. From the beginning, a number of developing countries feared that tougher environmental standards would be used as reasons for imposing trade restrictions which would limit their export potential to OECD countries. These basic concerns have been reflected in all subsequent UN negotiations on environmental issues or on sustainable development.

The compromise reached in Stockholm created a strong link between the environment and development that has since been the basis for the United Nations' approach to these issues. It was central to the twenty-six Stockholm principles that environmental problems arise from different sources, in industrialized countries primarily as a consequence of the existing patterns of production and consumption, and in developing countries primarily as a result of the lack of development and widespread poverty. This was clearly a political compromise and not a reflection of any detailed analysis of the world's environmental problems. Politically, it was essential to engage developing countries in international co-operation on environmental issues, and this could only be achieved by clearly linking environment and development.[1]

The decisive breakthrough came in 1987 with the publication of the Brundtland Report, *Our Common Future*, which launched the concept of sustainable development. Sustainable development means development that is sustainable economically, socially, and environmentally, and where these three pillars of development are in tune with each other. The Brundtland Commission's main conclusions are thus the same as those of the Stockholm Conference; that continued economic growth is a prerequisite for enabling developing countries to solve their problems of poverty, and that in order to pursue this course, economic growth should be both socially and environmentally sustainable.[2]

However, in practice over the more than twenty-five years since the publication of the Brundtland Commission's Report development has generally been characterized by there being a disconnection of the three supposedly connected aspects of sustainable development, with the consequence that the concept of sustainable development is often seen as being coterminous with only the environmental pillar and therefore as an issue primarily to be dealt with by ministries of the environment.

In terms of results, the UN Conference on Environment and Development in Rio de Janeiro in 1992 (the "Earth Summit") was probably the most important and successful UN summit ever. One of its results was the Rio Declaration on Environment and Development, which formulated the important rules of play for the area of the environment, including the principle of the "common but differentiated responsibilities" (principle 7) of industrialized and developing countries as the basis for various sets of rights and responsibilities, as well as the "precautionary principle" (principle 15) which requires states to act on the basis of reasonable suspicion and, for example, to prohibit the use of certain materials or production processes without necessarily having full scientific certainty that there is a potential serious threat to the environment. Another important outcome was the adoption of Agenda 21, a global action plan which focuses particularly on how to counteract a series of highly specific environmental problems.[3]

The Rio Conference also led to the adoption of two legally binding conventions: the UN Framework Convention on Climate Change (UNFCCC) and the Convention on Biological Diversity. Two years later, there followed the UN Convention to Combat Desertification. These three conventions introduced the concept of treaty-based comprehensive international collaboration on the environment. Today, there are more than 500 environmental or environment-related treaties between two or more parties. About 325 of these treaties are multilateral, and of these about 30 are global. Finally, the Conference led to the establishment of the UN Commission on Sustainable Development (CSD), which was formally initiated in December 1992.[4]

International co-operation on the environment has been considerably strengthened over the last twenty years since the Rio Conference in 1992. Conventions, ministerial meetings, CSD gatherings have followed in a steady stream. The United Nations also set up a special environment program, the UN Environment Programme (UNEP), after the Stockholm Conference and the UNDP's work on the environment and in relation to sustainable development has also been notably strengthened. The World Bank has provided strong technical support and funding in the area of the environment, and a new facility (the Global Environmental Facility [GEF]) has been established for financing measures in the fields of bio-diversity, climate change, agricultural degradation, water, and combatting toxins in the environment.

These two decades of enhanced international environmental co-operation has also produced one of the world's most successful examples of effective multilateral co-operation anywhere, namely the Montreal Protocol on Substances that Deplete the Ozone Layer. The background to the Montreal Protocol was the scientific discovery in the 1970s clearly identifying that the ozone layer, which is ten to sixteen kilometres above the Earth's surface and protects the Earth from strong ultraviolet rays, was being rapidly depleted by a number of commonly used industrial chemical products.

This depletion of the ozone layer appeared in the form of a growing ozone hole above Antarctica, and it was believed that it would spread rapidly. The consequences of the depletion and eventual disintegration of the ozone layer would be dramatic, both for humans (a great increase in the number of cases of skin cancer globally) and the environment (both for arable crops and for the growth of plankton in the sea). Even though it took some time to establish scientific proofs of cause and effect, the outlook was so alarming that many countries were willing to act on the basis of the precautionary principle. There were important indications, which later became clear proofs, that a number of chemical components (chlorofluorocarbons, or CFCs) were strongly implicated in the depletion of the ozone layer. These were chemicals that were widely used in refrigerators and freezers and in aerosol cans and other everyday products and processes, such as dry cleaning.

UNEP launched international negotiations on the issue. Scientific evidence soon disclosed the connection between CFCs and the damage to the ozone layer, and this convinced the industry, including major producers of CFCs, which decided to concentrate on the production of substitute products which did not have a negative effect on the ozone layer. The Montreal Protocol was signed in 1987 and entered into force on 1 January 1989. In the first instance, the aim was to restrict the use of eight chemicals, but the list has since been expanded to cover more than one hundred ozone-depleting products, including some of the original substitutes for CFCs which turned out to be even more dangerous. The original ambition was to halve the use of substances that deplete the ozone layer, but it was later agreed to phase them out completely.

The Montreal Protocol is an example of international goal-setting and a framework approach. Each country could develop its own approach to the phasing out the dangerous substances, as long as the agreed result was achieved. Naturally, the participation of the developing countries was essential. Unless the use of CFCs was stopped also in the developing countries, the efforts in the industrialized countries would not have been able to solve the global problem. In order to get the developing countries on board, a new international fund was set up to help cover the additional costs which these countries would incur in shifting to new technologies and new chemicals which would not have a negative effect on the ozone layer. For twenty years the industrialized countries have collectively paid an average of about us$120 million a year to the fund.

Today, the use of ozone-depleting chemicals has been almost totally phased out in the industrialized countries and is well on the way to be phased out also in the developing countries. There are clear indications that the depletion of the ozone layer has now been stopped, and that the ozone layer will most probably be fully restored by about 2050.[5]

As well as being a success in itself, the Montreal Protocol is also a model solution to a global environmental issue that has increasingly been seen as applicable in other fields, including climate change. The model is based on:

- scientific evidence of the dramatic negative effects at the global level of a "business as usual" approach;
- available technologies making possible a solution which mitigates and, in the long run, solves the problem without having a negative effect on economic growth;
- active involvement by industry in solving the problem. Many companies see new business opportunities in developing new technologies and materials which do not have negative effects on the environment; and
- access to (donor) financing and technology transfer which ensures that developing countries can leapfrog some stages of development without additional costs, moving straight to the newest state of the art technology.

Obviously one must not stretch the comparison too far. The ozone issue was and is much more straightforward than the problem of climate change, for example. The scientific challenge was much simpler, the technical problems much more easily solved, there were fewer actors involved, and the technological and financial implications were much less than in the case of climate change. The increase in global warming and the ensuing change in the global climate which the world will face in coming decades can only be partly countered and only with a very broad-spectrum approach, requiring much more innovation and change than finding substitutes for CFCs.

CLIMATE CHANGE

The enhanced international co-operation since the Rio Conference in 1992 has primarily focused on environmental issues, rather than on the broader agenda of sustainable development. The result has been that the economic and social dimensions of sustainable development have to a large extent been disregarded.

This has been most obvious in the work of the CSD, which was established in 1992, following the Rio Conference, with a view to considering the issue of sustainable development in its totality.

There were great expectations of the CSD, with participation at ministerial level from both industrialized and developing countries during its early years. As the CSD was unable to produce results and the broad concept of sustainable development was replaced in practice by a stronger focus on more limited environmental issues, interest in the CSD diminished and it is now broadly considered one of the United Nations' less important bodies.

The same applies to the United Nations Economic and Social Council (ECOSOC). As mentioned in chapter 2, ECOSOC is one of the principal organs of the United Nations (Article 7 of the UN Charter), but it has never been able to perform its intended coordinating function. For many years attempts have been made to reform ECOSOC, but with relatively limited interest from the member states. It is thus not surprising that the results have been modest.

Over time, the UN has been presented with a number of proposals to strengthen ECOSOC and to change it into a parallel to the Security Council in the social and economic areas, including proposals to transform ECOSOC into a global council for sustainable development or an "economic security council." However, ECOSOC's size (fifty-four members) is a practical obstacle to its effectiveness, and restricting the number of members is not an immediate prospect. There are not many who believe in the possibility of breathing new life into ECOSOC.

Focusing primarily on the environmental dimension of sustainable development also makes negotiations on climate change harder. Global warming and climate change is not an environmental issue; it is a question that can only be addressed in the context of sustainable development in all three of its dimensions.

This means that it will most probably not be possible to deal with climate change in a predominantly environmental context such as the

UNFCCC. From the very beginning, international negotiations in relation to the Climate Convention has been undertaken by environment ministries, environmental agencies and climate experts. The preparatory work for the fifteenth session of the Conference of Parties (COP 15) to the United Nations Framework Convention on Climate Change in Copenhagen in December 2009 confirmed that a narrow convention framework like the UNFCCC is not well suited institutionally to dealing with the broad social and economic challenges that climate change negotiations involve.

When the Climate Convention entered into force nearly twenty years ago, and even when the Kyoto Protocol was negotiated in 1997, climate change was by no means a serious enough concern for it to be dealt with by heads of states and government. Climate issues were something for the future. The scientific evidence was not yet conclusive and other global issues were thought to be more important.

For many years, climate change was an issue which countries kept on the back burner. It was something they would look into in due course, and the negotiating machinery was thought of merely as something that was nice to have in place for the future. International discussions were kept within the confines of environmental approaches which suited many environment ministries very well, but it also meant that governments were slow to address the wider social, economic and political problems which today are at the centre of the climate change discourse.

The *Fourth Assessment Report* of the Intergovernmental Panel on Climate Change (IPCC) in November 2007 was a turning point. The IPCC was set up in 1988 by UNEP and the World Meteorological Organization (WMO), and its *Fourth Assessment Report* was drawn up in with the collaboration of more than 3,000 scientists from a wide variety of scientific disciplines.

The Report made it clear that there was now a significant increase in scientific certainty about the risk and extent of climate change. The main message from the extensive analysis of climate data was that it would be necessary to halve emissions of greenhouse gases, primarily CO_2, by 2050 (in relation to 1990), and to keep the concentration of CO_2 in the atmosphere below 450 parts per million (ppm). Such a level of CO_2 in the atmosphere would most probably keep the increase of the median global temperature to no more than two degrees Celsius by the end of the twenty-first century. The level is now at about 430 ppm and it is growing by about 2.5 ppm every year.[6]

The next IPCC report is due in 2013–14, but the scientific preparations for the report are well under way. One of the most important changes resulting from the rise of median global temperature is the increased melting of the Arctic ice cap and the significance of this for the rise in sea levels. The *Fourth Assessment Report* concluded that we are on the way to a rise in the global sea level of between eighteen and fifty-nine centimetres by the end of the present century. More recent studies show that the Greenland ice cap is melting faster than expected, and that the rise in sea level will more probably be around one hundred centimetres or more. This means that about 17 per cent of the landmass of Bangladesh will be under water, as well as large parts of megacities like Lagos and Cape Town. Some small island states like the Maldives and Tuvalu will disappear altogether.[7]

Moreover, temperature increases in the arctic regions may also release quantities of old CO_2 and methane gases that are now trapped in the permafrost in the arctic tundra. If it really begins to thaw in these regions, this could release billions of tonnes of greenhouse gases. This is only one of the factors that threaten to develop into a global tipping point for climate change – where the negative developments become irreversible and where nothing can then be done to correct the situation.[8]

Much indicates that the alarming analysis in the IPCC's Report from 2007 is actually too optimistic by today's standard. The forecasts made by climate researchers and other scientists are changing all the time as new data are validated and interpreted. The IPCC has probably underestimated the negative effects of what will happen in the next decades if no new steps are taken to limit emissions of greenhouse gases. The IPCC uses a number of different scenarios, each of which has a degree of latitude for variations. The highest temperature increase in these scenarios lies between +2.9 and +6.4 degrees Celsius. As stated, the Report concludes that a concentration of atmospheric CO_2 of up to 450 ppm and a temperature increase of 2 degrees Celsius is acceptable, though with some risks. However, there is both scientific and political pressure, not least from those countries that are particularly threatened by climate change, to adopt a more conservative line and to restrict atmospheric CO_2 to 350 ppm. This will be one of the key issues in the coming report.[9]

Climate change is a fact, it has been going on for many years, and much of the change observed has been caused by human behaviour. The aim is not to put the clock back to the pre-industrial age, but to keep future change to a level which we think we can cope with.

The population of Africa will double in the next forty years, from about 1 billion people to about 2 billion. A temperature increase of just a few degrees will have a dramatic effect on the continent's food production. Changes in patterns of precipitation, widespread drought, and the intolerance of existing crops to increased temperatures will present sub-Saharan Africa with major challenges. These changes could affect political stability and give rise to considerable risks for new conflicts over access to the resources of the continent as well as increased migration pressure, not least toward Europe.

And this is not just a problem for Africa. There is a predicted increase in the world population from the present 7 billion to more than 9 billion by 2050, accompanied by a significant increase in urbanization and a comparable growth of the middle classes in many of the emerging economies.

In this situation, a global reduction of the emissions of CO_2 and other greenhouse gases will require a gradual but targeted and ambitious switch to global low-energy growth in the coming decades. This will necessitate fundamental changes to the way societies are organized and to the existing patterns of production, consumption, transportation, and housing.

All this calls for a far-sighted, long-term, and deep transformation process, from one economic growth paradigm to another, stretching far beyond the purviews of climate change negotiators and environment ministers.

Prior to the Climate Change Conference in Copenhagen (COP 15) in December 2009 this fundamental imbalance between the narrow basis for negotiation (the Climate Convention and the Kyoto Protocol) and the very broad economic and political agenda became obvious. Negotiators did not have a mandate to do anything about the real agenda, and those who could have done something about the broader agenda were not negotiating.

In an attempt to solve this problem, the Danish government, as host of the meeting, decided to encourage political leaders to participate in COP 15. More than one hundred heads of state and government had taken part in the Climate Summit which the UN's secretary-general hosted in New York as part of the opening of the General Assembly in September 2009. Three months later, around 115 heads of state and government attended COP 15 in Copenhagen. This was an unprecedented participation by world leaders in negotiations of a relatively technical nature. Their presence in Copenhagen was organized at short notice, in many cases causing political disharmony between those that had been responsible for the negotiations until then and those who now took over.

The traditions, procedures, language, and approach to solutions in international negotiations have developed over time and within an existing framework, and it is not always easy to jump into the middle of things, even for political leaders. Permanent international institutions, regular meetings, established practices, and professional secretariats which can properly prepare for meetings often create a better setting for international negotiations and decisions than ad hoc arrangements. There is no doubt that the lack of a well-established framework for the involvement of heads of state and government in climate change negotiations was part of the explanation for the chaotic situation witnessed at the COP 15 meeting.

But the most important explanation for the failure to reach a political breakthrough in Copenhagen was without a doubt the fact that the two main global actors, China and the United States, who between them account for about half the global CO_2 emissions, either would not or could not reach an agreement in the negotiations leading up to COP 15.

For China, there was clearly some reluctance to accept a global monitoring system which would have given other countries some insight into internal Chinese matters, and in any case China did not want to be a party to a binding agreement which might, in some circumstances, be perceived as limiting the country's growth ambitions. Everything indicates that the Chinese government fully understands the seriousness of the problems related to climate change and is willing to take an active part in solving these problems, apart from anything else also in order to get a head start in the technological developments that will in any event be part of the global response to climate change. But there is a big difference between doing something because it is in the country's own interest and accepting international obligations that might limit its freedom of action.

For the United States, it was to a large degree the financial and economic crisis, with the collapse of the financial and housing markets, together with a sharp increase in unemployment – every president's Achilles heel – that held back the Obama administration. The crisis especially hit some of the political swing states in the American "rust belt," where much of the traditional industrial production is concentrated (Indiana, Michigan, Ohio, Pennsylvania, etc.), and which in the mid-term election one year later was instrumental in installing a Republican majority in the House of Representatives.

It was already clear in the autumn of 2009 that many American business leaders who had been positive about getting to grips with the challenges of climate change had changed their views and now recommended waiting and concentrating instead on dealing with the economic crisis and in particular on saving as many jobs as possible. The Obama administration's arguments about the potential long-term gains and the millions of new jobs that would be created by adopting a pro-active and progressive climate change policy were submerged in the immediate concerns of the fact that many Americans view globalization as mainly leading to American jobs being shipped abroad, not least to China. In this political climate, it was impossible to get climate change legislation through the Senate.[10]

It was these political realities that created the real problems at COP 15, not the political views of some of the more extreme developing countries and their procedural difficulties in accepting the outcome of what had been negotiated among a small group of key political leaders.

The best evidence of this is that the following Climate Change Conference, COP 16 in December 2010 in Cancun, Mexico, to a large extent formalized the non-emission-related outcome of COP 15, against the declared opposition of Bolivia. The COP process is largely consensus-based, but in the long run a small minority of countries will not be able to maintain their opposition to what is agreed by the great majority of countries, including all the big players.[11]

Regardless of the form it ultimately takes, a global climate change agreement should include goals for limiting global emissions, presumably for 2020, 2030, and 2050, reflecting the principle of common but differentiated responsibilities, i.e., that demands for reductions of CO_2 emissions will be much more stringent for the industrialized countries, presumably in the order of 80 to 90 per cent by 2050, and less for the developing countries, perhaps only 20 per cent by 2050, compared with 1990.

The industrialized countries' CO_2 emissions are becoming an ever smaller proportion of the world's total emissions. Any future climate change agreement must thus cover *all* countries, i.e., *both* the industrialized countries which undertook specific obligations to reduce their emissions in the Kyoto Protocol in 1997 *and* all other countries, including the United States, China, and the rest of the new emerging economies which so far have not accepted specific commitments to reduce CO_2 emissions. The first period of binding commitments under the Kyoto Protocol expired at the end of 2012. A political condition for countries accepting new obligations after 2012 was that other countries which have so far stood outside the agreement should also accept similar obligations in the long run. At COP 17 in Durban, South Africa, in December 2011, it was decided to seek a new global climate change agreement by 2015, the specific formulation calling for a "protocol, another legal instrument or an agreed outcome with legal force under the Convention applicable to all Parties" to come into effect by 2020.[12]

The agreement will also have to contain commitments and mechanisms for financial transfers from the industrialized countries to the developing countries, similarly to the ones established in Montreal Protocol, so as to assist developing countries in making the technological leap from their present dependence on fossil fuels, such as coal, oil, and natural gas, to making greater use of renewable energy (i.e., forms of energy that do not emit CO_2), as well as making major improvements in their energy efficiency. Other areas where action must be taken include restricting deforestation and developing new farming methods, as well as adapting countries' economies to the changes to the climate which will occur even if measures to combat climate change are taken soon. The genie is already out of the bottle, and it is impossible to put it back in. Climate change is happening, as witnessed in changes to the patterns of precipitation and drought in many parts of the world; the challenge is to reduce future CO_2 emissions and as far as possible to limit their negative effects.

It will not be easy to reach a global climate agreement by 2015, whether in the form of a legally binding international agreement (which is hardly likely) or in the form of a political framework agreement such as that proposed prior to the COP 15 meeting (which is more likely). In reality, the difference between these two approaches is not great. A legally binding agreement is also a political agreement. No real sanctions can be applied if a country breaches is obligations. "Sanctions" will primarily mean that a non-compliant country is "named and shamed." It is also possible that a country that tries to wriggle out of its obligations could be "punished" in other international contexts.

Rather than sanctions, what drives international co-operation on climate change are the possibilities of technological innovation, export opportunities, and job creation connected with new climate change technology. A climate agreement would be a strong incentive for participating countries to invest in research and development, and a clear, unambiguous long-term signal to the business community about the direction for the future. It would be a strong message that it is time to climb aboard the train if one wishes to be among the first movers.[13]

This applies particularly to the energy sector where comprehensive changes will be of the utmost importance for reducing CO_2 emissions. The energy sector (production, transmission, and consumption of energy) is responsible for two-thirds of all CO_2 emissions. Limiting the increase in the global mean temperature to two degrees Celsius will require the rise in CO_2 emissions to peak in 2020 and then to decline. This will require massive investments in more environmentally friendly forms of energy and improvements in energy efficiency, not least in the emerging economies where CO_2 emissions will otherwise increase sharply in the coming years.

But there is another side to the global energy agenda. There are still 1.3 billion people who live without access to electricity, primarily in sub-Saharan Africa and in Asia. Without targeted measures, this number will only fall to 1.2 billion by 2030. However, with global investments in energy access in the order of us$48 billion per year, primarily from funds generated from the countries themselves and from private investors, it would be possible to provide access to electricity for virtually all households before 2030. It is important that this challenge, and the possibility of linking climate change interventions to measures aimed at reducing global poverty, should not be overshadowed by focusing only on the future energy policies of the emerging economies.[14]

CLIMATE CHANGE FINANCING

The costs involved in a climate agreement will be a matter for negotiation. The only thing that is entirely clear is that the sooner the decisions are taken the easier it will be to make the adjustments and the costs will be lower. This was the main conclusion of the report published in 2006 by a team led by the British economist Nicholas Stern. Stern has subsequently adjusted the figures in the report and in 2009 stated that the costs of stabilizing the CO_2 concentration in the atmosphere at 550 ppm – somewhat above the level of 450 ppm recommended in the IPCC report – would be about 1 per cent of the global GNI, and that the costs of stabilizing the concentration at 500 ppm would be 2 per cent of the global GNI every year for the next fifty years.

There is obviously considerable uncertainty about such figures. Costs of 1, 2, or 3 per cent of the global GNI represent a significant share of the world's annual economic growth. But these are not investments that will disappear. The money will be invested in climate adaptation, and in new forms of energy and new infrastructure projects which will in themselves create new and sustained economic growth. This is one side of the balance sheet. On the other side, the longer we wait the more expensive, drastic, and dramatic the necessary restructuring will have to be.[15]

The Copenhagen Accord from December 2009 contained two financial commitments. Altogether over a three-year period from 2010 to 2012 the industrialized countries would provide US$30 billion in new and additional funds for financing adaptation to climate change and emission restrictions in the developing countries, especially in the most vulnerable countries. Also, the industrialized countries would together provide US$100 billion a year from 2020 to assist developing countries adapt to and mitigate climate change. This assistance would be made conditional on meaningful reductions of emissions and full transparency of the implementation of such reductions; in other words, there would have to be something visible in return, a quid pro quo. The US$100 billion would be mobilized in the form of both private and public funds, from bilateral and multilateral sources, including from innovative sources of finance.[16]

The overall development assistance from the OECD countries to developing countries amounted to US$133 billion in 2011, corresponding to 0.31 per cent of the OECD countries' GNI. The internationally established goal for development assistance is 0.7 per cent of GNI, and meeting this goal will therefore in itself involve a doubling of aid (see chapter 9). The US$100 billion for climate change measures on top of this, knowing that it is difficult to distinguish in practice between development assistance and climate change assistance, will thus be a trebling of the existing level of development assistance. This is hardly possible in a situation where the national budgets of most, if not all, OECD countries are under severe pressure from the effects of the economic crisis and in the longer term also from demographic changes, especially in Europe, with relatively fewer young people compared to a large increase in the number of retirees.[17]

However, the financing need not necessarily come solely from traditional public budgets which Western countries finance from their tax revenues. The financing could also come from levies on certain financial transactions which could serve the dual purpose of both being a source of revenue and contributing to financial stability. This is the case with the proposed "Tobin Tax" on international financial transactions, named after the originator of the idea, the economist James Tobin. This proposal has been reviewed by the Leading Group, with the participation of about sixty countries and a number of international organizations and NGOs. The Leading Group provides one of the most important international frameworks for discussions of new and innovative financing mechanisms.[18]

The revenue from taxes on financial transactions naturally depends on how widely they are applied and on the level of the tax. In an EU Commission staff working document in 2010, it was stated that even a tax of 0.005 per cent on transactions in the world's most widely used currencies (the currency transaction levy, CTL), which is among the least ambitious proposals on the table from a revenue point of view, could generate US$33 billion per year. Under this proposal the revenue would be collected by individual countries which would be administratively easiest, but it also raises the question of whether it is at all feasible to introduce new taxes, which can create political problems in some countries.[19]

There are many proposals for taxes on international financial transactions, and the international financial crisis of recent years, and the financial sector's responsibility for it, has not reduced the number of proposals. What will be decisive for whether such international or internationally coordinated taxation on financial transactions can be successfully introduced is whether there is the political will to do so, whether such systems can be administered efficiently, and whether there would be a risk of major market distortion as a consequence of such new instruments. So far there has been limited political will in the economically dominant countries to look seriously at these issues.

Immediately following the COP 15 meeting, the UN secretary-general appointed a High-level Advisory Group on Climate Change Financing (AGF), under the leadership of the Norwegian prime minister Jens Stoltenberg and then Ethiopian prime minister Meles Zenawi, to find ways to raise the US$100 billion per year which the Copenhagen Accord promised the developing countries. The AGF included a number of finance ministers and heads of relevant international organizations, and it published its report in November 2010. The general conclusion was that it would be possible but not easy to raise the necessary funds. The funds would have to come from a broad range of different sources.

The report's starting point was that the largest part of the revenue should be obtained as revenue raised in connection with CO_2 emissions, on the basis that in 2020 the price per tonne of CO_2 would be us$20–25. It was estimated that significant income could be raised by auctioning national CO_2 quotas (emission permits for which companies would be required to pay more than in the past). If only 10 per cent of this revenue were put into international financing schemes, this alone would contribute about us$30 billion per year.

Other income could be raised by doing away with existing subsidies for fossil fuels and switching such funds to climate change financing (estimated revenue us$10 billion, which is a very small share of present global fossil fuel subsidies), taxes on CO_2 emissions emanating from air and sea transport (us$10 billion), increased transfers from international development banks (us$10 billion), increased private investments, and the positive effects for developing countries of quota trading (us$10–30 billion). The report states that there was not full agreement on all the proposals and projected revenue streams, and some of the proposals are therefore only outlined in very general terms. The main aim of the AGF report was to get some of the sceptics on board, and it succeeded in achieving the participation of China's vice-finance minister and President Obama's (then) chief economic adviser Lawrence Summers. The price which the United Nations had to pay was that the report was more vaguely phrased than is normally the case for reports from UN high-level advisory groups.[20]

Apart from the question of where the money is to come from, there is also the essential question of how the funds are to be spent and how they should be allocated; in other words, who decides how to use it?

The traditional financing of development, on which the OECD's Development Assistance Committee (DAC) keeps statistics, is technically a grant from the donor to the recipient. The donor government is entirely free to determine the extent and the allocation of its assistance. The United Nations goal of 0.7 per cent of GNI in development assistance is not binding and donors only release the funds when they actually transfer the allocation to a developing country or to an international organization of its choosing. The donors alone define the conditions under which the funds are to be used and they can stop their assistance programs at short notice or decline to provide further assistance if for any reason they are not satisfied with the way the assistance is handled. The donor's accountability is to their government auditors and ultimately to their taxpayers; the developing countries or the international organizations receiving the assistance have no formal claim to the funds.

In the eyes of most developing countries, climate change financing is different from development assistance, not least because the funds for climate action can be raised in new ways that are not so directly related to the tax revenues of industrialized countries. The international co-operation on countering or slowing down climate change takes place between countries which share a common purpose and with common benefits for all (lower emissions of CO_2, reduced climate change, and lower negative social, economic, and human costs). For these reasons the developing countries claim some entitlement to the funds raised and call for more influence on how the funds are allocated and the conditions for their use. This different approach to aid is part of the global power struggle about who decides what in the multilateral system.

Innovative financing is still on the drawing board in international negotiations, but the problem has begun to be directly addressed in a few cases. For example, France has imposed a tax on plane tickets which has been in force since 2006, and this approach has been taken up by Chile, Korea, Madagascar, and Mauritius, among others.

The tax is payable by all who fly from airports in the participating countries (though not by transit passengers). Its level can vary from country to country as it does not have a distortive effect on competition; for example, few passengers will drive from Paris to Brussels in order to save the relatively small amount payable on a transatlantic flight. Thus, France puts a tax of €1 per passenger on domestic flights and €4 on international departures, though the amount is ten times as much for travellers in business and first classes. The total revenue from this plane-ticket tax is around €160 million per year, and the accrued amount is paid to UNITAID (an international facility for the purchase of drugs against HIV/AIDS, malaria, and tuberculosis). The revenue from this tax is the most important source of income for UNITAID's activities in developing countries.[21]

SCARCITY OF NATURAL RESOURCES

When at the World Economic Forum in Davos, Switzerland, in January 2011, Secretary-General Ban Ki-moon was asked to provide the headlines for the current international development agenda, he did so specifically referring to climate change and sustainable development, and with a particular focus on three dominant resource challenges: energy, water, and food.[22]

In the coming decades, the world will encounter significant problems with regard to the allocation of resources in all three areas, as the world population grows from its present 7 billion to about 9.3 billion in 2050, and, according to current forecasts, to 10 billion before the upward curve finally breaks at the end of the century.[23]

This demographic development can be firmly predicted due to the current age distribution of the populations of individual countries, and although it may be slightly adjusted as time progresses it has to be accepted as a fact. There will also be strong growth of the global middle classes – some estimating it to grow from around 1.8 billion people in 2009 to almost 5 billion people in 2030. Of course, this is a positive development, but it will also lead to huge increases in expectations of increased consumption and higher standards of living across the globe.[24]

The United Nations forecasts increases in the global demand for food of 50 per cent up to 2030, and up to 100 per cent by 2050. This increased demand for food will occur at a time where growth in agricultural productivity has not increased significantly since the "green revolution" which took place from the 1950s to the 1980s. There will thus be greater pressure on land resources, not just to increase the share of arable land but also to limit deforestation in order to protect the climate. We may also see a competition between land needed for food production (in order to satisfy the increased demand from the middle classes for meat and other high-end products) and land needed for biofuels (to reduce CO_2 emissions).

The picture becomes even more clouded when the effects of climate change are taken into account, especially in Africa, where the changing patterns of precipitation will make some of the land that is currently cultivated less usable. There is little doubt that significant improvements in agricultural research and the development of more effective and more disease and drought resistant crop varieties will be essential to satisfy the increased demand for food.[25]

As for global access to fresh water, there has been a six-fold increase in water use during the twentieth century, and a further 33 per cent increase in demand is expected from 2000 to 2025. This will put increased pressure on supplies in some parts of the world already experiencing water shortages, and it is expected that by 2025 more than 1 billion people will be living in areas affected by some degree of water scarcity.

Here, too, climate change will drastically alter the situation. In some areas, there will be greater scarcity (for example, around the Mediterranean, in the Middle East, and in the Western parts of the United States). In other areas, there will be more water as a result of increased precipitation. The main problem will not be drinking water but the 70 per cent or so of all fresh water consumption that is used for irrigation in the agricultural sector. In some countries, artificial irrigation techniques are highly ineffective, and there is great scope for reducing water use with new technologies and more effective irrigation.

There is a real risk of conflict over access to water resources. About 145 countries have joint access to one or more rivers, either where rivers flow through more than one country (upstream versus downstream countries) or where the national borders are defined by a river. There is generally good collaboration between riparian states in managing such joint resources, but this may not continue if there are major changes in the future use of water from these rivers.

The risks from melting glaciers in the Himalayas are a special problem. Over one-sixth of the world's population live around rivers that rise in the Himalayas: the Ganges, Indus, Mekong, Yangtze, and Yellow River. Millions of people depend on the water from these shared resources, rivers running through several countries, and water extracted from shared aquifers. Many of these resources are not regulated by international agreements, and even where there are agreements, as in the case of the Nile, countries where these rivers rise (such as in Ethiopia) increasingly question whether to continue to allow so much water to flow down to Egypt. The Latin American countries whose fresh water comes from the Andes will also be exposed to water shortages as the glaciers melt.

In the energy sector, the International Energy Agency (IEA) predicts that the global demand for energy will increase by 36 per cent from 2008 to 2035, mainly because of the increased demand from Asia. Non-OECD countries will account for 93 per cent of the increase.[26]

Energy consumption is the primary cause of CO_2 emissions, and restrictions on energy use and the replacement of fossil fuels by renewable forms of energy will be a key part of any climate change discussion.

In 2010, the Secretary-General's Advisory Group on Energy and Climate Change (AGECC) proposed two new global goals in the energy field. First, the 1.3 billion people who do not have access to modern forms of energy should be able to have access to electricity by 2030, i.e., for both household and productive use. Second, energy intensity should be improved by 40 per cent up to 2030, which would require doubling the historical levels of improving energy efficiency.[27] A third goal was introduced in the spring of 2011, when it was decided also to seek a doubling of the share of renewable energy in the global energy mix by 2030.

At this stage, these are only proposals from the secretary-general. The three goals are closely connected and mutually supportive as parts of an overall goal of achieving Sustainable Energy for All by 2030 (SE4All). To achieve access to electricity for all will mean increased CO_2 emissions, even if only by a few percentage points, but this increase only underlines the need for simultaneous and substantial improvements in the effectiveness of energy consumption so the 1 billion more people who will live on this planet in twenty years' time, and the improvements in living standards which the growing middle class will call for, will not lead to a global increase in the use of fossil fuels, and especially of coal and oil (the CO_2 emissions from natural gas are only half of those of coal). On the contrary, there is a need for a much greater reliance on non-fossil fuels such as hydro, solar, wind, geothermal, or biomass. Increased use of such sources of renewable energy in itself underpins an overall climate change policy of reducing CO_2 emissions. Renewables are also much easier to use in a smaller scale – and with much less capital intensive investment – which means that these sources of energy are a better fit for those parts of the world that cannot be reached cost effectively through existing electricity grids. Perhaps up to half of the people presently without electricity will get access by way of mini-grid or off-grid solutions.

Investing in renewable energy has many positive side effects. It supports the basic policy objectives of climate change interventions. It creates greater security of supply and is more politically and economically independent (renewable energy is local energy, in contrast to the current Russian supplies of natural gas to Western Europe or the US reliance on oil imports from the Middle East, at least until the recent focus on national shale gas resources). And for poorer households, the use of new sources of renewable energy will significantly reduce respiratory disease that is the consequence of using firewood for cooking and heating without proper ventilation. Respiratory diseases are estimated to cause around 2 million deaths per year among the poorest people in the world.

As also indicated, geographical distances, lack of infrastructure, and low population densities in many areas are such that mini-grids or local off-grid solutions may be preferable to investing in transmission lines, linking up to national power grids. In such a situation, local sources of energy, be they solar panels, windmills, bio-gas, geothermal energy, or small hydroelectric turbines, will often be the most cost-effective solution. And if some renewable energy sources are not yet cost-effective, everything suggests that they soon will be. The price for solar panels is falling rapidly, and the same applies to other forms of renewable energy.

Renewable energy, especially traditional biomass and hydro power, provided about 13 per cent of total global energy and about 19 per cent of electricity in 2008. The IPCC believes that it is possible to expand this share significantly in the coming years. The IPCC has made calculations for a number of scenarios with considerable variations in renewable energy's share of global energy supply in 2030 and 2050. The scenario giving the highest share for renewable energy pointed to the possibility of reaching 43 per cent in 2030 and 77 per cent in 2050.[28]

The growing demands for food, water, and energy are interlinked, and together they constitute a significant problem of global resource scarcity. New kinds of food crops which require less freshwater will reduce the pressure on water supplies. The regulation of the major rivers in Africa and Asia which flow through different countries will create greater certainty of water supply, and the construction of joint hydroelectric power plants will be able to significantly increase electricity production for all the riparian states, but it may also have negative effects on traditional forms of fishing and agriculture. A coherent policy on biofuels and a stronger focus on second generation biofuels, using waste products rather than foodstuffs like maize and sugar cane, will allow increased production of food crops alongside the production of more energy from biomass.

Climate change is a crosscutting concern in all these areas and both creates new opportunities and imposes restrictions which will vary from region to region and country to country. Even a relatively modest rise in sea level will create enormous problems for a country like Bangladesh which has millions of its people living in low-lying delta areas.

Institutionally fragile or conflict-affected countries will face further and more difficult challenges in dealing with these problems. Their capacities are already under stress, and the new challenges will only add to this stress (see chapter 9). There will be an increased need for the UN system to take action to support these countries with capacity building over a broad front, and there will especially be a need for more cross-disciplinary cohesive strategic advice.

SUSTAINABLE DEVELOPMENT – VERSION 2.0

Global scarcities of food, water, and energy could very well prompt a race between better resourced and stronger global actors to secure their future supplies. The beginnings of this scramble for resources can already be seen in sub-Saharan Africa, where external investors, like Chinese companies, seek to position themselves by buying up or leasing arable land and by investing in extractive industries such as minerals, queuing up for access to exploit the continent's natural resources.

If this happens, we may find ourselves in a classic situation of social Darwinism, where the strong may be able to save themselves at the cost of the weak through unrestrained use of their market economy strength. A small preview of this was the food crisis in 2008, where in rapid succession more than thirty countries introduced export prohibitions or strict export limits in order to ensure their own food security. This created significant problems for other countries which were suddenly cut off from their normal sources of food supply.[29]

The solution to this lies not in increased competition but in closer international co-operation, and in the active use of multilateral systems in negotiations, including the UN system. In particular, the solution lies in seeing the problems in conjunction and as expressions of the global interdependence which has only been reinforced by globalization. This is a complex cluster of issues which must be addressed through the concept of sustainable development and within the scope of the Earth's carrying capacity.

The United Nations was created to do great things, or at least attempt them. It is part of the UN's DNA that it should try to meet such global challenges.

The immediate challenge will be to develop a political framework for relaunching the concept of sustainable development. We must go back to the roots of what sustainability really means and start by studying again the Brundtland Report. Sustainable development does not only concern the environment, or even primarily the environment. The concept integrates all three dimensions: economic, social, and environmental sustainability, as well as their interrelationship.

A relaunch of the concept of sustainable development as the main global growth paradigm could act as the basis for a global dialogue on: first, how to deal with the scarcity of key resources; second, how to revive global negotiations on reductions of CO_2 emissions; and third, how to define and raise the funds required to help the developing countries implement the necessary technological and social reforms. It will require much effort and a lot of political will to pave the way for such a global paradigm shift. A first step was taken at the Rio+20 Conference in Rio de Janeiro in June 2012, but it was only a beginning. The follow-up to Rio+20, the discussions on the post 2015 international development agenda (see chapter 9), and the Durban agreement on time-bound negotiations on a new climate change agreement by 2015, all indicate that the next few years, from 2012 to 2015 will be important for multilateral co-operation. Either we start to fix the problems, or we embark on a journey toward a very difficult and very risky future, where we may pass various points of no return along the way.

It is reasonably clear where the economic dimension of sustainable development is pointing – toward a fundamentally new paradigm for sustainable production, transport, and consumption in line with the carrying capacity of the planet. It is also clear where the environmental dimension is headed – toward restrictions on the depletion of finite resources and on the destruction of natural habitats, as well as on renewed efforts to effectively combat pollution and emissions of CO_2 and other greenhouse gases.

What it means for the social dimension of sustainable development is less clear. What remains clear is that social cohesion, globally, regionally, nationally, and locally, is important for dealing with the various kinds of societal stress that always accompany a major paradigm shift. The different processes of change which all countries will have to go through over the coming decades will require cohesion and solidarity, as well as social resilience. The question of how to deal with economic equality and inequality in a society and the challenges inherent in the establishment and maintenance of a social safety net may in the end turn out to be the essential elements in relation to whether we will be able to achieve sustainable development – version 2.0.

PART V

Perspectives

A spade hangs on the wall of my office at One Dag Hammarskjold Plaza. It is a fine, shiny new spade with a formal inscription. I usually say that it is for shovelling paper – to clear my office of all the official reports, pamphlets, printouts, and notes that are an inherent part of day-to-day bureaucratic life.

As is often the case, the truth is more prosaic. The spade was used in the groundbreaking ceremony for the temporary UN building in New York on 5 May 2008. It was a beautiful spring day, and it had fallen to me to be one of the five representatives of the member states who, together with the secretary-general and representatives for the United States and the City of New York, were to break the ground on the north lawn for the new temporary building.

This was not an honour due to me personally. I just happened to be the chair of the Western European and Other States Group of Member States. This is a job that rotates each month, and the responsibilities are usually limited to chairing the monthly meetings of the group to deal with electoral issues such as candidatures for UN commissions and executive boards, and to speaking on behalf of the group at memorial services and more ceremonial occasions of the General Assembly. However, on this occasion there was only action, and no words – a mark had to be made and a hole had to be dug. And the clean, polished, and shining spade is a reminder of the occasion and of the ongoing renovation of the UN Headquarters in New York.

The United Nations is much more than its seventeen acres of prime New York real estate and its many subsidiary offices in so many demanding places around the world. It is much more than the many institutions, agencies, departments, funds, and programs that constitute the UN system, and also much more than the considerable economic resources at its disposal and the tens of thousands of staff members who embody the challenging work of the organization, many of them in dangerous duty stations in conflict areas.

The United Nations is an idea. It is a belief that international co-operation makes sense, that co-operation is better than conflict, and that co-operation must be based on values, and on right rather than might. It is based on a strong conviction that it is only through international co-operation that solutions can be found to what Kofi Annan called the "problems without passports" – all the global problems that spread so easily without regard for national borders, and which no country can deal with on its own.

12

Perspectives

All nations conduct diplomacy to promote their national interests. Responsible stakeholders go further: They recognize that the international system sustains their peaceful prosperity, so they work to sustain that system.

World Bank president Robert Zoellick, 2005

Global change is proceeding at an ever increasing pace. Regardless of current economic downturns and crises in large parts of the world, the underlying structures are in constant movement. The economic and political map of the world is changing rapidly.

The new and emerging economies will continue to show impressive growth rates in the coming years. The United States will still be the leader of the orchestra, but countries such as Brazil, China, India, Indonesia, Mexico, and South Africa will increasingly set the tone. A number of European countries with proud histories will be sulking in the percussion section.

The world's economic centre of gravity is shifting eastward toward Asia. This means there will be more room for Asian perspectives and values, more emphasis on the collective rather than on the individual, and greater focus on harmony in society rather than on the dynamics created by the challenging of authority. This is not a matter of either/or, but the global dominance of Western values and norms could face more challenges in the future.

The monopoly which states have enjoyed as participants in inter-governmental co-operation will also come under increased pressure. In the globalized world there are many more international actors than just nation-states. Increasingly there are regional organizations with their own agendas (such as the EU and the African Union), major transnational companies, private foundations, think tanks, global civil society organizations, media conglomerates and NGO networks. These all have something to offer and want a place at the table, or at least within speaking distance, when global challenges are debated.

Our globalized world has many problems that do not respect national boundaries and which we can only solve by working together. This applies to problems such as poverty, climate change, scarcity of resources, lack of food security, dangerous pandemics, migration, complex armed conflicts with regional implications, gross violations of human rights, terrorism, trans-border crime, and the proliferation of weapons of mass destruction.

International co-operation has achieved incredible results since 1945. Some of these results are hard to prove: for almost seventy years we have avoided a nuclear war, and we are presumably further from such hostilities than ever. We have been able to deal with a number of national and international conflicts in a way that has ensured that they have not got entirely out of hand. We know that the threat of terrorism still hangs over us, but in this area too international collaboration has been intensified.

There have also been incredible results for which there is more positive proof: we have gradually reduced tariff barriers and trade restrictions between countries and created the basis for a massive increase in world trade. There are also regions, particularly Europe, where regional economic integration has been very successful. We have developed common standards for goods and services and have generally benefitted from the great potential of globalization. Global . economic growth in recent decades has ensured that even though the world population has grown, average living standards have clearly improved.

Nearly half a billion people were raised out of poverty between 1990 and 2005, and everything indicates that a further half billion people will be raised out of poverty by 2015. That is a lot of poor people now finding a foothold in the lower middle class. However, there will still be around 1 billion people living in abject poverty in 2015 (people living on less than US$1.25 per day).

Along the way we have also misjudged some of the fundamental conditions for the long-term sustainability of our planet. Rachel Carson's *Silent Spring* was published in 1962. Donnella Meadow's *The Limits to Growth* was a bestseller in the 1970s. The concept of sustainable development was introduced in the 1980s. The Climate Change Convention and the Kyoto Protocol came into effect in the 1990s, and with it the first attempts to deal more systematically with global warming. For nearly fifty years we have seen more and more signs that the sustainability of the planet is threatened. We know that this cannot continue in the long run, but we have been unable to fully convince ourselves of the seriousness of the situation and of our obligation to act on it, sooner rather than later.

We have also seen and exploited the potential which new technology continues to create and which may help us to reduce or solve the problems we encounter. We created a hole in the ozone layer with potential danger for millions of people. New knowledge, new technology, and effective international collaboration are enabling us to close the hole again, and we are well on the way to achieving this.

New technology will also help us solve other problems of sustainability. The use of natural gas generates much less CO_2 than coal or oil, and renewable energy sources are entirely free of CO_2 emissions. But the changes to production methods, transport, consumption, lifestyles, and housing that are necessary in order to limit the concentrations of greenhouse gases in the atmosphere go further than can be dealt with by technology alone. A more sweeping global paradigm shift is needed.

Where does the United Nations fit into this picture?

The UN is not a world government. It is part of the global decision-making structure. It is an important part, but it is only a part.

The United Nations has legitimacy. It can create the framework for international decisions so as to give them legitimacy and ensure that they more easily accepted by all countries and the great majority of their people.

The UN cannot enforce a global paradigm shift, but the organization can confirm its relevance by facilitating many of the discussions that will be necessary for establishing the proper balance between the various interests on the global stage. Ultimately the UN may also be able to nudge the process along and give its blessing to new paradigms as they emerge.

The imminent paradigm shift to a global low-carbon economy can be prepared and implemented in many forums, globally, in regional organizations, in discussions between the major economies (in particular the G20), in public-private partnerships and through increased interactions between governments and private companies. The United Nations will be able to intensify its participation in this broad cooperation if it exercises its convening power. When the UN calls, leaders usually come.

Metaphorically speaking, the global ship must chart an entirely different course from the one it has been sailing so far, but it must also make sure that all the passengers are aboard.

This is of particular concern to the fragile and conflict-affected countries which have had difficulties sharing in the gains from globalization and which risk being left further behind if they are not able to access the potential gains of the emerging paradigm shift. In relation to these countries, most of which are in sub-Saharan Africa, the United Nations will often have a more operational role implementing assistance activities, especially in capacity building, to help these countries cope with the emerging new global realities.

It is this aspect, the need for all to be on board, that has the potential to create synergies between the three potential transformative projects which are the focus of this book.

If the United Nations is to exploit its potential to support and to some extent to formulate these transformative projects, there will need to be some changes to the way the organization works.

The first UN, the United Nations as a negotiating forum between governments, must be made more effective, from the General Assembly and on down. With its universal status the UN system has achieved unique legitimacy which gives a strong backing to the decisions which the member states take collectively in the United Nations. For all its defects, the Security Council is reasonably capable of taking action and making things happen. The General Assembly is not.

A new negotiating culture is needed for the General Assembly and a number of subsidiary bodies in order to change this. Such a culture must be more oriented toward making real compromises, where there is genuine give and take in relation to the core interests of each country rather than a continuation of the existing consensus culture, where disagreements are smoothed out. In a new political culture the member states should be more focused on their substantive interests and less on their political power games.

It will not be easy. The global jockeying between countries for position and status and the desire of the emerging economies to turn their greater economic weight into more political power will inevitably be reflected at the United Nations. Even though the composition of the Security Council remains a pre-eminent issue, in this regard the issue is broader. There is also a desire for increased influence in the General Assembly and in its many subsidiary bodies. It is essential that states should not play power games for the sake of playing power games, but that power should be exercised in relation to substance and interests, and that the aim should be to create greater common welfare. The EU could have an important role in creating such a change of negotiating culture.

It is also important that the member states should be challenged. According to the UN Charter, the Secretariat (the second UN) is a principal organ in line with the General Assembly and the Security Council. The secretary-general and the Secretariat and the other UN organizations must seek an enhanced and stronger role vis-à-vis the member states. This requires better internal coordination, less bureaucracy, improved analytical skills, and firm political leadership of the whole organization. The United Nations must participate actively in informal debates and collaborate with representatives of the member states as well as with international think tanks and academia. From time to time, this will be politically risky for the UN and for the secretary-general, but it will be necessary if the organization is to provide leadership in the twenty-first century.

There is also a third UN, which reflects the interaction needed between the United Nations and the many new actors on the international stage. In future there will be a need for increased contact between the intergovernmental level, the UN Secretariat, and the various non-state actors which increasingly have an impact on development and influence world opinion. These are civil-society organizations, business organizations and private companies, and the academic world, as well as the many religious organizations, movements, and institutions across the world. Account must also be taken of news media. In the present day 24/7 global news stream, the media sometimes deviate from objective reporting and cool analysis and lead political decision makers down the wrong track. The influence and engagement of celebrities can create positive awareness and focus on the work of the United Nations which even the most engaged secretary-general can find hard to match.

But first and foremost there is a need for the United Nations to reinforce its collaboration with the rest of the international system, including the World Bank, the IMF, and the WTO. There is a significant potential for more joint analyses and proposals. The United Nations will also have to co-operate more closely with the regional organizations which will be increasingly important actors in the global decision-making structure. This applies in particular to the African regional and sub-regional organizations such as AU, ECOWAS, SADC, and the Intergovernmental Authority on Development (IGAD). And it applies equally to the EU and in some cases to NATO. And, finally, it is important to create good and smooth working relations between the UN and the G20, G8 and all the other G-groups.

Sovereign nation-states will continue to be the most important decision makers at the UN, but other actors will grow in importance. The international system is pliable and organic and will continue to find new ways of operating. We will see many more informal networks, ad hoc coalitions and coalitions of the willing on specific issues. The contest to set the agenda will be ever harder. The United Nations has a clear home advantage in this contest, but it can lose it if it does not play the game with determination and zest.

The UN Security Council will still be the most important international forum for resolving conflicts and for the international community to come together to address specific threats to international peace and security. The five permanent members have a firm grip on power in the council. The Security Council is as capable of action as the differing great power interests in the council allow. Its composition could be more representative and more accurately reflect the international power structure as it is today and as it will continue to develop. However, its composition is not entirely inappropriate, and any improvement of the representativeness of the council would have to be set against its effectiveness in taking action.

In future, the Security Council will most probably act more in alignment with regional organizations which will become more self-confident and continue to improve their effectiveness so as to exert more influence on Security Council decisions. The council will still have the last word, but there will be an increased need for it not to steer on a collision course with the regional organizations, above all in Africa and the Middle East. The recent role of the Arab League, both in Libya and in Syria, is a case in point.

While this may at first appear to limit the council's scope for action, it is clear that improved coordination with regional organizations also creates a considerable potential for extending the scope of the Security Council's influence and reinforcing its legitimacy, whether or not the council itself is enlarged.

The United Nations and the Security Council will continue to focus on the domestic situation in individual countries. The globalization of the media and the emergence of a global audience will put further pressure on political leaders to act, and to act quickly, in cases which they might otherwise have chosen to ignore or would wish to have had more time to analyze. Short-sighted tactical measures will become more prevalent at the expense of more long-term strategic perspectives. This is not necessarily a purely positive development.

One effect will be that greater attention will be given to human rights issues, especially genocide, war crimes, and other systematic and gross violations of human rights. Concepts such as sovereignty as responsibility and responsibility to protect will probably grow in importance and will emphasize that the social contract between a country's political leadership and its citizens is not a purely internal matter, but like so many other international problems must be seen from a cross-border perspective. When it comes to mass atrocities, all governments are ultimately accountable to the world at large.

This point will undoubtedly give rise to international debates and to various degrees of hypocrisy and denial. It may also provoke a debate about the pre-eminence of global values and about differing views on individual freedoms and their relevance to different cultures. This discussion may also be tempered by actual developments in individual countries. New digital media and global networks, such as Facebook, Twitter, and YouTube, and whatever the next global networking facility may be, will continue to make the world smaller and increase the possibilities for international mobilization of support for those who are fighting against systematic and systemic violence and repression.

The United Nations will have a central role in this development. The UN's fundamental values are clear and, in the eyes of the organization, universal. The UN's human rights instruments cover a very broad spectrum and deal with gross violations of human rights from widely differing perspectives. The possibility of holding political leaders to account for their crimes before the International Criminal Court clearly restricts the scope for dictatorial regimes to avoid criminal liability. This is of course a very positive development, but in practice it can sometimes make it more difficult to find a political solution to problems. Each situation must be dealt with on its own premises, always thinking one step ahead.

But the role of the United Nations goes further. For the UN, democracy and development are closely bound together. As Boutros Boutros-Ghali stated as secretary-general in 1994, a democratic form of government is the only form of government which, in the long

run, can accommodate proper interaction between the different ethnic, religious, social, and cultural interests within a country. Democracy is, thus, an essential element of governance – in the conduct of
national policies, in the formulation of political decision-making
processes and in the daily business of government: "Governance may
be the single most important development variable within the control of individual States."[1] Strengthening democratic political systems
and supporting the rule of law at all levels of society are among the
core mandates of the United Nations.

In the area of development the comparative advantage of the UN
system lies in three particular strengths.

The first is its global presence and the interrelationship between
the system's normative functions and its operational activities,
between the establishment of international norms and standards
where those are needed and practical measures to assist countries in
implementing these norms and standards. The operational activities
primarily take the form of capacity building and institutional development with a view to developing and strengthening public institutions and their staff. The organizations, agencies, funds, and programs
that are part of the UN system cover many different areas of competence and skills, from compiling and analyzing statistics to scientific
collaboration on meteorology, and to the development of national
health and educational systems.

The second is the UN system's central role in the area of humanitarian assistance, as the ultimate resort for issuing consolidated appeals
for emergency aid and in making overall assessments of needs, as
coordinator of international work in the field, and as one of the
biggest and most important providers of humanitarian assistance
through UNICEF, the WFP, and the UNHCR.

The third is the UN's special position in helping to put institutionally fragile and conflict-affected countries back on the right track.
These are countries that have a special need for the United Nations'
core competences of capacity and institution building, and where the
UN can also provide a unique spectrum of support measures by combining and tailoring the system's political, peacebuilding, peacekeeping, humanitarian, and development operations so as to create a
coherent strategy that can help countries move from war to ceasefire
and from there to a consolidated and robust state of peace, and finally to recovery and development.

It is a critical task to get everyone on board and ensure that even the institutionally weakest and most challenged countries become able to participate in the process of globalization and have the possibility of attracting private investment and know-how. Many countries in Africa have great economic potential, if only they were able to emerge from the embrace of conflict and civil war and stabilize their political and economic situation.

Continued economic growth is necessary in order to raise as many as possible of the world's 1 billion poor people out of extreme poverty. And economic growth is also necessary in order to provide a reasonable living standard for the billions of people who can just about manage to keep above the threshold of poverty. However, the ability of the planet to sustain growth sets some clear parameters for how it should be achieved in order not to compromise the possibilities for future generations to fulfill their needs. Future growth must be sustainable – economically, socially, and environmentally.

This takes us back to the imminent paradigm shift to a global economy based on low-carbon growth, and to a world which, by a combination of a political framework, the proper tools of economic management and technological advances will be able to at least halve CO_2 emissions by 2050. Since it does not appear that climate negotiations in the UNFCCC will lead to any real results, it will probably be better to shift the focus to the issue of scarcity of resources, and especially to the issue of energy.

One route that should be followed is the vigorous pursuit of sustainable energy for all, focusing on access to energy also for the poorest, on greater energy efficiency for all, and on the worldwide dissemination of renewable sources of energy. Here the United Nations could use its normative goal-setting function as well as its convening power by getting the relevant actors – governments, businesses, and civil society – together in a multi-stakeholder collaboration to make sustainable energy production and consumption a global transformative project. But the United Nations will only be able to implement such a project if the member states, and especially the biggest and economically most important of these (the G20), play an active and supportive role.

The UN system has many items on its agenda – political, social, economic, and environmental. They all converge in a global meta-agenda of striking an overall balance between winners and losers among the member states in specific areas. Such a balance has to be struck between the big and the small, between the many and the few, and between the short-term and the long-term perspectives.

This meta-agenda for the United Nations has changed over time. In the 1950s, it was predominantly seen from an East-West perspective, reflecting the ideological struggle between the United States and its allies and the Soviet Union and its allies. Through the 1960s, 1970s, and 1980s, it was still seen in the light of the East-West conflict, but also increasingly from a North-South perspective, with decolonization and the expansion of UN membership with the addition of dozens of new member states.

Since 1989, the North-South perspective has dominated the meta-agenda of the UN. However, the nature of the "South" has become less clear, both politically and economically. The new and emerging economies have largely outgrown the other developing countries. In many ways these emerging economies have more in common with the old industrialized countries, but they still face their own development challenges, and high levels of inequality. Today, most of the world's poor live in emerging economies. The new meta-agenda for the United Nations will not be bipolar but triangular – trying to mitigate the interests and concerns of the industrialized countries, the emerging economies and the poorer developing nations, and to take these interests and concerns into account when finding workable – and globally acceptable – solutions to the many "problems without passports," which remain at the core of the UN agenda.

Nearly seventy years after the San Francisco Conference in the spring of 1945, the UN Charter is still the organization's guiding light. The Charter still expresses a strong belief in people's good sense (at that time almost against better judgment), and in fundamental values and the rights of individuals, their dignity and worth.

It is often said that the UN is nothing more than the will of its 193 member states. In some respects this is of course true, but not entirely so.

The will of the member states is not immutable. Sometimes individual countries and even individual persons can make a difference and pull developments in a different direction. This can be by leadership, by putting forward clear arguments, creating alliances, taking advantage of shifting political constellations, formulating compromise solutions, and thus sometimes changing both the international rules of the game and the size of the playing field on which the game is played.

Nation-states will still be the dominant actors in the international system and in the United Nations. All countries have responsibilities under the UN Charter to maintain peaceful co-existence and to manage the world in a sustainable manner.

Over the next ten to fifteen years, the United Nations' ability to create an institutional framework for relevant, legitimate and effective international co-operation will largely be determined by whether its 193 member states recognize the unique opportunities to come together and to live up to their joint responsibilities.

UN SYSTEM

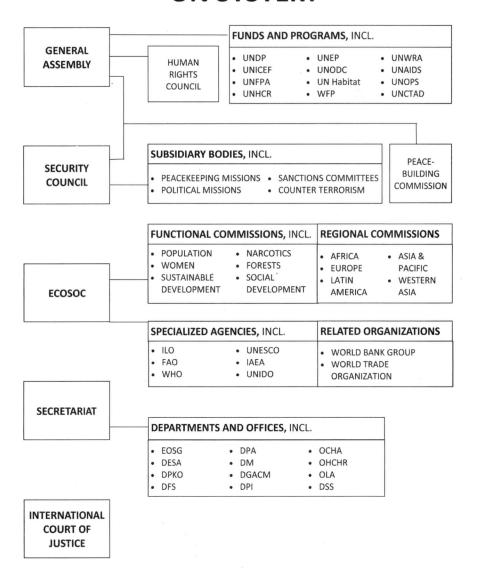

GENERAL ASSEMBLY

HUMAN RIGHTS COUNCIL

FUNDS AND PROGRAMS, INCL.
- UNDP
- UNICEF
- UNFPA
- UNHCR
- UNEP
- UNODC
- UN Habitat
- WFP
- UNWRA
- UNAIDS
- UNOPS
- UNCTAD

SECURITY COUNCIL

SUBSIDIARY BODIES, INCL.
- PEACEKEEPING MISSIONS
- POLITICAL MISSIONS
- SANCTIONS COMMITTEES
- COUNTER TERRORISM

PEACE-BUILDING COMMISSION

ECOSOC

FUNCTIONAL COMMISSIONS, INCL.
- POPULATION
- WOMEN
- SUSTAINABLE DEVELOPMENT
- NARCOTICS
- FORESTS
- SOCIAL DEVELOPMENT

REGIONAL COMMISSIONS
- AFRICA
- EUROPE
- LATIN AMERICA
- ASIA & PACIFIC
- WESTERN ASIA

SPECIALIZED AGENCIES, INCL.
- ILO
- FAO
- WHO
- UNESCO
- IAEA
- UNIDO

RELATED ORGANIZATIONS
- WORLD BANK GROUP
- WORLD TRADE ORGANIZATION

SECRETARIAT

DEPARTMENTS AND OFFICES, INCL.
- EOSG
- DESA
- DPKO
- DFS
- DPA
- DM
- DGACM
- DPI
- OCHA
- OHCHR
- OLA
- DSS

INTERNATIONAL COURT OF JUSTICE

UN System Organization Chart
Source: http://www.un.org/en/aboutun/structure/org_chart.shtml

Notes

CHAPTER ONE

1 Dadush and Stancil, "The World Order in 2050," *Carnegie Endowment for International Peace: Policy Outlook* (April 2010), and "How to Get a Date," *The Economist*, 31 December 2011. Accessed 4 May 2013, http://www.economist.com/node/21542155.

2 Karns and Mingst, *International Organizations*, 3–33. See also Ruggie, preface to *Global Governance and the UN: An Unfinished Journey*, eds. Weiss and Thakur, xv–xx. Weiss and Thakur define "global governance" as: "The sum of laws, norms, policies, and institutions that define, constitute, and mediate relations among citizens, society, markets, and the state in the international arena," 6.

3 On the Nordic countries and the UN, see: Götz, *Deliberative Diplomacy*.

4 Bolton, *Surrender is Not an Option*, quoted in Anne Applebaum, "Defending Bolton," *Washington Post*, 9 March 2005, accessed 4 May 2013, http://www.washingtonpost.com/wp-dyn/articles/A18706-2005Mar8.html. McKeever, *Adlai Stevenson*. 481–507; and Moynihan, *A Dangerous Place*, especially 169–95 on Zionism and racism.

5 On the proposed League of Democracies, see Carothers, "A League of Their Own," *Foreign Policy* (July/August 2008), 44–9; and Stedman, "America and International Cooperation," *Policy Analysis Brief*.

6 See National Intelligence Council, *Global Trends 2025*, Washington, November 2008, accessed 2 May 2013, http://www.acus.org/files/publication_pdfs/3/Global-Trends-2025.pdf.

7 Zakaria, *The Post-American World*, 1–5.

8 UN Secretary-General Kofi Annan, *We the Peoples*, report to the Millennium Summit in 2000, http://www.un.org/millennium/sg/report/cho.pdf; and *In*

Larger Freedom, report to the World Summit in 2005, http://www.un.org/ largerfreedom/contents.htm.
9. Power, *Chasing the Flame*, 526.

<h3 style="text-align:center">CHAPTER TWO</h3>

1 Groom, "Getting to 'Go,'" in *The United Nations at the Millennium: The Principal Organs*, eds. Taylor and Groom, 1–20; Henig, *Versailles and After 1919–1933*; Macmillan, *Peacemakers*; Claude, *Swords into Plowshares*, 41–56.
2 On Wilson and the League of Nations, see John Milton Cooper Jr., *Woodrow Wilson*, 454. On the similarities between the League of Nations and the UN, see Mazower, *No Enchanted Palace*, 1–28; and for the Covenant of the League of Nations, see http://avalon.law.yale.edu/20th_century/leagcov.asp, accessed 4 May 2013.
3 On the Atlantic Charter, see Borgwardt, *A New Deal for the World*, 14–45.
4 On the Yalta Conference, see Plokhy, *Yalta*, in particular chapters 9 and 14 (the Roosevelt quotation is on p. 191). On the San Francisco Conference, see Schlesinger, *Act of Creation*, in particular chapters 12 and 14. See also McCullough, *Truman*, 398; and Meisler, *United Nations*, 1–20.
5 For an overview of all the organizations and more detailed information about each, see United Nations: *Basic Facts about the United Nations*.
6 Weiss, introduction to *What's Wrong with the United Nations*, 1–11.
7 The G77 is named after the number of signatories to the developing countries' joint declaration in connection with the first UN Conference in Trade and Development (UNCTAD I) in 1964. The group is usually referred to as G77 and China, as China is not formally part of the G77.
8 The G77 and NAM have a common platform in the Joint Coordination Committee. Chile became a member of the OECD in 2010, but remains a member of the G77. The same is the case with Bosnia-Herzegovina, which is the last European G77 country. See Swart and Lund, *The Group of 77*, 26ff.
9 UN Secretary-General's High-Level Panel on Global Sustainability, *Resilient People, Resilient Planet*, 30 January 2012, accessed 4 May 2013, http://www. un.org/gsp/report.
10 On the Global Compact, see www.unglobalcompact.org. See also Sagafi-Nejad and Dunning, *The UN and Transnational Corporations*, 195ff.
11 For the General Assembly Resolution on the status of the EU, see: Res A/65/276 of 3 May 2011, daccess-dds-ny.org/doc/UNDOC/LTD/N11/309/ 29/PDF/N1130929.pdf?OpenElement.

CHAPTER THREE

1 Lipsey, *Hammarskjöld. A Life*, and Urquhart, *Hammarskjold*.

2 Traub, *The Best Intentions*; Annan, *Interventions*.

3 The US was slow to describe the situation in Darfur as "genocide," primarily out of fear that this could trigger domestic demands for military intervention in Sudan. When Secretary of State Colin Powell did so, it was with reference to the UN Convention for the Prevention and Punishment of the Crime of Genocide, which does not include provisions on intervention.

4 See http://www.theglobalfund.org, accessed 4 May 2013. Pisani, *The Wisdom of Whores*, 295ff., gives a more critical view of the start up of GFATM. The author was a member of the GFATM board from 2005 to 2007, representing the Netherlands, Ireland, Luxembourg, and the Nordic countries.

5 Urquhart, "The Evolution of the Secretary-General," in *Secretary or General?*, ed. Chesterman, 32.

6 Keating, "Selecting the World's Diplomat," in *Secretary or General*, ed. Chesterman, 47–66.

7 Albright, *Madam Secretary*, 261; Boutros-Ghali, *Unvanquished*, 258; and Gharekhan, *The Horseshoe Table*, 280.

8 Urquhart, *Hammarskjold*, 54.

9 Myint-U and Scott, *The UN Secretariat*, 126.

10 UN Secretary-General, *Safety and Security of United Nations and Associated Personnel*, dok. A/65/344, 3 September 2010, paras 6, 10, and 24.

11 Urquhart, *Hammarskjöld*, 521. Hammarskjöld's speech in Oxford on 30 May 1961 is at: http://www.un.org/Depts/dhl/dag/docs/internationalcivilservant.pdf (accessed 4 May 2013).

12 Weiss, *What's Wrong with the United Nations*, 173–90. On the oil-for-food scandal, see Meyer and Califano, *Good Intensions Corrupted*.

13 Four Nations Initiative, *Towards a Compact*. Report of final proposals by the Four Nations Initiative, published 13 September 2007, accessed 4 May 2013, http/www.centerforunreform.org/node/275.

14 Claude, *Swords into Plowshares*, 191.

15 In recent years a number of very important researchers have carried out a project on the UN's political thinking and development of concepts, within the framework of the UN Intellectual History Project. Indiana University Press has published fourteen volumes. *UN Ideas That Changed the World* (2009) summarizes the results of this research project which has been led by professor Thomas G. Weiss of the Ralph Bunche Institute at City University of New York.

16 Jolly, Emmerij, Ghai, and Lapeyre, *UN Contributions to Development Thinking and Practice*, 11. On UN Women, see www.unwomen.org.

17 UNDP, *Human Development Report 2013*, 144–7.

18 Toye and Toye, *The UN and Global Political Economy*. Commodity prices may be going up at present, but structurally there has been a decline over time.

19 UNCTAD, *The Financial and Economic Crisis*.

CHAPTER FOUR

1 Bosco, *Five to Rule Them All*, 92ff.; and McKeever, *Adlai Stevenson*, 522ff.

2 Bosco, 3.

3 On Security Council mandates, see David M. Malone, "Security Council," in *The Oxford Handbook on the United Nations*, eds. Weiss and Daws, 117–35; Adam Roberts, "The Use of Force," 133–52 in Malone ed., *The UN Security Council*; and Gharekhan, "Procedures and Practices of the Security Council," in *The Horseshoe Table*, 13–43.

4 In connection with the adoption of the first resolution, the then US ambassador to the UN, John Negroponte, said among other things that "this resolution contains no 'hidden triggers' and no 'automaticity' with respect to the use of force" (8 November 2002). On the UN and the two Iraq wars in general, see Malone, *The International Struggle Over Iraq*; and Munoz, *A Solitary War*.

5 Bosco, 231.

6 On 16 September 2004, in response to a direct question from the BBC, Kofi Annan answered, "Yes, if you wish. I have indicated it was not in conformity with the UN charter from our point of view, from the charter point of view, it was illegal." "Iraq war illegal, says Annan," BBC News, updated 16 September 2004, http://news.bbc.co.uk/go/pr/fr/-/2/hi/middle_east/3661134.stm. David Bosco calculates that of the ten elected members, only Spain and Bulgaria clearly supported the United States and the United Kingdom. Germany and Syria, like France, Russia, and China, were clearly against, while Chile, Mexico, Angola, Cameroon, Guinea, and Pakistan were also leaning toward the negative side. A vote would therefore have revealed that only four of the fifteen members supported a resolution authorizing the use of force (Bosco, 238). See also: Annan, *Interventions*, 357.

7 Bosco, 115.

8 Security Council Resolution 1970 of 26 February 2011.

9 One EU country (Cyprus) is even a member of the Asian group. Israel, not being able to actively participate in its geographical group (Asia), has been admitted to WEOG until the situation in the region may change.

CHAPTER FIVE

1 Bellamy and Williams, *Understanding Peacekeeping*, 71–92 and 173–92; Urquhart, *Hammarskjold*, 159–94; and *A Life in War and Peace*, 131–9, shows how Hammarskjöld developed the concept and the terms of reference for UNEF.

2 See the overview in Bellamy and Williams, *Understanding Peacekeeping*, 86.

3 UN, *Report of the Panel on United Nations Peace Operations* (the Brahimi Report), UN documents A/55/305 and S/2000/809, 21 August 2000, para. 48, accessed 4 May 2013, http://www.un.org/peace/reports/peace _operations/. See also Doyle and Sambanis, "Peacekeeping Operations," in *The Oxford Handbook on the United Nations*, eds. Weiss and Daws, 323–48.

4 Each year there is a review of the UN's peacekeeping operations and political missions in the *Annual Review of Global Peace Operation* (most recently 2012), published by the Center on International Co-operation (CIC), New York University. See also CIC's analysis: *Peacekeeping: Current and Future Trends*; and Richard Gowan, Megan Gleason, and Morgan Hughes *UN Peacekeeping: The Next Five Years*.

5 The fifteen peacekeeping missions and the numbers provided here (as of March 2013) do not include UNAMA in Afghanistan which is technically a special political mission and not a peacekeeping mission. UNAMA staff was around 1,500 in March 2013.

6 Information on DPKO obtained in March 2013. South Sudan's independence as from 9 July 2011 meant that the UN Mission in Sudan (UNMIS), with 10,000 personnel, was replaced by two new missions: UN Mission in the Republic of South Sudan (UNMISS) with up to 8,000 personnel (established by Security Council Resolution 1996 of 8 July 2011) and UN Interim Security Force for Abyei (UNISFA) with up to 4,200 personnel (Resolution 1990 of 27 June 2011).

7 Among others in DR Congo; see Security Council Resolution 1925 of 28 May 2010.

8 On mass rape in the eastern Congo, see report from Harvard University and Oxfam: "Now the world is without me" of 15 April 2010, www.oxfam.org/ en/policy/now-world-without-me, accessed 4 May 2013.

9 This section is based on the author's visit to Liberia in 2010. Some of the statistics have been subsequently updated.

10 Helene Cooper, *The House at Sugar Beach*, 28–36.

11 For the peacekeeping scale of assessment, see UN document A/67/224 of 3 August 2012, Annex 3, accessed 4 May 2013, www.un.org/en/peacekeeping/ operations/financing.shtml. The five permanent members of the Security

Council pay 48.7 per cent of peacekeeping expenses, as compared to 40.3 per cent of the regular budget.

12 The total number of fatalities among UN peacekeepers in all missions since 1948 amounted to 3,091, as of March 2013.

CHAPTER SIX

1 On Liberia, see Roland Paris, "Post-Conflict Peacebuilding," in *The Oxford Handbook on the United Nations*, eds. Weiss and Daws, 414.

2 Mikulaschek, Cockayne, and Perry, *The United Nations Security Council and Civil War*. The definition of civil war used here, which is commonly used, means that the conflicts in Timor-Leste (independence from Indonesia), Namibia (independence from South Africa), South Lebanon, Gaza/The West Bank, and Western Sahara (Morocco's occupation of the former Spanish colony) are not included. However, these conflicts were, of course, on the Security Council's agenda in 1989–2006.

3 UN Secretary-General's High-Level Panel on Threats, Challenges and Change, *A More Secure World* accessed 6 May 2013, http://www.un.org/secure world/report2.pdf.

4 World Summit Outcome, September 2005, para. 97. (doc. A/RES/60/1) The mandate was decided in Security Council Resolution 1645 (2005) and General Assembly Resolution 60/180, both from 20 December 2005, accessed 4 May 2013, un.org/en/peacebuilding/mandate.stmhl.

5 In 2010–11 the United Kingdom carried out an analysis of multilateral organizations in relation to the UK's foreign policy interests. The PBF came out of this well. See Department of International Development, *Multilateral Aid Review: Assessment of UN Peacebuilding Fund (PBF)*, 1 March 2011, accessed 4 May 2013, https://www.gov.uk/government/publications/uploads/system/uploads/attachment_data/file/67627/pbf.pdf.

6 Review report of 21 July 2010: A/64/868. Security Council Resolution 1947 (2010), adopted 29 October 2010.

7 Henrik Jespersen, "Study of UNDP, UNICEF and UNFPA's engagement in fragile and post-conflict states," November 2010, Annex on UNDP in Liberia; accessed 4 May 2013, http://reliefweb.int/sites/reliefweb.int/files/resources/857F0FFEA723D03F85257831005B7979-Full_Report.pdf.

8 On Sergio Vieira de Mello, see Power, *Chasing the Flame.*

9 There is no official list of fragile or conflict-affected countries. Such a list would change over time, and in any case in the view of many countries there is some stigmatization associated with such lists. Definition of "fragili-

ty": World Bank, "Conflict, Security, and Development," *World Development Report*, (2011), xvi.

10　See Lars Engberg-Pedersen, Louise Andersen, and Finn Stepputat, *Fragile Situations*, DIIS Report, (2008), 9; Ghani and Lockhart, *Fixing Failed States*, 169–97; Doyle and Sambanis, *Making War and Building Peace*, 337–42; Fukuyama, *State Building*, 43–91; and Dobbins, Crane, and DeGrasse, *The Beginner's Guide to Nation-Building*.

11　Jones, Pascual, and Stedman, *Power and Responsibility*, 177.

12　Report of the Secretary-General on Peacebuilding in the Immediate Aftermath of Conflict (A/63/881 of 11 June 2009); OECD, *Principles for Good International Engagement in Fragile States and Situations*, (April 2007), accessed 4 May 2013, www.oecd.org/data oecd/61/45/38368714.pdf; and International Dialogue on Peacebuilding and Statebuilding, *Dili Declaration* (April 2010), accessed 4 May 2013; http://www.g7plus.org/news-articles/2010/4/10/dili-declaration.html.

13　Doyle and Sambanis, "Peacekeeping Operations," chapter 8. See also Jones et al., *Power and Responsibility*, 189.

14　*World Development Report 2011: Conflict, Security and Development*, Washington, 2011.

15　Civilian capacity in the aftermath of conflict, Independent report by a Senior Advisory Group under the chairmanship of the former under-secretary-general Jean-Marie Guehenno (doc. A/65/747-S/2011/85 of 22 February 2011). Accessed 4 May 2013, www.civcapreview.org.

CHAPTER SEVEN

1　Human rights are referred to in Articles 1, 55, and 62 of the UN Charter, Normand and Zaidi, *Human Rights at the UN*, 107–42. On the history of human rights, see Hunt, *Inventing Human Rights* and Ishay, *The History of Human Rights*.

2　Glendon, *A World Made New* Hunt, 176–214; and Normand and Zaidi, 117. The eight countries which abstained were Belarus, Czechoslovakia, Poland, the Soviet Union, Ukraine, Yugoslavia, Saudi Arabia, and South Africa.

3　René Cassin's views are referred to in Normand and Zaidi, 189.

4　See the UN Treaty Collection: http://treaties.un.org – status for ratification checked on 13 August 2012. There are probably several reasons why the United States has not ratified the Convention on the Rights of the Child. It normally takes the United States many years to ratify a human rights convention. The Convention on the Elimination of All Forms of Discrimination against Women from 1979 has still not been ratified by the United States, because it wants to be sure that all the obligations can be met, both at federal and at state levels (the United States is the only one of 188 countries signing the convention which has not yet ratified it). Both in relation to this convention and in relation to the Convention on the Rights of the Child there are also conservative political forces and Christian fundamentalist groups in the United States which have deep-rooted objections to the UN Conventions, which they – mistakenly – see as both undermining national sovereignty and parents' rights to decide for their children.

5 Office of the High Commissioner for Human Rights, UN-Habitat, and WHO, "The Right to Water", fact sheet no 35, Geneva, (August 2010). One hundred and twenty-two countries voted in favour, 41 abstained, and none voted against the draft resolution (A/64/L63) in the UN General Assembly on 28 July 2010. The UN Human Rights Council adopted Resolution A/HRC/RES/15/9 without a vote on 30 September 2010. Accessed 4 May 2013, http://daccess-dds-ny.un.org/doc/UNDOC/GEN/G10/166/33/PDF/ G1016633.pdf?OpenElement.

6 Vienna Declaration and Programme of Action, 25 June 1993, adopted as GA Resolution 48/121.

7 Joined cases C-402/05 P and C-415/05 P *Yassin Abdullah Kadi v Council and Commission*, accessed 4 May 2013, http://eur-lex.europa.eu/LexUriServ/Lex UriServ.do?uri=CELEX:62005CJ0402:EN:HTML. In addition to Article 48 of the UN Charter on the binding nature of Security Council resolutions, Article 103 also states that the provisions of the UN Charter shall prevail over other international obligations.

8 Security Council Resolution 1904 of 17 December 2009; the mandate for the ombudsperson is in Annex II. The office of the ombudsperson has gradually asserted itself, as demonstrated in the fifth report to the Security Council: "Report of the Office of the Ombudsperson pursuant to Security Council resolution 2083 (2012)" of 31 January 2013 (doc. S/2013/71), available at the website of the ombudsperson: http://www.un.org/sc/ombuds person.

9 Security Councils Resolutions 1988 and 1989 of 17 June 2011.

10 The definition of torture is in Article 1 of the convention. As for the "ticking bomb," see: Association for the Prevention of Torture, *Defusing the Ticking Bomb Scenario*, (Geneva: APT, 2007), which refutes all the arguments for torture in detail. See also Richardson, *What Terrorists Want*, 236; and Fisher, *Morality and War*, 166–90. Among those who argue that torture often does not give reliable and usable information is John McCain, the Republican candidate in the 2008 US presidential election, who himself suffered severe

torture as a prisoner of war in the Vietnam War: Michael Scherer and Bobby Ghosh, "McCain Denies Giving O.K. to CIA Torture Tactic," *Time* 31 August 2009, accessed 4 May 2013, http://www.time.com/time/nation/article/0,8599,1919523,00.html.

11 Committee Against Torture, *Selected Decisions of the Committee Against Torture*, vol. 1, (Geneva, United Nations Publications, 2008).

12 Office of the High Commissioner of Human Rights, "Special Rapporteur on Torture and Other Cruel, Inhuman or Degrading Treatment or Punishment," United Nations Human Rights, http://www2.ohchr.org/english/issues/torture/rapporteur/index.htm. On the general significance of the special rapporteur, see Piccone, *Catalysts for Rights*.

13 Fukuyama, *The End of History*, xi–xxiii.

14 Freedom House data, obtained from www.freedomhouse.org on 14 August 2012. There have not been changes to the numbers even in Africa, but this is not to say that there has been no change, merely that the plusses and minuses have cancelled each other out.

15 Declaration on the Right to Development, GA Resolution 41/128 of 4 December 1986. Bertrand G. Ramcharan, "Norms and Machinery," in *The Oxford Handbook on the United Nations*, eds. Weiss and Daws, 439–62.

16 Amartya Sen, "Human Rights and Asian Values," Morgenthau Memorial Lecture, New York, 1997, www.sph.emory.edu/media/IPHR/Readings/sen%20-%20asianvalues.pdf, accessed 6 May 2013. Amartya Sen, *Development as Freedom*, 227–48.

17 The view of most Western countries that the basic approach to the debate about offending religious sensibilities is already covered by Article 20 of the ICCPR is somewhat hampered by the fact that the United States has a legal (constitutional) reservation in respect of this provision and is therefore reluctant to refer to it. For the OIC argument in the form of a United Nations draft resolution, see A/C.3/65/L.46/Rev.1, accessed 4 May 2013, http://daccess-dds-ny.un.org/doc/UNDOC/LTD/N10/644/89/PDF/N1064489.pdf?OpenElement.

18 Freedom House, *Policing Belief*, accessed 4 May 2013, http://www.freedomhouse.org/report/special-reports/policing-belief-impact-blasphemy-laws-human-rights.

19 Dennison and Dworkin, "Toward an EU Human Rights Strategy."

CHAPTER EIGHT

1 Bass, *Freedom's Battle*: on Lord Russell, see 180; on the Armenian genocide, see 315. See also Balakan, *Armenian Golgatha*.

2 Evans, *The Responsibility to Protect*, 24; and Bellamy, *Global Politics and the Responsibility to Protect*, 1–7.

3 Bellamy and Williams, *Understanding Peacekeeping*, 214–29; Dallaire, *Shake Hands with the Devil* and Power, *A Problem from Hell*, 329–442.

4 Dansk Udenrigspolitisk Institut, *Humanitarian Intervention*, 128.

5 On Kosovo, see Fisher, *Morality and War*, 104.

6 International Commission on Intervention and State Sovereignty, *The Responsibility to Protect*.

7 Secretary-General's High-Level Panel on Threats, Challenges and Change, *A More Secure World*; UN Secretary-General, *In Larger Freedom*. On Kofi Annan's role, see Traub, *The Best Intentions*, 50.

8 UN Secretary-General, *Implementing the Responsibility to Protect*, January 2009 (doc. A/63/677). On the basis of the debate, on 14 September 2009 the General Assembly unanimously adopted a resolution (A/RES/63/308), which took note of the report and decided to continue the discussion on R2P.

9 Asia-Pacific Centre for the Responsibility to Protect, *Cyclone Nargis and the Responsibility to Protect*, Myanmar/Burma briefing no. 2, accessed 4 May 2013, http://responsibilitytoprotect.org/legacyDownload.php?module=uploads&func=download&fileId=539.

10 Mark Schneider, "Implementing the Responsibility to Protect in Kenya and Beyond" (address to the World Affairs Council of Oregon, Portland State University, Portland, OR, 5 March 2010), accessed 4 May 2013, http://www.crisisgroup.org/en/publication-type/speeches/ 2010/implementing-the-responsibility-to-protect-in-kenya-and-beyond.aspx.

11 Information given by the Secretary-General's adviser on R2P, Ed Luck, to the author in July 2011.

12 Security Council Resolutions 1970 of 26 February 2011 and 1973 of 17 March 2011, both on Libya.

13 Report of the Secretary-General on the Responsibility to Protect: Timely and Decisive; 24 July 2012 (UN Document S/2012/578).

14 Paragraphs 4 to 8 of Security Council Resolution 1970 of 26 February 2011. See also Security Council Resolution 1593 of 31 March 2005, which refers the situation in Darfur to the Prosecutor for the International Criminal Court.

15 For general information on the ICC, see its website: http://www.icc-cpi.int.

16 See the internal UN papers prior to the secretary-general's retreat in Alpbach, 5–6 September 2010, 32ff., accessed 4 May 2013, at http://www.foxnews.com/projects/pdg/austria_retreat_papers.pdf.

17 On Kenya after Moi, see Wrong, *It's Our Turn to Eat*.

18 See http://www.icty.org/sid/24; http://www.unictr.org/cases/tabid/204/ Default.aspx; ; http://www.sc-sl.org/MOREINFO/tabid/75/Default.aspx; and http://www.cambodiatribunal.org/trial-proceedings. All websites accessed 4 May 2013.

19 Hayner, *Unspeakable Truths*, 32ff., 114.

20 Report of the Secretary-General, *The Role of Regional and Subregional Arrangements in Implementing the Responsibility to Protect*, Doc. A/65/877 of 28 June 2011. For the secretary-general's speech of 12 July 2011, see: http://www.un.org/apps/ news/infocus/sgspeeches/statments_full.asp?statID= 1246#. On Libya, see also Simon Adams, *Libya and the Responsibility to Protect*, October 2012, accessed 4 May 2013, http://www.globalr2p.org/ media/files/libyaandr2poccasionalpaper-1.pdf.

CHAPTER NINE

1 The United Nations' 0.7 per cent goal was set out in "International Development Strategy for the Second United Nations Development Decade," General Assembly Resolution 2626 (XXV) of 24 October 1970 (para. 43), accessed 7 May 2013, http://www.un-documents.net/a25r2626.htm. The United States and Switzerland stated that they did not consider themselves bound by the 0.7 per cent goal. The percentage was originally linked to gross national product (GNP), but today, following the global changes to national accounting systems in 1993, it is calculated in relation to gross national income (GNI). See Stokke, *The UN and Development*, 520.

2 The OECD defines and registers aid transfers for its members. For the OECD's definition of development aid, see: http://www.oecd.org/document/4/0, 3746,en_2649_34447_46181892_1_ 1_1_1,00.html (accessed 7 May 2013).

3 On the *World Summit for Children* in 1990, see Weiss and Thakur, *Global Governance and the UN*, 179. On UN conferences in general, see Karns and Mingst, *International Organizations*, 126; and Schechter, *United Nations Global Conferences*, 107ff. For the Declaration from the World Food Summit in 1996, see: http://www.fao.org/wfs/index_en.htm (accessed 7 May 2013).

4 Millennium Declaration (General Assembly Resolution A/RES/55/2, para. 19), accessed 7 May 2013, http://www.un.org/millennium/declaration/ares552e.pdf.

5 *The Millennium Development Goals Report 2012*, New York, July 2012. For the goals, targets and indicators, see: http://mdgs.un.org/unsd/mdg/Host .aspx?Content=indicators/officiallist.htm, accessed 4 May 2013.

6 Singh and Darroch, *Adding It Up*, 30.

7 The UN Millennium Project's comprehensive report was presented in 2005

and is available at: http://www.unmillenniumproject.org/reports/index
_overview.htm (accessed 4 May 2013). For the Gleneagles Declaration, see:
http://www.unglobalcompact.org/docs/about_the_gc/government_support/
PostG8_Gleneagles_Communique.pdf (accessed 7 May 2013). On development aid 2004–09, see UN Development Programme, *What Will It Take to
Achieve the Millennium Development Goals?*, 40.

8 *The Millennium Development Goals Report 2012*, 58–65.

9 UNICEF: Diverse countries are making rapid progress in child survival –
   UNICEF reports, press release 13 September 2012, accessed 4 May 2013,
   http://www.unicef.org/media/media_65823.html.

10 The latest global data for infant mortality are in the *Millennium Develop-
   ment Goals Report 2012*, 26–9. UNICEF's new equity strategy is described in
   UNICEF, "Social Protection: Accelerating the MDGs with Equity," August 2010;
   UNICEF, "Progress for Children – Achieving the MDGs with Equity," Septem-
   ber 2010, interactive website: http://www.devinfo.info/pfc/index.html; and
   UNICEF, "Narrowing the Gaps to Meet the Goals," September 2010. See also
   The Lancet, special release on 20 September 2012, including Mickey Chopra,
   Alyssa Sharkey, Nita Dalmiya, David Anthony, and Nancy Binkin, "Strategies
   to Improve Health Coverage and Narrow the Equity Gap in Child Survival,
   Health, and Nutrition," accessed 4 May 2013, http://www.ncbi.nlm.nih.gov/
   pubmed/22999430.

11 The various results are given in, among others, the UN's "We Can End
   Poverty" campaign, prior to the MDG Summit in September 2010, see:
   http://www.endpover ty2015.org. The earlier calculation of the extent of
   global death in childbirth of more than 500,000 a year was adjusted down-
   wards on the basis of expert criticism. See also Richard Horton, "Maternal
   Mortality: Surprise, Hope, and Urgent Action," *The Lancet*, 375 (8 May
   2010): 1581. The latest aggregated figures are in the *Millennium Development
   Goals Report 2012*, 30.

12 UN, "The Global Partnership for Development at a Critical Juncture," MDG
   Gap Task Force Report 2010, 20 and figure 4. See also Andy Summer and
   Meera Tiwari, "Global Poverty Reduction to 2015 and Beyond," *Institute of
   Development Studies, Working Paper*, 2010, no. 348 (October 2010): 16.

13 Declaration of interest: Together with my Senegalese colleague Paul Badji, I
   was co-chair of the negotiations, first on the modalities of the summit, and
   then on the drafting of the Summit declaration "Keeping the Promise: United to achieve the Millennium Development Goals," which is available as
   A/RES/65/1, (accessed 6 May 2013),_http://www.un.org/en/mdg/summit
   2010/pdf/outcome_documentN1051260.pdf.

14 In 2010, the OECD countries' total aid was about US$129 billion, correspond-

ing to 0.32 per cent of GNI: see OECD, "Development: Aid Increases, but with Worrying Trends," press release,6 April 2011, accessed 4 May 2013, The Gleneagles promises would have resulted in aid in 2010 of 0.37 per cent of the OECD countries GNI: see UNDP, "What Will It Take," 40. See also UNDP, "Unlocking Progress"; and UNDP, "The Path to Achieving the Millennium Development Goals."

15 UNDP, "What Will It Take," 20. Other studies suggest that these proportions may be a bit on the high side.

16 See paras. 30–4 and 49–50 of the outcome document A765/1.

17 See the Every Woman Every Child website: http://www.everywomanevery child.org.

18 See: http://www.everywomaneverychild.org/commitments (accessed 4 May 2013).

19 UN, "Ban Names High-Level Panel to Map Out 'Bold' Vision for Future Global Development Efforts," United Nations press release, 31 July 2012, accessed 4 May 2013, http://www.un.org/apps/news/story.asp?NewsID=42597 &Cr=mdgs&Cr1=&Kw1=postper cent2D2015+development+agenda&Kw2 =&Kw3=. See also UN, "The Future We Want," Rio+20 outcome document, 22 June 2012, accessed 4 May 2013, http://www.uncsd2012.org/content/ documents/727The%20Future%20We%20Want%2019%20June%201230pm .pdf.

20 For background: the Secretary-General's Advisory Group on Energy and Climate Change (AGECC), "Energy for a Sustainable Future," New York, 28 April 2010, accessed 4 May 2013, http://www.un.org/wcm/webdav/site/ climatechange/shared/Documents/AGECC%20summary%20report%5B1%5D .pdf.
    The three energy targets for 2030 are in line with the overall climate targets to limit the global temperature increase to two degrees Celsius by 2100.

21 Andy Sumner, "Global Poverty and the New Bottom Billion," IDS Working Paper 349, November 2010. In this context, "poverty" is understood as "extreme poverty," i.e., living conditions where people live on less than US$1 per day (now up-rated to US$1.25 per day).

CHAPTER TEN

1 Harry S. Truman, inaugural address, 20 January 1949, quoted in Weiss and Thakur, *Global Governance and the UN*, 174; and Behrman, *The Most Noble Adventure*, 51.

2 The figures given here are from the Secretary-General's report, "Analysis of Funding of Operational Activities for Development of the United Nations

System for the year 2010," advance unedited version, 31 May 2012, accessed 7 May 2013, http://www.un.org/en/development/desa/oesc/pdf/2012 _funding_report-figures_and_tables.pdf. The report probably underestimates the OECD countries' share of the voluntary contributions by not including financing via other funds that are financed by the OECD countries. See also OECD/DAC, 2010 Report on Multilateral Aid DCD/DAC (2010) 32, 17 June 2010, accessed 4 May 2013, http://www.oecd.org/development/ effectiveness/45828572.pdf; and Development Co-operation for the MDG, Maximizing Results, DESA 2010 (ST/ESA/326), accessed 4 May 2013, http://www.un.org/en/ecosoc/newfunct/pdf/10-45690(e)(desa)development _cooperation_for_the_mdgs_maximizing_results.pdf.

3 In the United Nations, member states lose their right to vote if they are in arrears to more than two years of assessed contributions.

4 *Analysis of the Funding of Operational Activities for Development of the United Nations System for 2010*, 25 (note 2). According to the World Bank's definition, middle-income countries are countries with an average annual per capita income of between US$1,000 and $4,000. Countries with an average per capita income of between US$4,000 and about $12,000 are upper-middle-income countries, and countries with above about US$12,000 are high-income.

5 UNDP, *Capacity Development*, in which there are references to many other tools. See also: Udenrigsministeriet [the Danish Foreign Ministry], *Addressing Capacity Development in Danish Development Co-operation: Guiding Principles and Operational Steps* (Technical Advisory Services, 2011).

6 UN, *At Work Together*, accessed 4 May 2013, http://www.unliberia.org/doc/ atworktogether_uninliberia.pdf. The number of staff members is naturally changing all the time.

7 The generally agreed phrase is *sexual and reproductive health and rights* (SRHR). Reproductive rights are recognized in UN resolutions; sexual rights are not explicitly acknowledged in agreed UN resolutions.

8 Singh and Darroch, *Adding It Up*.

9 There is a very detailed review of what this means in practice in *A Human Rights–Based Approach to Programming. Practical Implementation Manual and Training Materials*, prepared by the UNFPA and Harvard School of Public Health, 2010. There is also a UN website for rights-based development at http://hrbaportal.org. On reproductive rights, see the ICPD chapter 7 and in particular para. 7.3, accessed 7 May 2013, http://www.unfpa.org/webdav/site/ global/shared/documents/publications/2004/icpd_eng.pdf. See also Singh and Darroch, *Adding It Up*. On the question of abortion, see ICPD paras. 7.24 and 8.25.

10 For the CEB members and their mandates, see: http://www.unsceb.org/
content/ceb/and http://www.undg.org (accessed 6 May 2013).

11 UN, *Analysis of the Funding of Operational Activities for Development of the
United Nations System for 2008* (A/65/79, 14 May 2010), 46. UNDG, *Delivering
as One Lessons Learned from Pilot Countries: Prepared by Coordination Officers
from Albania, Cape Verde, Mozambique, Pakistan, Rwanda, Tanzania, Uruguay
and Vietnam*, June 2009. United Nations, *Independent Evaluation of Lessons
Learned from Delivering as One*, July 2012, accessed 4 May 2013, http://www
.un.org/en/ga/deliveringasone/pdf/mainreport.pdf.

12 The first international financial institutions, the World Bank and the International Monetary Fund, were established in July 1944, though it was only
after the end of the Second World War that they became operational. In
contrast to the UN, the World Bank and the IMF were predominantly Western institutions up until the end of the Cold War. Russia first became a
member of the World Bank in 1992.

13 For the shares of voting rights in the World Bank, see "International Bank
for Reconstruction and Development Subscriptions and Voting Power of
Member Countries," accessed 4 May 2013, http://siteresources.worldbank
.org/BODINT/Resources/278027-1215524804501/IBRDCountryVotingTable
.pdf.

14 Weiss and Thakur, *Global Governance and the UN*, 160.

15 The G20 co-operation originally included Argentina, Australia, Brazil, Canada, China, France, Germany, India, Indonesia, Italy, Japan, Mexico, Russia,
Saudi Arabia, South Africa, South Korea, Turkey, the United Kingdom, and
the United States – altogether nineteen countries plus the European Union.
Subsequently, the Netherlands and Spain have participated in some meetings, and as have Ethiopia (as representative for NEPAD), Malawi (AU), Vietnam (ASEAN), and Singapore. In addition to the UN, the World Bank, the
IMF, the OECD, and the WTO take part. See David Shorr, *Making the G-20 a
Reservoir of Global Leadership*, April 2011, accessed 4 May 2013,
http://www.stanleyfoundation.org/resources.cfm? id=449.

16 Mallaby, *The World's Banker*, 232ff.

17 On the 2009 conference see: http://www.un.org/ga/econcrisissummit
(accessed 4 May 2013).

18 High-Level Task Force on the Global Food Security Crisis, *Comprehensive
Framework for Action*, New York, July 2008, accessed 4 May 2013, www.un
.org/en/issues/food/taskforce/pdf/OutcomesAndActionsBooklet_v9.pdf.

19 Richard Gowan, "A Second Chance for Ban Ki-moon," *IP Journal*, 30 April
2011, accessed 4 May 2013, https://ip-journal.dgap.org/en/ip-journal/topics/
second-chance-ban-ki-moon.

20 Henrik Jespersen, Study of UNDP, UNICEF and UNFPA's engagement in fragile and post-conflict states; November 2010, Annex on UNDP in Liberia; accessed 4 May 2013, http://reliefweb.int/sites/reliefweb.int/files/resources/857F0FFEA723D03F85257831005B7979-Full_Report.pdf.).

CHAPTER ELEVEN

1 Rachel Carson's *Silent Spring*, (1962) was one of the main impetuses for the environmental movement. Donnella Meadow's *The Limits to Growth* (1972) also informed the Stockholm Conference and contributed to many developing countries' fear of that they would be forced to limit their growth out of concern for the environment. The "Report of the United Nations Conference on the Human Environment" is available at: http://www.unep.org/Documents.Multilingual/Default.asp?DocumentID=97 (accessed 4 May 2013). See also Nico Schrijver, "Natural Resources and Sustainable Development," in *The Oxford Handbook on the United Nations*, eds. Weiss and Daws, 600; and Weiss and Thakur, *Global Governance and the UN*, 204.

2 The World Commission on Environment and Development (Brundtland Commission), *Our Common Future*, 1–23.

3 For the Rio Declaration, see "Report of the United Nations Conference on Environment and Development," 14 August 1992, http://www.un.org/documents/ga/conf151/aconf15126-3.htm (accessed 4 May 2013).

4 On international environmental conventions in general, see Najam, Papa, and Taiyab, *Global Environmental Governance*.

5 On the Global Environmental Facility (GEF), see: http://www.thegef.org/gef. On the Montreal Protocol, see UNEP's account in: http://ozone.unep.org/Publications/MP_A_Success_in_the_making-E.pdf (accessed 4 May 2013).

6 The increase in the global temperature is measured against the temperature in the pre-industrial age; see IPCC, "Climate Change 2007: Synthesis Report" (AR4) http://www.ipcc.ch/pdf/assessment-report/ar4/syr/ar4_syr.pdf (accessed 4 May 2013). See also Victor, *Global Warming Gridlock*; and Stern, *A Blueprint for a Safer Planet*, 39.

7 On the increase in sea levels, see the "Synthesis Report for the Climate Change Conference in Copenhagen," 10–12 March 2009, accessed 4 May 2013, http://climatecongress.ku.dk/pdf/ synthesisreport; and Arctic Monitoring and Assessment Programme (AMAP), Snow, Water, Ice and Permafrost in the Arctic," 2011, accessed 4 May 2013, http://amap.no/swipa/SWIPAOverviewReport.pdf.

8 NEP executive director Achim Steiner statement to UN Security Council, UN webcast. 20 July 2011, accessed 4 May 2013, http://www.unmultimedia

.org/tv/webcast/2011/07/achim-steiner-unep-security-council-meeting-part-1
.html.

9 The IPCC's temperature and sea-level scenarios: http://www.ipcc.ch/publica
   tions_and_data/ar4/syr/en/spms3.html (accessed 4 May 2013).

10 This analysis is primarily based on the author's impressions of the climate
   change debate in the United States and on discussions with US diplomats,
   business people, and climate experts in the course of 2009.

11 UNFCCC, Copenhagen Accord, accessed 4 May 2013, http://unfccc.int/
   resource/docs/2009/cop15/eng/l07.pdf. The Copenhagen Accord was not
   adopted at the meeting; a decision was merely taken to take note of it. However, over the fifteen months following the Copenhagen Summit, 114 countries signed up to the agreement.

12 See Outcome of COP 17, accessed 4 May 2013, http://unfccc.int/resource/
   docs/2011/cop17/eng/09a01.pdf.

13 On the climate change economy in general, see Newell and Paterson, *Climate Capitalism*.

14 International Energy Agency, *World Energy Outlook 2010*, 237–71.

15 Stern, *The Economics of Climate Change*; and Stern, *A Blueprint for a Safer
   Planet*, 48.

16 UNFCCC, Copenhagen Accord, para. 8. For more on the individual countries'
   contributions to fast start finance, see http://www3.unfccc.int/pls/apex/
   f?p=116:8:3430607776235347::NO::: (accessed 4 May 2013).

17 For information about ODA transfers in 2011, see OECD, "Development: Aid
   to Developing Countries Falls Because of Global Recession," press release, 4
   April 2012, accessed 4 May 2013, http://www.oecd.org/newsroom/
   developmentaidtodevelopingcountriesfallsbecauseofglobalrecession.htm.

18 See the Leading Group's website: http://www.leadinggroup.org/rubrique20
   .html (accessed 4 May 2013).

19 EU Commission staff working document, 1 April 2010, accessed 4 May
   2013, http://ec.europa.eu/economy_finance/articles/international/
   documents/innovative_financing_global_level_se c2010_409en.pdf; the revenue estimate is on p. 22. See also the Leading Group, "Globalizing Solidarity: The Case for Financial Levies, Report of the Committee of Experts to
   the Taskforce on International Financial transactions and Development,"
   June 2010, 19 (leadinggroup.org/article668.html, accessed 4 May 2013).

20 Report of the Secretary-General's High-level Advisory Group on Climate
   Change Financing, 5 November 2010, accessed 4 May 2013, http://www.un
   .org/wcm/webdav/site/climate change/shared/Documents/AGF_reports/AGF
   _Final_Report.pdf, paras. 40–7. See also the EU Commission staff working
   document referred to in note 19 above, p. 32.

21 Leading Group, "Globalizing Solidarity," 12; EU Commission staff working document, p. 35. On UNITAID, see: http://www.unitaid.eu; and Douste-Blazy, *From the Solidarity Contribution on Air Tickets to the Financial Transaction Tax.*

22 World Economic Forum, Davos, secretary-general's introduction to the press conference, 28 January 2011, accessed 4 May 2013, : http://www.un.org/apps/sg/offthecuff.asp?nid=1687.

23 See UNDESA,"World Population Prospects, the 2010 Edition," 3 May 2011, updated 6 December 2012, accessed 4 May 2013, http://esa.un.org/unpd/wpp.

24 McKinsey Global Institute, *Resource Revolution.*

25 This section is primarily based on a report published by the Center on International Co-operation (CIC) at New York University, drawn up by Alex Evans, *Globalization and Scarcity. Multilateralism for a World with Limits,* November 2010, accessed 4 May 2013, http://cic.es.its.nyu.edu/sites/default/files/evans_multilateral_scarcity.pdf.

26 IEA, *World Energy Outlook 2010,* 77.

27 Secretary-General's Advisory Group on Energy and Climate Change (AGECC): *Energy for a Sustainable Future,* New York, April 2010.

28 IPCC, *Special Report Renewable Energy Sources (SRRES), Summary for Policymakers,* May 2011, 18, accessed 4 May 2013, http://www.ipcc-wg3.de/special-reports/srren.

29 Evans, 11.

CHAPTER TWELVE

1 An Agenda for Development. Report of the Secretary-General (A/48/935), 6 May 1994, accessed 4 May 2013, globalpolicy.org/component/content/article/226/32314.html.

Suggestions for Further Reading

A great number of books and articles have been written about the United Nations and there is a lot of additional material available on various websites. The following list is therefore only intended to be a starting point for further reading on the topics discussed in the individual chapters of this book. The list is mainly restricted to relatively recent publications.

CHAPTER ONE: INTRODUCTION

There is a short introduction to the United Nations in Jussi M. Hanhimäki, *The United Nations. A Very Short Introduction*, Oxford: Oxford University Press, 2008. *The Oxford Handbook on the United Nations*, edited by Thomas G. Weiss and Sam Daws, Oxford: Oxford University Press, 2007, is a reference work giving a comprehensive overview of the whole UN system. A corresponding German work (translated into English) is: *A Concise Encyclopedia of the United Nations*, edited by Helmut Volger, 2nd ed., Leiden: Martinus Nijhoff Publishers, 2010.

In connection with the work on this book I have drawn heavily on the *United Nations Intellectual History Project*, a research project which, since 2000, has resulted in a series of monographs published by Indiana University Press under the general editorship of Louis Emmerij, Richard Jolly, and Thomas G. Weiss. In relation to the topics discussed in this chapter, the following is particularly relevant: Thomas G. Weiss and Ramesh Thakur, *Global Governance and the UN. An Unfinished Journey*, Bloomington, IN: Indiana University Press, 2008.

In addition, references can be made to the following UN websites:

- United Nations: http://www.un.org

- UN Security Council (SC): http://www.un.org/Docs/sc
- UN General Assembly (GA): http://www.un.org/en/ga
- UN Peacebuilding Commission (PBC): http://www.un.org/peace/peacebuilding
- UN Human Rights Council (HRC): http://www2.ohchr.org/english/bodies/hrcouncil
- The International Criminal Court (ICC): http://www.icc-cpi.int/EN_Menus/icc/Pages/default.aspx
- UN Department of Peacekeeping Operations (DPKO): http://www.un.org/en/peacekeeping
- UN Department of Political Affairs (DPA): http://www.un.org/wcm/content/site/undpa
- UN Department of Economic and Social Affairs (DESA): http://www.un.org/en/development/desa/index.html
- UN High Commissioner for Human Rights (OHCHR): http://www.ohchr.org/EN/Pages/WelcomePage.aspx
- UN Development Programme (UNDP): http://www.undp.org/content/undp/en/home.html
- UN Children's Fund (UNICEF): http://www.unicef.org
- UN Population Fund (UNFPA): http://www.unfpa.org

CHAPTER TWO:

UNITED NATIONS: ORGANIZATION AND METHODS OF WORK

The history of the United Nations's creation is described in Stephen C. Schlesinger, *Act of Creation: The Founding of the United Nations*, Boulder, CO: Westview Press, 2003. Mark Mazower, *No Enchanted Palac: The End of Empire and the Ideological Origins of the United Nations*, Princeton: Princeton University Press, 2009, gives an interpretation of the ideological basis which emphasizes the continuity from the League of Nations; while Elizabeth Borgwardt, *A New Deal for the World. America's Vision for Human Rights*, Cambridge, MA: Belknap Press of Harvard University Press, 2005, gives an interpretation which emphasizes the differences.

Another broad overview which is generally positive about the UN is Paul Kennedy, *The Parliament of Man: The Past, Present, and Future of the United Nations*, New York: Random House, 2006. Thomas G. Weiss, *What's Wrong with the United Nations and How to Fix It*, Cambridge, UK: Polity, 2008, is more critical of the UN and the UN system.

CHAPTER THREE: THE SECRETARIAT

The office of Secretary-General is the topic in Simon Chesterman, ed. *Secretary or General? The UN Secretary-General in World Politics*, Cambridge, UK: Cambridge University Press, 2007. The history of the UN Secretariat is given in Thant Myint-U and Amy Scott, *The UN Secretariat*, New York: International Peace Academy, 2007. There is a description of how the UNDP has gradually developed into the organization we know today in Craig N. Murphy, *The United Nations Development Programme: A Better Way*, Cambridge, UK: Cambridge University Press, 2006.

The most recent biography of Dag Hammarskjöld is Roger Lipsey, *Hammarskjöld. A Life*, Ann Arbor, MI: University of Michigan Press, 2013. James Traub, *The Best Intentions. Kofi Annan and the UN in the Era of American World Power*, New York: Farrar, Strauss and Giroux, 2006, is one of several biographies of the Ghanaian former secretary-general. Recently Kofi Annan issued his own memoirs: Kofi Annan. *Interventions. A Life in War and Peace*. With Nader Mousavizadeh. New York: The Penguin Press, 2012. Samantha Power, *Chasing the Flame. Sergio Vieira de Mello and the Fight to Save the World*, New York: The Penguin Press, 2008, is a fascinating portrait of one of the UN's senior diplomats.

CHAPTER FOUR: THE SECURITY COUNCIL

The history of the Security Council is excellently described in David L. Bosco, *Five to Rule Them All: The UN Security Council and the Making of the Modern World*, Oxford: Oxford University Press, 2009, which also contains a comprehensive bibliography.

Chinmaya R. Gharekkan, *The Horseshoe Table. An Inside View of the UN Security Council*, New Delhi: Pearson Longman, 2006, gives a view of the work of the council from the perspective of someone who has both been a delegate on the council and worked in the UN Secretariat. The former Canadian ambassador to the UN, David M. Malone, has written about the Security Council, including how the council dealt with the question of Iraq: David M. Malone, *The International Struggle over Iraq: Politics in the UN Security Council 1980–2005*, Oxford: Oxford University Press, 2006.

CHAPTER FIVE: PEACEKEEPING OPERATIONS

There is a thorough review of the UN's peacekeeping operations in Alex J. Bellamy and Paul D. Williams, *Understanding Peacekeeping*, 2nd ed., Cambridge, UK: Polity, 2010.

Each year the Center on International Cooperation (CIC) at New York University publishes a survey of all UN operations. The latest version is *Annual Review of Global Peace Operations 2012*, Boulder, CO: Lynne Rienner, 2012. A corresponding survey is made of the UN's political missions: *Review of Political Missions 2011*, Boulder, CO: Lynne Rienner, 2011. The CIC's website gives an excellent introduction to a number of more detailed analyses of peacekeeping work: http://www.cic.nyu.edu/.

CHAPTER SIX: PEACEBUILDING

Many books and articles on peacebuilding have appeared in recent years, including Michael W. Doyle and Nicholas Sambanis, *Making War and Building Peace*, Princeton: Princeton University Press, 2006; James Dobbins, Seth G. Jones, Keith Crane, and Beth Cole DeGrasse, *The Beginner's Guide to Nation-Building*, Santa Monica, CA: Rand Corporation, 2007; Ashraf Ghani and Clare Lockhart, *Fixing Failed States*, Oxford: Oxford University Press, 2008; and Francis Fukuyama, *State-Building: Governance and World Order in the Twenty-first Century*, Ithaca, NY: Cornell University Press, 2004.

On the UN as a builder of states, for example in Kosovo and Timor-Leste, see Carolyn Bull, *No Entry without Strategy*, Tokyo: United Nations University Press, 2008.

CHAPTER SEVEN: HUMAN RIGHTS

On human rights in general, see Micheline R. Ishay, *The History of Human Rights*, 2nd ed., Berkeley, CA: University of California Press, 2008. On the UN's work on human rights, see Roger Normand and Sarah Zaidi, *Human Rights at the UN*, Bloomington, IN: Indiana University Press, 2008. On how the Universal Declaration came into being, see Mary Ann Glendon, *A World Made New: Eleanor Roosevelt and the Universal Declaration of Human Rights*, New York: Random House, 2001.

The New Zealand Handbook on International Human Rights, Wellington: New Zealand Ministry of Foreign Affairs and Trade, 2008 reviews the most important human rights conventions. The historical texts can be found in Jon E. Lewis, ed., *A Documentary History of Human Rights: A Record of the*

Events, Documents and Speeches that Shaped Our World, New York: Carroll and Graff, 2003.

CHAPTER EIGHT: GENOCIDE AND WAR CRIMES

Much has been written in recent years about the responsibility to protect. Alex J. Bellamy, *Global Politics and the Responsibility to Protect: From Words to Deeds*, London: Routledge, 2011, gives a good overview of the subject. Gareth Evans, *The Responsibility to Protect: Ending Mass Atrocity Crimes Once and For All*, Washington, DC: Brookings Institution Press, 2008 also covers a wide area. There is a very interesting discussion of earlier examples of humanitarian intervention in Gary J. Bass, *Freedom's Battle: The Origins of Humanitarian Intervention*, New York: Alfred A. Knopf, 2008.

The ICISS report, *The Responsibility to Protect: Report of the International Commission on Intervention and State Sovereignty*, Ottawa: International Development Research Centre, 2001, is still the best foundation for understanding the concept. It is accessible via http://responsibilitytoprotect.org/ICISS Report.pdf.

CHAPTER NINE: GLOBAL DEVELOPMENT GOALS

The United Nations MDGS and the status of progress toward the achievement of the goals are dealt with in the annual report: *The Millennium Development Goals Report 2012*, New York: United Nations, 2012.

In connection with the Millennium Development Goals Summit in September 2010, the UNDP published a number of analyses covering the work being done to achieve the goals: *Beyond the Midpoint. Achieving the Millennium Development Goals*, New York, United Nations, 2010; *What Will It Take to Achieve the Millennium Development Goals? An International Assessment*, New York: United Nations, 2010; *Unlocking Progress: MDG Acceleration on the Road to 2015*, New York: United Nations, 2010; and *The Path to Achieving the Millennium Development Goals: A Synthesis of Evidence from around the World*, New York: United Nations, 2010. See also the UNDP's website on this: http://www.undp.org/content/undp/en/home.html.

CHAPTER TEN:
OPERATIONAL ACTIVITIES FOR DEVELOPMENT

The best impression one can get of what the UN's funds, programs and specialized agencies actually do in the field can be got by visiting their respective websites.

There is a broad introduction to the UN's development activities in Olav Stokke, *The UN and Development: From Aid to Cooperation.* United Nations Intellectual History Project Series, Bloomington, IN: Indiana University Press, 2009. The basis for the UN's development activities is described in Richard Jolly, Louis Emmerij, Dharam Ghai, and Frederic Lapeyre, *UN Contributions to Development Thinking and Practice*, Bloomington, IN: Indiana University Press 2004; and in Richard Jolly, Louis Emmerij, and Thomas G. Weiss, *The UN Ideas That Changed the World*, Bloomington, IN: Indiana University Press, 2009.

CHAPTER ELEVEN: SUSTAINABLE DEVELOPMENT

The Brundtland Commission Report is still worth reading: World Commission on Environment and Development, *Our Common Future*, Oxford: Oxford University Press, 1987.

On the issue of climate change, the best introductions are Nicholas Stern, *A Blueprint for a Safer Planet: How We Can Save the World and Create Prosperity*, London: Vintage Books, 2010; Mark Maslin, *Global Warming: A Very Short Introduction*, Oxford: Oxford University Press, 2009; and Lael Brainard, Abigail Jones, and Nigel Purvis, eds., *Climate Change and Global Poverty*, Washington, DC: Brookings Institution Press, 2009.

Bibliography

Acemoglu, Daron and James A. Robinson. *Why Nations Fail: The Origins of Power, Prosperity, and Poverty*, New York: Crown Publishers, 2012.

Adebajo, Adekeye. *UN Peacekeeping in Africa. From the Suez Crisis to the Sudan Conflicts*, Boulder, CO: Lynne Rienner Publishers, 2011.

Albright, Madeleine. *Madam Secretary: A Memoir*. With Bill Woodward. New York: Miramax Books, 2003.

Annan, Kofi. *Interventions: A Life in War and Peace*. With Nader Mousavizadeh. New York: The Penguin Press, 2012.

Antholis, William and Strobe Talbott. *Fast Forward: Ethics and Politics in the Age of Global Warming*, 2nd ed. Washington, DC: Brookings Institution Press, 2011.

Ash, Timothy Garton. *Free World*. New York: Penguin Books, 2004.

Baehr, Peter R. and Leon Gordenker, *The United Nations. Reality and Ideal*, 4th ed. New York: Palgrave Macmillan, 2005.

Balakan, Grigoris. *Armenian Golgatha: A Memoir of the Armenian Genocide 1915–1918*. New York: Alfred A. Knopf, 2009.

Bass, Gary J. *Freedom's Battle: The Origins of Humanitarian Intervention*. New York: Alfred A. Knopf, 2008.

Behrman, Greg. *The Most Noble Adventure: The Marshall Plan and the Time When America Helped Save Europe*. New York: Free Press, 2007.

Bellamy, Alex J. and Paul D. Williams. *Understanding Peacekeeping*, 2nd ed. Cambridge, UK: Polity, 2010.

Bellamy, Alex J. *Global Politics and the Responsibility to Protect: From Words to Deeds*. London: Routledge, 2011.

Bolton, John. *Surrender Is Not an Option: Defending America at the United Nations and Abroad*, New York: Threshold Editions, 2007.

Borgwardt, Elizabeth. *A New Deal for the World. America's Vision for Human Rights*. Cambridge, MA: Belknap Press of Harvard University Press, 2005.

Bosco, David L. *Five to Rule Them All: The UN Security Council and the Making of the Modern World*. Oxford: Oxford University Press, 2009.

Boutros-Ghali, Boutros. *Unvanquished: A U.S.-U.N. Saga*. New York: Random House, 1999.

Brainard, Lael, Abigail Jones, and Nigel Purvis eds. *Climate Change and Global Poverty*. Washington, DC: Brookings Institution Press, 2009.

Brock, Lothar, Hans-Henrik Holm, Georg Sørensen, and Michael Stohl. *Fragile States: Violence and the Failure of Intervention*. Cambridge, UK: Polity, 2012.

Bull, Carolyn. *No Entry without Strategy*. Tokyo: United Nations University Press, 2008.

Carothers, Thomas. "A League of Their Own," *Foreign Policy* (July/August 2008): 44–9.

Carr, Edward Hallett. *The Twenty Year's Crisis 1919–39*. 1939. Reprint, New York: Harper Perennial, 2001.

Casella, Alexander. *Breaking the Rules*. Geneva: Editions du Tricorne, 2011.

Chesterman, Simon, ed. *Secretary or General? The UN Secretary-General in World Politics*. Cambridge, UK: Cambridge University Press, 2007.

Chesterman, Simon, Michael Ignatieff, and Ramesh Thakur. *Making States Work: State Failure and the Crisis of Governance*. Tokyo: United Nations University, 2005.

Claude, Inis L. Jr. *Swords into Plowshares: The Problems and Progress of International Organization*, 4th ed. New York: Random House, 1971.

Coicaud, Jean-Marc, Michael W. Doyle, and Anne-Marie Gardner, eds. *The globalization of human rights*. Tokyo: United Nations University Press, 2003.

Collier, Paul. *The Bottom Billion*. Oxford: Oxford University Press, 2007.

– *Wars, Guns, and Votes: Democracy in Dangerous Places*. New York: Harper, 2009.

– *The Plundered Planet: How We Must – and How We Can – Manage Nature for Global Prosperity*. Oxford: Oxford University Press, 2010.

Cooper, Helene. *The House at Sugar Beach*. New York: Simon and Schuster, 2008.

Cooper, John Milton, Jr. *Woodrow Wilson: A Biography*. New York: Vintage, 2009.

Cronin, Bruce and Ian Hurd, eds. *The UN Security Council and the Politics of International Authority*, New York: Routledge, 2008.

Dadush, Uri and Bennett Stancil. "The World Order in 2050," *Carnegie Endowment for International Peace: Policy Outlook* (April 2010).

Dallaire, Roméo. *Shake Hands with the Devil: The Failure of Humanity in Rwanda*. London: Arrow Books, 2003.

Dansk Udenrigspolitisk Institut. *Humanitarian Intervention: Legal and Political Aspects*. Copenhagen: DUPI, 1999.

Dennison, Susi and Anthony Dworkin. "Toward an EU Human Rights Strategy for a Post-Western World" *European Council on Foreign Relations* (September 2010)

Dobbins, James, Seth G. Jones, Keith Crane, Andrew Rathmell, Brett Steele, Richard Teltschik, and Anga Timilsina. *The UN's Role in Nation-Building: From the Congo to Iraq*. San Francisco, CA: Rand Corporation, 2005.

– Keith Crane, and Beth Cole DeGrasse. *The Beginner's Guide to Nation-Building*. San Francisco, CA: Rand Corporation, 2007.

Dobbs, Richard, Jeremy Oppenheim, Fraser Thompson, Marcel Brinkman, and Marc Zornes. *Resource Revolution: Meeting the World's Energy, Materials, Food, and Water Needs*. New York: McKinsey Global Institute, 2011.

Douste-Blazy, Philippe. *From the Solidarity Contribution on Air Tickets to the Financial Transaction Tax*. Toulouse: Éditions Privat, 2011.

Doyle, Michael W. and Nicholas Sambanis. *Making War and Building Peace*. Princeton: Princeton University Press, 2006.

Eckhard, Frederick. *Kofi Annan. A Spokesperson's Memoir*. New York: Ruder Finn Press, 2012.

Emmerij, Louis, Richard Jolly, and Thomas G. Weiss. *Ahead of the Curve? UN Ideas and Global Challenges*. United Nations Intellectual History Project Series. Bloomington, IN: Indiana University Press, 2001.

Evans, Alex. *Globalization and Scarcity: Multilateralism for a World with Limits*. New York: Center on International Cooperation, New York University, 2010.

Evans, Gareth. *The Responsibility to Protect: Ending Mass Atrocity Crimes Once and for All*. Washington, D.C.: Brookings Institution Press, 2008.

Farris, Stephan. *Forecast: The Consequences of Climate Change, from the Amazon to the Arctic, from Darfur to Napa Valley*. New York: Henry Holt and Company, 2009.

Fasulo, Linda. *An Insider's Guide to the UN*. 2nd ed. New Haven, CN: Yale University Press, 2009.

Ferguson, Niall. *Civilization.The West and the Rest*. New York: Penguin Books, 2011.

Fisher, David. *Morality and War: Can War Be Just in the Twenty-first Century?*. Oxford: Oxford University Press, 2011.

Floto, Inga. *Colonel House in Paris: A Study of American Policy at the Paris Peace Conference 1919*. Aarhus, Denmark.: Aarhus Universitetsforlag, 1973.

Four Nations Initiative. *Towards a Compact: Proposals for Improved Governance and Management of the United Nations Secretariat.* Report of final proposals by the Four Nations Initiative. 13 September 2007. Accessed 4 may 2013,ttp/www.centerforunreform.org/node/275.

Freedom House. *Policing Belief: The Impact of Blasphemy Laws on Human Rights.* Washington, DC: Freedom House, 2010.

Fukuyama, Francis. *The End of History and the Last Man.* New York, Free Press, 1992.

– *Trust: The Social Virtues and the Creation of Prosperity.* New York: Free Press, 1995.

– *State-Building: Governance and World Order in the Ttwenty-first Century.* Ithaca, NY: Cornell University Press, 2004.

– *The Origins of Political Order.* New York: Farrar, Straus, and Giroux, 2011.

Gareis, Sven Bernhard and Johannes Varwick. *The United Nations: An Introduction.* New York: Palgrave Macmillan, 2005.

Genocide Prevention Task Force. *Preventing Genocide. A Blueprint for U.S. Policymakers,* Washington, DC: American Academy of Diplomacy, 2008.

Ghani, Ashraf and Clare Lockhart. *Fixing Failed States.* Oxford: Oxford University Press, 2008.

Gharekhan, Chinmaya R. *The Horseshoe Table: An Inside View of the UN Security Council.* New Delhi: Pearson Longman, 2006

Giddens, Anthony. *The Politics of Climate Change,* 2nd ed. Cambridge, UK: Polity, 2011.

Glendon, Mary Ann. *A World Made New: Eleanor Roosevelt and the Universal Declaration of Human Rights.* New York: Random House, 2001.

Gore, Al. *The Future: Six Drivers of Global Change.* New York: Random House, 2013.

Gourevitch, Philip: *We Wish to Inform You That Tomorrow We Will Be Killed with Our Families: Stories from Rwanda.* New York: Farrar, Straus, and Giroux, 1998.

Götz, Norbert. *Deliberate Diplomacy: The Nordic Approach to Global Governance and Societal Representation at the United Nations.* Dordrecht, The Netherlands: Republic of Letters, 2011.

Groom, A.J.R. "Getting to 'Go'." In *The United Nations at the Millennium: The Principal Organs,* edited by Paul Taylor and A.J.R. Groom, 1–20. London: Continuum, 2000.

Hamburg, David A. *Preventing Genocide: Practical Steps toward Early Detection and Effective Action.* Boulder, CO: Paradigm Publishers, 2008.

Hammarskjöld, Dag. *To Speak for the World: Speeches and Statements.* Stockholm: Atlantis, 2005.

Hanhimäki, Jussi M. *The United Nations: A Very Short Introduction*. Oxford: Oxford University Press, 2008.

Hayner, Priscilla B. *Unspeakable Truths: Facing the Challenge of Truth Commissions*. New York: Routledge, 2002.

Henig, Ruth. *Versailles and After 1919–1933*. New York: Routledge, 1995.

Henley, Mary-Lynn and Henning Melber, eds. *Dag Hammarskjöld Remembered*. Uppsala, Sweden: Dag Hammarskjöld Foundation, 2011.

Hoopes, Townsend and Douglas Brinkley. *FDR and the Creation of the U.N.* New Haven, CT: Yale University Press, 1997.

Hunt, Lynn. *Inventing Human Rights: A History*. New York: W.W. Norton, 2007.

Ignatieff, Michael. *Empire Light: Nation-building in Bosnia, Kosovo and Afghanistan*. New York: Vintage, 2003.

Independent International Commission on Kosovo. *The Kosovo Report*. New York: Oxford University Press, 2000.

International Commission on Intervention and State Sovereignty. *The Responsibility to Protect*. Ottawa: International Development Research Centre, 2001.

International Energy Agency. *World Energy Outlook 2010*. Paris: IEA, 2010.

– *World Energy Outlook 2011*. Paris: IEA, 2011.

IPCC, *Special Report Renewable Energy Sources (SRRES), Summary for Policymakers*, May 2011. Accessed 4 May 2013 (http://www.ipcc-wg3.de/special-reports/srren).

Ishay, Micheline R. *The History of Human Rights*, 2nd ed. Berkeley: University of California Press 2008.

Johnson, Hilde F. *Waging Peace in Sudan: The Inside Story of the Negotiations That Ended Africa's Longest Civil War*. Eastbourne, UK: Sussex Academic Press, 2011.

Jolly, Richard, Louis Emmerij, Dharam Ghai, and Frederic Lapeyre. *UN Contributions to Development Thinking and Practice*. United Nations Intellectual History Project Series. Bloomington, IN: Indiana University Press, 2004.

– and Thomas G. Weiss. *The UN Ideas That Changed the World*. United Nations Intellectual History Project Series, Bloomington, IN: Indiana University Press, 2009.

Jones, Bruce, Carlos Pascual, and Stephen John Stedman. *Power and Responsibility: Building International Order in an Era of Transnational Threats*. Washington, DC: Brookings Institution Press, 2009.

Karns, Margaret P. and Karen A. Mingst. *International Organizations*. Boulder, CO: Lynn Rienner Publishers, 2010.

Keating, Colin. "Selecting the World's Diplomat." In *Secretary or General? The UN Secretary-General in World Politics*, ed. Chesterman, 47–66. Cambridge, UK: Cambridge University Press, 2007.

Kennedy, Paul. *Preparing for the Twenty-first Century*. New York: Vintage Books, 1993.

– *The Parliament of Man: The Past, Present, and Future of the United Nations*. New York: Random House, 2006.

Klare, Michael T. *Rising Powers, Shrinking Planet: The New Geopolitics of Energy*. New York: Metropolitan Books/Henry Holt and Co., 2008.

Lash, Joseph P. *Dag Hammarskjold: Custodian of the Brushfire Peace*. New York, Doubleday and Co., 1961.

Lewis, Jon E., ed. *A Documentary History of Human Rights*. New York: Carroll and Graff, 2003.

Liebling, Alvin, ed. *Adlai Stevenson's Lasting Legacy*. New York: Palgrave Macmillan, 2007.

Lipsey, Roger. *Hammarskjöld. A Life*. Ann Arbor, MI: University of Michigan Press, 2013.

Luck, Edward C. *Mixed Messages: American Politics and International Organization 1919–1999*. Washington, DC: Brookings Institution Press, 1999.

Mahbubani, Kishore. *The Great Convergence. Asia, the West, and the Logic of One World*. New York: PublicAffairs, 2013.

MacFarlane, S. Neil and Yuen Foong Khong. *Human Security and the UN: A Critical History*. United Nations Intellectual History Project Series. Bloomington, IN: Indiana University Press, 2006.

Macmillan, Margaret. *Peacemakers:. Six Months that Changed the World*. London: John Murray, 2001.

Mallaby, Sebastian. *The World's Banker*. New York: The Penguin Press, 2004.

Malloch-Brown, Mark: *The Unfinished Global Revolution*. New York: The Penguin Press, 2011.

Malone, David M. *The International Struggle over Iraq*. Oxford: Oxford University Press, 2006.

Malone, David M., ed. *The UN Security Council. From the Cold War to the twenty-first Century*, Boulder, CO: Lynne Rienner Publishers, 2004.

Mancini, Francesco and Adam C. Smith, eds. "Partnerships: A New Horizon for Peacekeeping?" *International Peacekeeping* 18, no. 5 (Special Issue, November 2011).

Manning, Richard. *Using Indicators to Encourage Development – Lessons from the Millennium Development Goals*. DIIS Report 2009:1. Copenhagen: Danish Institute for International Studies, 2009.

Maslin, Mark. *Global Warming:. A Very Short Introduction.* Oxford: Oxford University Press, 2009.

Mazover, Mark. *No Enchanted Palace: The End of Empire and the Ideological Origins of the United Nations.* Princeton: Princeton University Press, 2009.

Mazover, Mark. *Governing the World. The History of an Idea.* New York: The Penguin Press, 2012.

McCullough, David. *Truman.* New York: Simon and Schuster, 1992.

McDonald, Kara C. and Stewart M. Patrick. *UN Security Council Enlargement and U.S. Interests,* Council on Foreign Relations Special Report no. 59, December 2010.

McKeever, Porter. *Adlai Stevenson: His Life and Legacy.* New York: William Morrow and Co., 1989.

McKinsey Global Institute, *Resource Revolution: Meeting the World's Energy, Materials, Food, and Water Needs,* 2011. Accessed 6 May 2013, http://www.mckinsey.com/Features/Resource_revolution.

MDG Gap Task Force. *The Global Partnership for Development: Time to Deliver.* New York: United Nations, 2011.

– *The Global Partnership for Development: Making Rhetoric a Reality.* New York: United Nations, 2012.

Meadows, Donella, Jorgen Randers, and Dennis Meadows. *Limits to Growth: The Thirty-Year Update.* White River Junction, VT: Chelsea Green Publishing, 2004.

Meisler, Stanley. *United Nations: A History,* rev. ed., New York: Grove Press, 2011.

Meyer, Jeffrey A. and Mark G. Califano. *Good Intentions Corrupted: The Oil-for-Food Scandal and the Threat to the U.N.* New York: Public Affairs, 2006.

Mikulaschek, Christoph, James Cockayne, and Chris Perry. *The United Nations Security Council and Civil War: First Insights from a New Dataset.* New York: International Peace Institute, 2010.

Monbiot, George. *Heat: How to Stop the Planet from Burning.* Cambridge, MA: South End Press, 2007.

Moynihan, Daniel Patrick. *A Dangerous Place.* With Suzanne Weaver. Boston: Little, Brown and Co., 1978.

Munoz, Heraldo. *A Solitary War: A Diplomat's Chronicle of the Iraq War and Its Lessons.* Golden, CO: Fulcrum, 2008.

Murphy, Craig P. *The United Nations Development Programme.* Cambridge, UK: Cambridge University Press, 2006.

Myint-U, Thant and Amy Scott. *The UN Secretariat: A Brief History (1945–2006).* New York: International Peace Academy, 2007.

Najam, Adil, Mihaela Papa, and Nadaa Taiyab. *Global Environmental Governance: A Reform Agenda*. Winnipeg, MB: International Institute for Sustainable Development, 2006.

National Intelligence Council. *Global Trends 2025: A Transformed World*. Washington DC, November 2008. Accessed 6 May 2013, http://www.acus.org/files/publication_pdfs/3/Global-Trends-2025.pdf.

National Intelligence Council. *Global Governance 2025: At a Critical Juncture*. Washington DC, September 2010. Accessed 6 May 2013, http://www.acus.org/files/publication_pdfs/403/Global_Governance_2025 .pdf.

National Intelligence Council. *Global Trends 2030: Alternative Worlds*. Washington DC, January 2013. Accessed 6 May 2013, http://www.scribd.com/doc/115962650/Global-Trends-2030-Alternative-Worlds.

Newell, Peter and Matthew Paterson. *Climate Capitalism: Global Warming and the Transformation of the Global Economy*. Cambridge, UK: Cambridge University Press, 2010.

New Zealand Handbook on International Human Rights. Wellington: New Zealand Ministry of Foreign Affairs and Trade, 2008.

Normand, Roger and Sarah Zaidi. *Human Rights at the UN*. United Nations Intellectual History Project Series. Bloomington, IN: Indiana University Press, 2008.

OECD. *Perspectives on Global Development 2010*. Paris: OECD, 2010.

Piccone, Ted. *Catalysts for Rights: The Unique Contribution of the UN's Independent Experts on Human Rights*. Washington D.C., Brookings Institution Press, 2010.

Pisani, Elizabeth. *The Wisdom of Whores*. New York: W.W. Norton, 2008.

Plokhy, S.M. *Yalta: The Price of Peace*. New York: Penguin Books, 2010.

Power, Samantha: *A Problem from Hell: America and the Age of Genocide*. New York: Harper Perennial, 2002.

– *Chasing the Flame: Sergio Vieira de Mello and the Fight to Save the World*. New York: The Penguin Press, 2008.

Ramcharan, Bertrand G. *Preventive Diplomacy at the UN*. United Nations Intellectual History Project Series. Bloomington, IN: Indiana University Press, 2008.

Richardson, Louise. *What Terrorists Want*. New York: Random House, 2006.

Roberts, Callum. *The Ocean of Life: The Fate of Man and the Sea*. New York: Viking, 2012.

Robertson, Geoffrey. *Crimes against Humanity: The Struggle for Global Justice*, rev. ed. New York: The New Press, 2002.

Ruggie, John, ed. *Multilateralism Matters: The Theory and Practice of an Institutional Form*. New York: Columbia University Press, 1993.

Ruggie, John. Preface to *Global Governance and the UN: An Unfinished Journey*. Edited by Thomas G. Weiss and Ramesh Thakur. Bloomington: Indiana University Press, 2010, xv–xx.

Sachs, Jeffrey. *The End of Poverty*. New York: Penguin Books, 2005.

Sagafi-Nejad, Tagi and John H. Dunning. *The UN and Transnational Corporations*. United Nations Intellectual History Project Series. Bloomington, IN: Indiana University Press, 2008.

Schechter, Michael G. *United Nations Global Conferences*. London: Routledge, 2005.

Schlesinger, Stephen C. *Act of Creation: The Founding of the United Nations*. Boulder, CO: Westview Press, 2003.

Sen, Amartya. *Development as Freedom*. New York: Anchor Books, 1999.

Singh, Susheela and Jacqueline E. Darroch. *Adding It Up: Costs and Benefits of Contraceptive Services – Estimates for 2012* New York: Guttmacher Institute and UNFPA, 2012, accessed 4 May 2013, http://www.guttmacher.org/pubs/AIU-2012-estimates.pdf.

Steger, Manfred B. *Globalization: A Very Short Introduction*. Oxford: Oxford University Press, 2009.

Stedman, Stephen J. "America and International Cooperation: What Role for a League of Democracies?," *Policy Analysis Brief*. The Stanley Foundation, November 2008.

Stern, Nicholas. *The Economics of Climate Change*. Cambridge, UK: Cambridge University Press, 2007.

– *A Blueprint for a Safer Planet: How We Can Save the World and Create Prosperity*. London: Vintage Books 2010.

Stokke, Olav. *The UN and Development: From Aid to Cooperation*. United Nations Intellectual History Project Series. Bloomington, IN: Indiana University Press, 2009.

Sumner, Andy. "Global Poverty and the New Bottom Billion," *IDS Working Paper* 349, November 2010.

Swart, Lydia and Jakob Lund. *The Group of 77: Perspectives on Its Role in the UN General Assembly*. New York: Center for UN Reform Education, 2010.

Talbot, Strobe. *The Great Experiment: The Story of Ancient Empires, Modern States, and the Quest for a Global Nation*. New York: Simon and Schuster, 2008.

Taylor, Paul and A.J.R. Groom, eds. *The United Nations at the Millennium: The Principal Organs*. London: Continuum, 2000.

Timber, Craig and Daniel Halperin *Tinderbox: How the West Sparked the AIDS Epidemic and How the World Can Finally Overcome It*. New York: Penguin Press, 2012.

Toye, John and Richard Toye. *The UN and Global Political Economy*. United Nations Intellectual History Project Series. Bloomington, IN: Indiana University Press, 2004.

Traub, James. *The Best Intentions. Kofi Annan and the UN in the Era of American World Power*. New York: Farrar, Straus and Giroux, 2006.

UN. *Report of the Panel on United Nations Peace Operations* (the Brahimi Report). UN documents A/55/305 and S/2000/809. 21 August 2000. http://www.un.org/peace/reports/peace_operations/.

– *The United Nations Today*. New York: United Nations, 2008.

– *Basic Facts about the United Nations*. New York: United Nations, 2011.

– *The Millennium Development Goals Report 2010*. New York: United Nations, 2010.

– *The Millennium Development Goals Report 2011*. New York: United Nations, 2011.

– *The Millennium Development Goals Report 2012*. New York: United Nations, 2012.

– *The Security Council: Working Methods Handbook*. New York: United Nations, 2012.

– *In Search of New Development Finance: World Economic and Social Survey 2012*. New York: United Nations, 2012.

– *World Economic Situation and Prospects 2012*. New York: United Nations, 2012.

United Nations Handbook 2012/2013. Wellington, Ministry of Foreign Affairs and Trade, New Zealand, 2012.

UNCTAD. *The Financial and Economic Crisis of 2008–09 and Developing Countries*. New York: United Nations, 2010.

UNDP. *Capacity Development: A UNDP Primer*. New York: United Nations, 2009.

– *Beyond the Midpoint: Achieving the Millennium Development Goals*. New York: United Nations, 2010.

– *Unlocking Progress: MDG Acceleration on the Road to 2015*. New York: United Nations 2010.

– *The Path to Achieving the Millennium Development Goals: A Synthesis of Evidence from around the World*. New York: United Nations, 2010.

– *Human Development Report 2010: The Real Wealth of Nations*. New York: Palgrave Macmillan/United Nations, 2010.

– *Human Development Report 2013: The Rise of the South: Human Progress in a Diverse World*, New York, Palgrave Macmillian: 2013.

– *Governance for Peace: Securing the Social Contract*. New York: United Nations, 2012.

– *What Will It Take to Achieve the Millennium Development Goals? An International Assessment*. New York: United Nations, 2010.

UNEP. *Climate in Peril. A Popular Guide to the Latest IPCC Reports*. Arendal, Norway: GRID-Arendal, 2009.

– *Keeping Track of Our Changing Environment: From Rio to Rio+20 (1992–2012)*. Nairobi: UNEP 2011.

– *UNEP Yearbook 2011: Emerging Issues in Our Global Environment*. Nairobi: UNEP, 2011.

– *Towards a Green Economy: Pathways to Sustainable Development and Poverty Eradication*. Nairobi: UNEP, 2011.

UN Secretary-General. *We the Peoples*. New York: United Nations, 2000.

– *In Larger Freedom*. Report to World Summit in 2005.

UN Secretary-General's Advisory Group on Energy and Climate Change (AGECC). *Energy for a Sustainable Future*. New York. April 2010.

UN Secretary-General's High-Level Panel on Global Sustainability. *Resilient People, Resilient Planet: A Future Worth Choosing*, 30 January 2012. Accessed 4 May 2013, http://www.un.org/gsp/report.

UN Secretary-General's High-Level Panel on Threats, Challenges and Change, *A More Secure World: Our Shared Responsibility*, December 2004, http://www.un.org/secureworld/report2.pdf.

UN System CEB. *The Global Financial Crisis and Its Impact on the Work of the UN System*. United Nations: CEB Issues Paper 2009

Urquhart, Brian. *Hammarskjold*. New York: W.W. Norton, 1972.

– *A Life in Peace and War*. New York: W.W. Norton, 1987.

– *Ralph Bunche: An American Odyssey*. New York, W.W. Norton, 1993.

– "The Evolution of the Secretary-General." In *Secretary or General? The UN Ssecretary-General in World Politics*, edited by Chesterman, 32. Cambridge, UK: Cambridge University Press, 2007.

Van Genugten, Wilem, Kees Homan, Nico Schrijver, and Paul de Waart. *The United Nations of the Future: Globalization with a Human Face*. Amsterdam, KIT – Publishers, 2006.

Victor, David. *Global Warming Gridlock*. Cambridge, UK: Cambridge University Press, 2011.

Volger, Helmut, ed. *A Concise Encyclopedia of the United Nations*. Leiden, The Netherlands, Martinus Nijhoff Publishers, 2010.

Ward, Michael. *Quantifying the World: UN Ideas and Statistics.* United Nations Intellectual History Project Series. Bloomington, IN: Indiana University Press, 2004.

Weiss, Thomas G., Tatiana Carayannis, Louis Emmerij, and Richard Jolly. *UN Voices: The Struggle for Devlopment and Social Justice.* United Nations Intellectual History Project Series. Bloomington, IN: Indiana University Press, 2005.

– and Sam Daws, eds. *The Oxford Handbook on the United Nations.* Oxford: Oxford University Press, 2007.

– *What's Wrong with the United Nations and How to Fix It.* Cambridge, UK: Polity, 2008.

– Tapio Kanninen, and Michael K. Busch. *Sustainable Global Governance for the Twenty-first Century,* Bonn, Germany: Friedrich Ebert Stiftung, 2009.

– and Ramesh Thakur. *Global Governance and the UN.* United Nations Intellectual History Project Series. Bloomington, IN: Indiana University Press, 2010.

– David P. Forsythe, Roger A. Coate, and Kelly-Kate Pease. *The United Nations and Changing World Politics,* 6th ed. Boulder, CO: Westview Press, 2010.

– *Thinking about Global Governance: Why People and Ideas Matter.* London: Routledge, 2011.

– *Humanitarian Business.* Cambridge, UK: Polity, 2013.

Williams, Paul D. *War and Conflict in Africa.* Cambridge, UK: Polity, 2011.

World Bank. *A Case for Aid. Building a Consensus for Development Assistance.* Washington, DC: World Bank, 2002.

– *Development and Climate Change.* World Development Report 2010. Washington, DC: World Bank, 2010.

– *Improving the Odds of Achieving the MDGs.* Global Monitoring Report 2011. Washington, DC: World Bank, 2011.

– *Conflict, Security, and Development.* World Development Report 2011. Washington, DC: World Bank, 2011.

World Commission on Environment and Development. *Our Common Future.* Oxford: Oxford University Press, 1987.

Wrong, Michela. *It's Our Turn to Eat.* New York: Harper, 2009.

Yergin, Daniel. *The Quest: Energy, Security, and the Remaking of the Modern World.* New York: The Penguin Press, 2011.

Youde, Jeremy. *Global Health Governance.* Cambridge UK: Polity, 2012.

Zakaria, Fareed. *The Future of Freedom.* New York: W.W. Norton, 2008.

– *The Post-American World.* New York: W.W. Norton, 2008.

Index

0.7 per cent ODA target, 20, 185–6, 205, 246, 248
4 Ones, the, 219
Advisory Group on Climate Change Financing (AGF), 247–8
Advisory Group on Energy and Climate Change (AGECC), 252
Afghanistan, 97, 108, 127, 144, 152, 232
African Union (AU), 14, 34, 47, 97, 108–9, 224, 264
Agenda 21 (1992), 235
Ahtissari, Martti, 125
al Qaeda, 143–5
Alianza Bolivariana para los Pueblos de Nuestra América (ALBA), 33, 37
al-Bashir, Omar, 175
Amin, Idi, 161, 177
AMISOM (Somalia), 97
Annan, Kofi, 16, 46, 47, 49, 65, 73, 114, 169, 173, 187, 258
Arab League, 14, 77, 264
Arab Spring, 77, 158
Armenian genocide, 160
ASEAN, 14, 151, 224
Asian values, 153–4
assistant-secretary-general (ASG), 57

Atlantic Charter (1941), 25

Ban Ki-moon, 46, 47, 48, 51–2, 55, 65, 171
Benghazi, 76–7
Black Hawk Down (Somalia), 162
Bolton, John, 7
Boutros-Ghali, Boutros, 46, 52, 65
Brahimi, Lakhdar, 93
Brahimi Report, 93–94, 104, 163
Brazil, 4, 11–12, 31, 80, 84–5, 88, 199, 213
Brundtland Report (1987), 234, 255
Bunche, Ralph, 90
Bureau of Crisis Prevention and Recovery (BCPR), 123
Burundi, 116, 118
Bush, George H.W., 72
Bush, George W., 72

CANZ (Canada, Australia, New Zealand), 38
capacity building, 215–6
cartoon crisis, 154
Cassin, René, 135
Chief Executives Board (CEB), 28, 218

chlorofluorocarbons (CFCS), 236
child mortality, 191–2
Chile, 180
China, 3–5, 11, 26, 31, 47, 52, 72, 74,
    78, 87–8, 97–8, 153–4, 174–5, 181,
    199, 204, 242–3
Churchill, Winston S., 25, 135
civil wars, 113
civilian capacity, 129
climate change, 15, 35, 238–45
climate financing, 245–49
Clinton, Bill, 5, 52, 162
CO₂ emissions, 21, 239–42, 248, 267
Cold War, 5, 13, 51, 91, 112, 149,
    186–7, 227
Conference on the World Financial
    and Economic Crisis (2009),
    228–9
conflict-affected countries, 22,
    230–2, 254, 262, 266
Convention of the Rights of the
    Child, 136–7
COP 15 (Copenhagen), 15–6, 30, 55,
    241–2, 244, 246–7
COP 16 (Cancun), 243
COP 17 (Durban), 244
Cote d'Ivoire, 48, 76–7, 102, 107
Cyclone Nargis, 172

Dallaire, Roméo, 162
Darfur, 47–8, 106, 175
de Cuellar, Javier Peréz, 46, 52, 65
death penalty, 41
decolonization, 31, 36
defamation of religion, 154
Delivering as One, 20, 218–20, 231
Deng Xiaoping, 8
democratic governments, 150–1
Democratic People's Republic of
    Korea (DPRK), 34, 152, 214

Department of Economic and
    Social affairs (DESA), 54, 62
Department of Peacekeeping Opera-
    tions (DPKO), 97
Department of Political Affairs
    (DPA), 54, 106
development financing, 205
Dili Declaration (2010), 127
Doha Development Round, 191
Dumbarton Oaks Conference
    (1944), 26, 134

Earth Summit (Rio 1992), 234, 238
Economic and Social Council
    (ECOSOC), 27, 28, 39, 64, 227, 238
Economic Commission for Latin
    America and the Caribbean
    (ECLAC), 62
Economic Community of West
    African States (ECOWAS), 48, 76,
    112, 120, 151, 168, 263
Education for All (1990), 187, 192
emerging economies, 4, 11, 199, 226
energy, 203, 245, 251–3, 267
equity strategy, 192
European Convention on Human
    Rights (ECHR), 136, 140
European Force (EUFOR – Chad), 104
European Union (EU), 14, 37, 43–4,
    104, 109, 198, 224, 263
Every Woman Every Child, 41,
    200–1, 210
executive boards of funds and pro-
    grams, 211, 230
Expanded Programme of Technical
    Assistance (EPTA), 208
Extraordinary Chamber in the
    Court of Cambodia (ECCC), 179

Fifth Committee (budget), 53, 58

food, 213, 250
Food and Agricultural Organization
(FAO), 28, 209
Fourth World Conference on
Women (Beijing 1995), 149, 187
foundations, 13–14, 198, 206
fragility, 22, 126, 204
France, 47, 67, 70, 73, 78–81, 104,
190, 249
Freedom House, 150, 156
freedom of expression, 154
funding of operational activities,
210–1

G20, 14, 223–6, 228, 261
G4, 80–3
G7+, 127
G77, 32–3, 36–9, 43, 200, 206, 227
Gaddafi, Muammar, 69, 76–7, 167,
173
Gbagbo, Laurent, 48, 76, 178
General Assembly, 9, 17, 20, 26–37,
42–43, 49, 64, 151–2, 162, 171,
185, 195, 202, 227, 262
Genocide Convention, 136–7, 160
Gleneagles Summit (G8, 2005), 190,
197
Global Compact, 41
Global Environmental Facility
(GEF), 235
global food crisis (2008), 229–30,
254
Global Fund to Fight AIDS, Tuberculosis and Malaria (GFATM), 49
global governance, 6, 12
global power structure, 11–12
global public goods, 10
globalization, 12
good offices, 176
governance, 196, 214–5

Group of 77. *See* G77
Groups of Friends, 40–1

Hammarskjöld, Dag, 45, 46, 53, 56;
international civil service, 65,
90–1
High-Level Panel on Global Sus-
tainability (2012), 40
High-Level Panel on the Post-2015
Development Agenda (2012),
202
High-Level Panel on Threats, Chal-
lenges and Change (2004), 114
High-Level Panel on United
Nations System-wide Coherence
(2006), 219
High-Level Plenary Meeting (World
Summit 2005), 39
Holmes, John, 229
Holocaust, 160
human development, 62
Human Development Report
(HDR), 62
human rights, 12, 19, 33, 133–145
Human Rights Commission, 134
human rights conventions, 136
Human Rights Council (HRC), 28,
136, 148, 151, 167
humanitarian assistance, 113, 126,
09, 211, 266
Hussein, Saddam, 72–3

IBSA (India, Brazil, South Africa), 85
India, 4, 11–12, 31, 80, 86, 88, 204
Intergovernmental Panel on Cli-
mate Change (IPCC), 21, 239–40,
253
International Atomic Energy
Agency (IAEA), 28
International Commission on Inter-

vention and State Sovereignty
    (ICISS), 165–7
International Conference on Popu-
    lation and Development (ICPD),
    149, 187, 217
International Covenant on Civil
    and Political Rights (ICCPR), 135,
    155–6
International Covenant on Eco-
    nomic, Social and Cultural
    Rights (ICESCR), 135, 137
International Criminal Court (ICC),
    19, 60, 170, 174, 177–8, 265
International Criminal Tribunal for
    Rwanda (ICTR), 179
International Criminal Tribunal for
    the former Yugoslavia (ICTY), 178
International Energy Agency (IEA),
    251
International Labor Organization
    (ILO), 28, 134, 209
International Security Assistance
    Force (ISAF – Afghanistan), 97,
    108
Iran, 34, 84–5, 87, 152, 171
Iraq, 72–4
Islamophobia, 156
Israel, 67, 75

Janjaweed militia (Darfur), 47
Johannesburg World Summit
    (2002), 188
just war, 167

Kadi case, 143–4
Kenya, 31, 107, 173, 175, 178
Khalilzad, Zalman, 67
Khmer Rouge, 161
Korean War (1950–3), 74, 90
Kosovo, 65, 164–5

Kouchner, Bernard, 67, 172
Kyoto Protocol, 243, 260

Leading Group, 247
League of Democracies, 7, 8
League of Nations, 24–5, 56
Least Developed Countries (LDC),
    229
Lebanon, 160, 176
LGBT agenda, 13, 131–2
Liberia, 100–2, 112, 117, 119–24,
    130, 183, 216, 232
Libya, 76–7, 167, 173–5, 180, 264
Lie, Trygve, 45, 46, 65
Lisbon Treaty (2011), 43

Malloch-Brown, Mark, xiii, 188
McCain, John, 7
MDG Summit (2010), 194–202
membership of the United Nations,
    4, 7
Menkerios, Haile, 124, 177
Millennium Development Goals
    (MDGS), 19, 188–94
Millennium Summit (2000), 187–8
MINURCAT (Chad), 104
MINUSTAH (Haiti), 104, 124
Montreal Protocol, 235–7, 244
MONUSCO (DR Congo), 97, 99, 106,
    108
Moynihan, Daniel Patrick, 7
Myanmar, 34, 172, 214

NATO, 14, 165, 264
negotiations, 17, 36–43, 194–202
    (MDG Summit 2010)
Non-Aligned Movement (NAM),
    32–3, 36, 43
non-governmental organizations
    (NGOS), 13, 33, 148, 198, 206

North Korea, *see*: Democratic People's Republic of Korea (DPRK)
Nuremberg Trials, 134, 175–6

Official Development Assistance (ODA), 20, 186, 194, 205, 227
official languages, 59
Oil-for-Food program (Iraq), 58
Optional Protocol (Torture Convention), 146–7
Organisation for Economic Co-operation and Development (OECD), 20, 32, 186, 248
Organization of Islamic Cooperation (OIC), 154–5
Ouattara, Alassane, 48, 76, 178
Our Common Future (1987), 234
ozone layer, 236

P5, 53, 71, 74, 81–4,
Palestine, 67, 75–6
partnerships, 199, 206
Peacebuilding Commission (PBC), 28, 114–19
Peacebuilding Fund (PBF), 115
Peacebuilding Support Office (PBSO), 118
peacekeeping, 18, 89–92, 96–8, 102–5; strengthened mandates, 94–5, 104–6, 108
Pearson Report, 185
permanent missions at the UN, 31
plane ticket tax, 249
Policy Committee, 58
population, 4, 241
poverty, 204
Powell, Colin, 73
private sector, 198, 206
protection of civilians, 98–9

regional groups, 32
resident coordinator (RC), 212–13, 220, 232
responsibility to protect (R2P), 19, 22, 165–74, 180–1
Rice, Condoleezza, 67
right to development, 152–3
right to water, 137–9
rights-based approach, 213, 216
Rio-principles (1992), 234–5, 243
Roosevelt, Eleanor, 135
Roosevelt, Franklin D., 25, 135
Russia, 5, 47, 70, 78, 80, 174–5, 181, 190
Rwandan genocide, 10, 162–3, 169

San Francisco Conference (1945), 26, 268
sanctions, 72, 142
SARS, 8, 29
Second World War (1939–45), 3, 25, 36
Secretariat, 27, 29, 25–9, 60–6
secretary-general, 17, 45–50; functions, 50–53; appointment of, 59–60, 263
Security Council, 3, 9, 16; Climate Change, 17, 19, 26; creation of, 27, 29, 35–7, 47, 50–3; election of SG, 57; senior appointments, 70–1; membership, 72–3; mandate, 73–5; Iraqi wars, 75–6; Middle East, 76–8; Libya, 78–87; enlargement of, 84–6; prospective members, 87–8; US and China, 95–6; mandating peacekeeping, 106, 168; R2P, 262–4
Sen, Amartya, 153
Sexual and Reproductive Health and Rights (SRHR), 189, 217–8

Sexual Orientation and Gender Identity (SOGI), 131, 141
sexual violence in conflict, 99
SHIRBRIG, 107–08
Sierra Leone, 116
Sirleaf, Ellen Johnson, 120, 202
South Africa, 11–12, 85–6, 88, 180
South-South co-operation, 129, 216
South Sudan, 4, 100, 107
Southern African Development Community (SADC), 34, 151, 263
Soviet Union (USSR), 3, 26, 69–70, 74–5
Special Court for Sierra Leone (SCSL), 101, 179
Special Rapporteur (on torture), 147
Special Representative of the Secretary-General (SRSG), 57, 95
Srebrenica (Bosnia), 163
Stalin, Josef, 26
Stern, Nicholas, 245
Stevenson, Adlai, 7, 69
Stockholm Conference (1972), 233–4
Sudan, 47–8, 100, 107, 232
Suez Crisis (1956), 90
Summer, Lawrence, 248
sustainable development, 20, 22, 234–5, 255
sustainable development goals (SDGS), 202,
Sustainable Energy for All, 42, 203, 252
Syria, 34, 77, 85, 141, 152, 160, 173, 264

Taliban, 142–3
Taylor, Charles, 101, 112, 121
technical assistance, 208, 216

terrorism, 142–4
Timor-Leste, 112–3, 117, 127, 192
Tobin Tax, 205, 247
torture, 145–9
Torture Convention, 136–7, 145–9
transitional justice, 179, 181
troop contributing countries (TCCS), 105
Truman, Harry S., 23, 27, 207

U Thant, 46
UN Charter, 3, 6, 12–13, 21, 35, 46; article 2(7), 88, 134, 159, 164; article 27, 70–1; article 99, 50; article 97, 56; articles 100 and 103, 64, 71; article 51, 89–90; Chapter VII, 159, 164
UN conferences, 186–7
UN Development Group (UNDG), 58, 218
UN Educational, Scientific and Cultural Organization (UNESCO), 28, 209
UN Framework Convention on Climate Change (UNFCCC), 15, 235, 239
UN Millennium Project, 190
UN Women, 27, 61
UNAMID (Darfur), 47, 97
UNAMIR (Rwanda), 162
UNCTAD, 62–3
under-secretary-general (USG), 57
UNDOF (Golan Heights), 91
UNDP, 20, 27, 55, 61, 123, 188, 196, 209, 212, 230–1
UNEF (Gaza), 90–1
UNEP, 235–6
UNFICYP (Cyprus), 91, 94
UNFPA, 27, 55, 61, 209, 217, 230
UNHCR, 20, 27, 126, 209

UNICEF, 20, 27, 55, 61, 123, 126, 186, 192, 209, 230
UNIFIL (Lebanon), 91, 97, 104
UNITAF (Somalia), 161
UNITAID, 249
United Kingdom, 3, 26, 32, 35, 47, 70, 78, 81, 103, 190, 200, 224
United States, 3–4, 26, 32, 37, 47, 54, 62, 70, 75–6, 78, 80, 87–8, 103, 123, 141, 173–4, 190, 222, 242–3
Uniting for Consensus, 81–2
Universal Declaration of Human Rights, 12–13, 19, 133–6, 140, 149, 155–7
UNMIL (Liberia), 97, 101–2
UNPROFOR (Bosnia), 93, 163
UNRWA, 27
urbanization, 204, 241
Urquhart, Sir Brian, 50

Versailles Conference (1919), 24
veto powers, 3, 70–1, 82–3
Vienna Declaration and Programme of Action (1993), 140
Vieira de Mello, Sergio, 17, 124

Waldheim, Kurt, 46, 52
Washington Consensus, 223

water, 137–9, 193, 251
Western European and Others Group (WEOG), 44, 71
WFP, 20, 27, 126, 209
Wilson, Woodrow, 24
Wolfensohn, Jim, 226
women, peace, and security (res. 1325), 98
World Bank, 28, 112, 123, 128–9, 222–4, 263
World Development Report (WDR) 2011, 128–9
World Health Organization (WHO), 8, 28, 209
World Summit (2005), 114, 169–70
World Summit on Sustainable Development ("Rio+20" – 2012), 202–3, 255
World Trade Organization (WTO), 28, 63

Yalta Conference (1945), 26

Zakaria, Fareed, 12
Zimbabwe, 107, 132, 176–7
Zoellick, Robert, 189, 259
Zorin, Valerian, 70